GETTING INTO AMERICA

About the Author

HOWARD DAVID DEUTSCH, B.A. CCNY; LLB and J.D. Yale Law School; International Law, Cantab., is the senior partner of Deutsch and Salberg, a New York law firm specializing in International and Immigration Law.

Mr. Deutsch has extensive knowledge and experience in the fields of International and Immigration Law. As such, he has recently been called up by the United States Senate to advise on immigration policy. He has travelled extensively in the pursuit of his profession and has advised thousands of individuals and institutions on investments and relocation of staff to the United States.

As a recognized expert in the fields of International and Immigration Law, Mr. Deutsch has appeared and lectured on radio and television more than fifty times since *Getting Into America* was first published in the United States in 1984.

In 1964, Mr. Deutsch received his first university degree from the City University of New York (B.A., Phi Beta Kappa, Magna Cum Laude). His majors at the City University were Economics and English Literature. In 1970, he received his first law degree from the Yale Law School in New Haven, Connecticut; in 1974 he received a diploma in International Law from the University of Cambridge in England.

Mr. Deutsch was admitted to the California Bar in 1971, and to the New York Bar in 1972. He is now working on an Immigration Law Text for practitioners and students.

Deutsch and Salberg
One East 57th Street
New York, NY 10022
Tel: (212) 759-8373

Getting Into America

The United States Visa and
Immigration Handbook

Howard David Deutsch

With a Foreword by the former
President of the European
Commission on Human Rights

CORONET BOOKS
Hodder and Stoughton

To my wife, Jessica

Copyright © 1984 by Howard David Deutsch
First published in the United States of America by Random
House Inc., New York, and simultaneously in Canada by
Random House of Canada Limited, Toronto

First published in Great Britain in 1985 by Coronet Books
Third impression 1986

British Library C.I.P.

Deutsch, Howard David
   [The United States visa and immigration handbook].
   Getting into America: the United States visa and
   immigration handbook
   1. United States——Emigration and immigration
   I. Title   II. Getting into America: the United
   States visa and immigration handbook
   325.73   JV6493
ISBN 0–340–36935–3

Printed and bound in Great Britain for
Hodder and Stoughton Paperbacks, a
division of Hodder and Stoughton Ltd.,
Mill Road, Dunton Green, Sevenoaks,
Kent (Editorial Office: 47 Bedford
Square, London, WC1 3DP) by
Richard Clay (The Chaucer Press) Ltd,
Bungay, Suffolk

AUTHOR'S
NOTE

This book is not a legal text on immigration but, rather, a practical guide. It tells you how the system actually works rather than what the laws that govern the system state. This is an important distinction to bear in mind when reading the pages that follow.

When I began work on this book approximately two years ago, there was a great deal of talk about changes in the immigration laws and an amnesty for illegal aliens. There have, in fact, been several attempts to introduce and pass such laws, all of which have failed. I would like to point out that this book confines itself to a discussion of the laws as they stand now.

ACKNOWLEDGMENTS

I wish to thank my family and colleagues who assisted me during the two years it took me to prepare this book for publication. My partner, Libby D. Salberg, reviewed each chapter as it was written and made many helpful comments and suggestions. Also, without her cooperation, I would not have been free to spend so much time away from my practice writing this book.

Karen Shackman and Malin Blomqvist, who typed and proofread every page of the manuscript two or three times, deserve my admiration and gratitude.

I am especially indebted to Professor John Tebbel for his expert assistance and collaboration. Without his help, I would have been unable to bring this project to fruition.

My wife, Jessica, deserves special thanks for her patience and for her decision to temporarily set aside her own career to help me. My children, Rebecca and Jeremy, are to be congratulated for their forbearance during those long periods of time when I was writing and proofreading the manuscript rather than spending time with them.

HOWARD DAVID DEUTSCH
New York, 1983

CONTENTS

PART IV: SPECIAL CATEGORIES

PART V: TAXATION AND NATURALIZATION

APPENDIXES

FOREWORD

The United States of America is generally held to be the land of opportunity. It is a haven where dreams are realised and ambitions fulfilled. A free country where all men are equal.

Entering the United States, however, is no simple matter, whether for the immigrant or for the casual visitor or businessman. Immigration rules are necessarily tough and the business of obtaining temporary or permanent visas for the United States is a procedure fraught with complexity and red tape.

GETTING INTO AMERICA is a practical handbook to the problems of entry into the United States, based upon the author's expert knowledge of immigration law. This book can help in two ways: directly, should the reader seek to enter for one of the recognised purposes—business, holiday, study, long-term residence etc.; indirectly, by describing in concrete

terms the obstacles and demands that must be encountered
in all immigration including that across the frontiers of
Europe.

As GETTING INTO AMERICA indicates, movement
across the frontiers of the United States can range from
sneaking across the borders to legal entry for business or
pleasure or for longer periods of study. Whether coming to
America as a migrant worker under contract or with the aim
of achieving permanent residence symbolised by the coveted
"green card", different problems arise.

Enter illegally at your own risk! Forgery of documents may
result in prosecution, working as an illegal entrant could
mean deportation, and the phoney marriage to a national for
the purpose of securing a visa can entail its own complications. GETTING INTO AMERICA advocates honest
entry, suggesting short-cuts round the lengthy immigration
process which do not resort to bribery or fraud. Obtaining a
work permit involves establishing into which of the preferred
categories one falls and whether any special conditions are
attached to this, as for manual workers, engineers, doctors,
domestics, businessmen, students. In the case of someone
who is unwilling or unable to return to his country of origin
because of a well-founded fear of prosecution or ill-treatment
it may be possible to obtain refugee status; however, the circumstances permitting this are narrowly defined and restricted to the most urgent of cases, usually political. Should a
prolonged, even permanent residence be secured, the reunification of the family becomes a primary concern. Practice
varies as to who and how many qualify as "family", and the
criteria are necessarily harsh.

The author, Howard Deutsch, addresses himself to each of
these questions and many others in turn, illustrating his
material with samples of numerous official forms and documents which can be enough to baffle even the most intelligent
and worldly-wise of applicants. He does not pretend that
application for entry to the United States is a simple process,
nor that it is always concluded satisfactorily. In many cases a

reassessment of one's goals and status may be advisable, particularly in the case of the political refugee.

Even in this most democratic of countries—a melting-pot of different races and religions—prejudice is rife. Government officials are not immune to the current of resentment against the unchecked flux of immigrants, to the feeling that if allowed to continue without stricter controls, it could lower the standard of living of those already in America.

This said, fifty million people from all over the world will enter the United States each year on temporary visas. Many of them will embark on the process of achieving permanent residence after they arrive; a process which may take years to complete. The purpose of this handbook is to help them fulfil their ambition quickly and painlessly, to ease the process as far as possible. Written with the uninitiated layman in mind, it is lucid, comprehensive and always accessible—an invaluable work of reference not only for the unsuspecting first-time applicant, but also for all those, government officials and lawyers alike, whose task it is to implement the business of "getting into America".

Professor Sir James Fawcett
President of the European Commission on
Human Rights
1972–1981

INTRODUCTION

For millions of people throughout the world, the United States of America represents the land of dreams fulfilled, a country of great wealth and opportunity. Those of us fortunate enough to live here sometimes forget that many in the world would give almost anything to trade places with us. But like most other countries, the United States has rules and regulations that determine who may enter, for how long, and under what conditions. It's well known that our immigration rules are very tough, and so the desires of many of those who want to come here are often not realized.

As a lawyer, I've helped thousands of foreigners enter this country. I have shared the frustrations of my clients in dealing with complicated rules, with changing regulations, with interlocking bureaucracies, and sometimes with prejudice and ignorance on the part of those who administer the immigration laws. But I've also been surprised and encouraged by many cases of kindness and generosity among some of these officials.

I have found that a thorough understanding of immigration law plays only a small part in the successful outcome of many cases; often, it's more important to find out what actually works, rather than what is written.

In this volume I intend to give you practical solutions to the problems many of you have now or may encounter as you try to unravel the difficulties of getting into America. The book is intended not only for those who want to enter the United States permanently, or who want to become citizens, but also to help those who want to come here for business, study, pleasure, or any other purpose besides permanent residence. Many readers will want the information so they can help others—relatives, friends, clients, employees—and some will simply be trying to understand all the rules so they can accomplish their own immigration goals, whatever they may be.

To put it plainly, this book tells you how to get here and how to stay here if you want to. As you'll see soon enough, that isn't always easy to do. After you've finished reading, you may find you'll have to alter your goals to conform to what is possible. But at the least, I hope to explain to you how you can make the process of entry, immigration, and possibly naturalization relatively painless.

It is not an easy subject. The U.S. government isn't exempt from failings that are common to governments elsewhere in the world. The immigration laws themselves are sometimes confusing, often illogical, and generally outdated. Worse, the governmental machinery that administers the laws is grotesquely confused, under-staffed, and supplied with its share of ill-informed, often prejudiced people. As we all know, corruption exists in governments everywhere, and it exists here, too. All these factors further complicate the immigration process.

Nevertheless, millions of foreigners still want to come here. Fifty million people a year arrive just to visit, and more than three hundred thousand come annually to stay. These figures account only for legal immigration. No one knows how many aliens sneak into American illegally every year, but some estimates run to hundreds of thousands, and the figures may actually be higher.

Clearly, getting into America is different from getting into any other country. For a great many people, coming to America and staying here is not only the realization of a dream, but it can be a matter of desperation as well. That's especially true for those trying to avoid starvation or political persecution, and for those who are victims of war.

As a specialist in immigration and international law, I've seen all kinds of people in my office, and I have come to know many of them well. I know what successful immigration means to them, and I've learned that it isn't a subject to be approached casually. So the first questions I ask a prospective client are "What do you want to accomplish?" and "What are your goals?" This book is organized to answer these questions.

At the very beginning of the book, I'll give you an insight into the system with which we must deal—primarily, the Immigration and Naturalization Service, and other government agencies, the State Department, and the Department of Labor. I won't pretend that the system is either benevolent or fair, but it *is* the system within which you and I will have to work. I'll tell you something about the history of immigration and naturalization laws. After that, I'll introduce you to the individual government agencies involved and provide you with a bird's-eye view of how the system works.

From your standpoint, it would be nice if I could tell you that you won't need a lawyer to accomplish your objectives, but I have to say honestly that this isn't always the case. Often a lawyer *is* required, and so I've devoted chapter 2 to working with an attorney and the difficulties you are both likely to encounter. There are circumstances, however, in which you won't need a lawyer, and I'll describe these, too.

Everyone who wants to get into America, for whatever purpose, must have permission from the government to enter the United States. That permission results in a visa. Most people aren't aware that the word "visa" applies not only to temporary entry but also to permanent residence. A temporary, or nonimmigrant, visa (the words are interchangeable) is the red-white-and-blue stamp in your passport or travel document. A permanent resident visa is a group of documents authorizing permanent residence in the

United States. Nearly everyone who wants to come here, however, must first have a temporary visa. Consequently, I'll tell you what you need to know about the different types of temporary visas before I begin to explain how to apply for permanent residence.

Some temporary visas give permission to remain in the United States for a long time, perhaps as much as ten years. Other temporary visas, however, may permit a visitor to stay only for a day. Yet both are described as nonimmigrant, which is confusing and misleading to many people. In part 2 of the book, I'll explain this apparent contradiction.

Many—perhaps most—of the people who think of coming to America for a limited period eventually want to stay on permanently. Some authorities estimate that between six and twelve million illegal aliens are living in this country right now. Everyone who deals with immigrants knows that, and I'm well aware that many people who will read this book intend to use the temporary visa as a stepping stone toward permanent residence. Quite a few may even be thinking about entering illegally. Part 3 of this book is for those of you who wish to stay in this country permanently.

After I've explained the subject of permanent residence in its several forms, I'll talk about specific kinds of immigrants and nonimmigrants who have special problems—problems so broad in scope and so common that they deserve to be discussed individually. I will also devote a chapter to the problems of taxation faced by foreigners intending to come to America. And in the final chapter, when I discuss the subject of naturalization, I'll cover most of the rules and regulations, and the pros and cons, of obtaining American citizenship.

Immigration law is a complicated field, and the rules and regulations covering it are essentially exclusionary. Consequently, many people who want to immigrate believe at the outset that they will be unsuccessful. That's why so many resort to illegal measures, with a resulting chain of risk and corruption. A good deal of the corruption occurs because some aliens, in a desperate desire to obtain a "Green Card," or resident alien visa, are willing to pay an extremely high price, in money and personal safety, to get it. The Green Card—it's now white—is proof that you're a permanent resident of the United States. The abuse thus fostered is greater than many American authorities want to admit. Over the years, government officials, immigration lawyers, and the petitioners themselves have been implicated.

It's no secret that most of the people who abuse the laws get away with it, but there are severe penalties for such violations, and I intend to spell them out.

Early in my practice, I learned a valuable lesson that may help you avoid errors leading to frustration and, in extreme situations, to illegality. The lesson is that everything you do and everything you say during the immigration process becomes part of a record, which will be very difficult to eradicate later on. Every time you fill out an immigration form, then, remember that the information you provide may have consequences years later.

Unfortunately, the immigration process is littered with forms and documents. If you're applying for a nonimmigrant visa, your first step will be to fill out a nonimmigrant visa form and file it with an American embassy or consulate somewhere in the world. This form immediately becomes part of your permanent record. If you make false or misleading statements on it, it's possible they will come back to haunt you in the future.

As I've observed earlier, you may begin the immigration process out of a simple desire to visit the United States, and later on change your mind about becoming a resident. That's why it's necessary to fill out with great care and discretion every form you encounter. Needless to say, you must be truthful. You must also be wise enough to understand that bureaucracies deal badly with too much information, so don't write or say more than is absolutely necessary to answer the questions asked.

Since the United States is viewed increasingly as a haven—a place where people can invest their money, advance their careers, and fulfill their dreams—it has also become clear that the American government can't let in everyone who wants to come here. It's also understandable that Americans want to protect what they have, especially in a time of economic trouble and high unemployment. Many Americans worry that the country can't indefinitely continue to absorb large numbers of immigrants, some of whom may take jobs from American citizens or become public charges. They feel that continued immigration will lower the living standard of those already established here—paradoxically, the same standard the immigrants want to achieve for themselves.

Immigration officials themselves aren't immune to some of these feelings. It may be unfair and unjust, but it's a fact that such prejudices may sometimes affect the outcome of immigration applications. The prejudices are directed against the poor, for the most part, but what about the affluent? What about immigrants who come to the United States with a great deal of money, or temporary residents who want to invest here, to build businesses that will provide jobs for Americans? You might think the Immigration Service would welcome them with open arms. But that is not the case. Rich and poor alike, it appears, are affected by prejudice, and if there is any equality involved, it is in the fact that they're affected in about equal measure.

My goal is to help people get into this country, and I believe that the best way to avoid the pitfalls on the road to residence is to come to a clear understanding of the immigration law and of the people who administer it. In this book, I intend to provide you with that understanding. If what you're trying to do is illegal, I'll tell you so, and advise you what the risks are and what may happen if you're caught. But more important, this book can guide you through some perfectly legal shortcuts that you can take that may save you thousands of dollars and years of waiting.

Unfortunately, it won't be possible to address everyone's problems in this book; the subject is simply too large. I'll confine myself, then, to discussing those matters that affect the majority of readers, and I'm confident that most of your questions will be answered.

PART I

THE IMMIGRATION PROCESS

A GENERAL
VIEW OF
IMMIGRATION

I wrote this book to better your chances for success when you apply for American residence (Green Cards), visas, and citizenship. Competition for these objectives is sometimes stiff. The subject of immigration, which deals not only with residence, but with temporary visas and citizenship as well, often creates from your point of view an adversary relationship. Consequently, it's important to know as much as possible about your adversary, and about who or what may stand in the way of getting what you want.

This chapter discusses three subjects, each one of which is basic to a proper understanding of what you'll be reading later in this book:

1. A history of immigration in America.
2. Government departments.
3. How the immigration law operates.

Many of you will bring strong emotions to the reading of this book. Don't let them blind you to the reality that the United States government, like most (if not all) others, is usually insensitive to individual cases of suffering and abuse.

A HISTORY OF IMMIGRATION IN AMERICA

America has always been a nation of immigrants. Since the fifteenth century, people have been coming here from all over the world. Each new wave of immigration invited the suspicion and fear of those already here. Yet all these immigrants, taken together, built the United States and together made it what it is. Only when we understand this paradox can we also understand the problems immigrants face in getting into America today.

The very first immigrants were a mixed bag of landowners, slaves, merchants, indentured servants, victims of religious persecution, and fortune seekers. After the Founding Fathers devised the Constitution, a grass-roots revolt in the ratifying conventions compelled them to add a Bill of Rights. Yet neither the Constitution nor the Bill of Rights made any distinction between citizens and noncitizens.

In the nineteenth century, white, Anglo-Saxon Protestant politicians and businessmen, descended from the original settlers, controlled the country. They regarded most immigrants as cheap labor, doing the worst jobs for the lowest wages. While some states passed laws restricting their entry, the federal government recognized the country's tremendous need for such laborers.

From 1860 to 1920, more than twenty-eight million immigrants arrived in America. For many of these people, life became a deadly irony. It was clear that immigrants were absolutely essential to the expanding economy, but it was equally clear that their presence was producing wave after wave of anti-immigrant hysteria.

In response to this conflict, Congress enacted the first general immigration law in 1882. It provided for a head tax of fifty cents per immigrant, to be collected by the Treasury Department, which regulated immigration at that time. Moreover, "idiots, lunatics, convicts, and persons likely to become public charges" were barred from entering the country.

In 1888 another federal law was enacted that placed a limit on the length of time alien workers could stay in America. Under the terms of the law, alien contract workers had to be deported within a year after their entry. With one hand the government extended a carrot—the opportunity to work for low wages in the land of liberty—and with the other it held a stick that beat the workers back home again before they could establish roots.

Congress went on to enact even more restrictive legislation. In 1891 it passed a general immigration bill providing for the exclusion of "paupers" and all aliens who had come in illegally. "Anarchists" were added to the list of those excluded by a law of 1903, along with others, and in 1907 the list was again expanded to include people suffering from mental or physical conditions that might affect their ability to earn a living.

Nevertheless, between 1900 and 1910, there began a new wave of immigration from southern and eastern Europe. These people were not as easily assimilated as earlier arrivals, and consequently there were demands for further restrictions. The method chosen was a literacy test.

Another immigration law was enacted in 1917, with Congress overriding President Wilson's veto. It was a comprehensive law that went well beyond literacy tests to codify all the previous kinds of excludable immigrants and to create what was called euphemistically an "Asiatic Barred Zone," the effect of which was to exclude most Asians from the United States. Not until 1952 did Japanese immigrants become eligible for American citizenship.

In the depression that followed the First World War there were renewed demands for anti-immigration laws to protect jobs from foreigners. These demands resulted in the notorious Quota Act of 1921, a law that set up a system limiting the annual immigration of any nationality to 3 percent of the number of such people already in the United States in 1910. The purpose of the law was clear enough. Behind the figures was the intent to preserve northern and western European preponderance in the nation's composition. Great Britain, for example, had only 2 percent of the world's population, but it got 43 percent of the quota. The language of subsequent quota laws made it plain that the lawmakers considered immigrants from southern and eastern Europe to be innately inferior.

The quota system was reinforced by a new law in 1924, one that established annual quotas for every nationality group, based on the number of people of any particular national origin who were in the country as of 1920; at the same time, it continued the total exclusion of Asians and residents of the Pacific islands. These laws became hardy survivors of changing times: exclusion on racial grounds was not abolished until 1952. The quota system, as established in 1924, did not come to an end until 1968, and variations of it remained in force into the 1970s.

The cumulative effect of these laws was to curtail sharply the increasing flow of immigrants, which had gone on relatively unimpeded for a century. The figures told the story. Between 1931 and 1940, only 0.5 million people immigrated to the United States; 8.8 million had come between 1901 and 1910, and 5.7 million between 1911 and 1920. After 1930, there were some years when there were more people leaving the United States than entering it.

A new surge of anti-immigration feeling occurred in 1940, when the Alien Registration Act added "subversive" people to those who could be excluded and for the first time required registration and fingerprinting of all aliens in the United States, or those who were trying to come in as immigrants. There were also changes in the administration of the immigration law. What until 1906 had been the province of the Treasury Department subsequently came under the wing of the Department of Labor and, in 1940, was passed on to the Department of Justice.

In the McCarthy era, several bills were passed affecting immigration policy. Through the Internal Security Act of 1950, another echo of earlier legislation, noncitizens who were considered "politically dangerous" to national security could be excluded or deported. Then, in 1952, the Immigration and Nationality Act was again completely revised. This bill, better known as the McCarran-Walter Act, retained the national origins quota, established severe grounds for exclusion and deportation, and placed serious restrictions on available equitable relief in hardship cases. President Truman vetoed it, but his veto was overridden by Congress and the law passed.

Various technical changes were made in the immigration laws between 1954 and 1962. Then, in 1965, Congress broke new ground with a law that abolished the national origins quota system and ended restrictions on Asians. The changes made further distinctions as to place of birth, however. Those born in the Western Hemisphere were given special quotas of 120,000 annually, and those in the Eastern Hemisphere 170,000. It was the first time in our history that numerical restrictions had been placed on Western Hemisphere immigrants.

This 1965 act established the preference system, intended to make it easier for relatives of American citizens and residents to enter. It also assisted those who had professional qualifications, as well as workers whose skills were in short supply in the United States.

During the past several years, there have been repeated attempts on the part of Congress to change the immigration law. To date, none of these attempts have been successful, and even though there are many in Congress who are discouraged about the prospects for the passage of a new law, it is certainly my belief that before too long one will be passed. One of the key components of the bills that have been introduced to date has been the promise of amnesty to illegal aliens. The hopes for the passage of an amnesty bill have misguided many into the erroneous belief that they should therefore delay their attempts to become legal in favor of waiting for the bill to pass. However, when I had a look at the last version of the bill that failed some months ago, it was clear that only a quarter of a million out of the many millions of illegal aliens in the United States would have actually benefited from the proposed amnesty.

GOVERNMENT DEPARTMENTS

The immigration and visa situation in the United States is complicated to an undue extent by the fact that it is administered by many different branches of government. Too often they don't cooperate, and sometimes the rules that govern one contradict the rules of the other.

To some extent, this conglomeration of governmental agencies and departments affecting the immigration process results from one of America's greatest strengths—the separation of powers. This concept protects one branch of government from abuse by the others, and it has been widely imitated in other modern democracies. Yet the system has defects, one of them being confusion of purposes and methods.

Not all the inconsistencies result from a lack of intergovernmental coordination. Sometimes our government may issue orders to consulates and embassies because of requests and directives issued by the host government. Some countries, for example, are afraid that if their highly trained specialists are able to obtain visas easily that would permit them to work in the United States, many would never return. Consequently, these governments may suggest to ours that our embassies be particularly strict when it comes to issuing visas. Sometimes when I've asked consuls to explain a harsh decision, they have told me that they were operating under State Department directives, resulting from a concern expressed by the host government.

Let's take a look at the principal branches of government that administer our complex immigration laws. You'll certainly encounter most or all of them in your effort to get into America. The agencies are:

1. The Department of State, and its embassies and consulates around the world.
2. The Immigration and Naturalization Service, a branch of the United States Department of Justice. (I'll often refer to it subsequently by its initials, INS.)
3. The United States Department of Labor.

There are also other bureaucracies you may encounter, such as the Department of Health and Human Resources, or labor unions. I'll consider the role of the former in the chapter about doctors and of the latter where relevant.

The Department of State

For most prospective immigrants, the immigration process begins in a U.S. consulate or embassy. Almost all visas, whether temporary or permanent, are granted there initially. Interested applicants should check with the embassy or consulate closest to their place of residence to establish where, and to whom, their applications should be made.

It's important to know, at the start, that the treatment you get from a consulate or embassy will vary widely from one country to another, and from one consulate or embassy to another. Even within an individual consulate or embassy the treatment you get may vary widely from one official to another.

To cite an extreme example of these variations, it's unfortunately true that applications for temporary visas from residents of certain Central American and South American countries are viewed with suspicion and sometimes with derision. That's because our representatives in those countries don't believe for a minute that applicants for temporary visas will leave America once they get into it. That's also true for Israel and, during the summer months, for Sweden as well. When young girls from Sweden apply for temporary visas during the summer, our government believes they intend to stay and work as housekeepers and child attendants.

The Immigration and Naturalization Service

This is often referred to as the Immigration Service, or the INS, and it's part of the Justice Department. As with most federal governmental organizations, the Service's rules apply uniformly across the United States, regardless of which state you may happen to be in. Consequently, lawyers who practice immigration law can do so in any state, without regard to where they've been licensed. Applicants, however, don't enjoy such benefits of uniformity, so in your dealings with the Service, don't expect to be treated with any degree of consistency. In New York, Miami, Los Angeles, or any other city that is overcrowded and has a large alien population, the offices of the Immigration Service are understaffed and more or less demoralized. They simply can't do the job they've been hired to do. As a result, staff members are often irritable, unfriendly, even hostile—and they frequently lose applications. In smaller cities, however, you will usually get prompt responses to your applications. It's worth mentioning that this difference of response time among cities can sometimes be used to your advantage, if you're in a position to choose your place of filing.

There's one common denominator, however. When an immigration application of any kind is filed in the United States, it will be handled by the Immigration Service, and that applies to both immigrant and nonimmigrant matters. In appendix 1 you'll find a list of every Immigration Service district office in America, with relevant addresses.

All local Immigration Service offices have equal power. If you believe that you (or your application) have been treated unfairly, you will sometimes have recourse in the form of an appeal to a regional office of the Service. These regional offices are listed in appendix 2. There is also the option of a final appeal to the Board of Immigration Appeals in Washington. Such appeals, however, should be handled only by competent professionals, whose help you would be well advised to seek.

It may be worth mentioning that the federal court system is also available to you if you think the Service hasn't dealt fairly with your application, even at the highest level. But again, using the federal courts should be the work of a lawyer.

The Department of Labor

Like State and Justice, this department is a primary branch of government. In 1984, as this book is published, it is an unhappy branch as far as immigration is concerned because of the large number of people who are unemployed in America. Naturally, that fact has a negative impact on applications made by aliens who want permission to work in the United States.

Approval by this department is essential to at least one nonimmigrant visa category, the H-2, or temporary work permit. If the Labor Department says yes, you can be confident that you will ultimately prevail; but if it refuses, you have almost no chance at all.

If immigration is what you want, you'll find that a large number of those who immigrate do so on the basis of permission granted by the Department of Labor to work here permanently. This permission takes the form of a labor certification.

Although the Department of Labor's headquarters are in Washington, your application for certification will usually not be processed there. The department has offices in every state, and these state offices have branch offices in many cities, so your application will be filed initially in one of these branch offices.

In my experience, there is much less prejudice in the Labor Department than in the other departments I have discussed. Its people are both competent and conscientious. That doesn't mean they work rapidly. As always, there are more applications than an overworked staff can handle. But it helps to know that if there's any difficulty about your application, it will usually be for good reason and not the result of prejudice or sloppy handling.

HOW THE IMMIGRATION LAW OPERATES

In general, aliens who make application for any benefit under the immigration and naturalization laws fall into two categories: immigrants and nonimmigrants. Immigrants are people who want to come here permanently. Nonimmigrants are those who can prove they're coming here for a temporary stay. Our immigration system nevertheless assumes that everyone wants to come here permanently, because experience has shown that this is nearly always the case. Consequently, if you want a temporary visa, you'll have to prove to an immigration official that you *don't* want to come here permanently. Otherwise, it will be assumed that you don't really intend to leave. This is true not only at American ports of entry, but also when you apply for a temporary visa at an embassy or a consulate abroad.

Most immigrants begin as nonimmigrants, so it makes sense to talk about that category first.

Nonimmigrants

These are people entering the United States for a temporary stay. If you can prove such an intention to an official of the government when you apply for a visa, and later when you enter the United States, you'll be admitted for a specific period of time. Most nonimmigrant visas, such as the B-2, or visitor's visa, are applied for at an American embassy or consulate in the applicant's country of residence.

Certain kinds of nonimmigrant visas can be applied for only in the United States, however, and these are mostly visas that permit either study or work. After an application is filed, in the city where the job or study is to take place, the alien waits for approval, which will be sent to the embassy or consulate abroad in the country where the applicant is waiting.

For other nonimmigrant visas, there is no requirement that an application be made in the United States. To secure such visas, it's necessary for the alien to apply at an American embassy or consulate in the country where he or she is living.

Temporary visas will be covered in part 2 of this book.

Permanent Residence

Many people who want the Green Card never set foot in this country until they're granted permission to live here permanently. These people are probably in the minority, however. Most would-be United States residents first enter the country on a temporary visa of some kind and then begin the process of making application for permanent residence. It's often possible for them to change their status while they're here, a process called "adjustment of status," which I'll cover later.

A major obstacle to permanent residence is the quota and preference system. This is a system regulated overall by the number of nonresident aliens permitted to immigrate to the United States in any calendar year. Some categories of people are exempt from the quota, especially immediate relatives of United States citizens. Immigrants subject to numerical limitations are divided into categories, each one of which is given a certain percentage of the quota numbers available. These categories are known as "preferences," and I'll explain them later.

Getting a quota number may be difficult for those who come

from certain countries that have exceeded the overall number of people who can immigrate to the United States in any one year. The number is twenty thousand. For certain categories of aliens in certain countries, this benchmark may already have been exceeded by the time you apply. In appendix 3 you'll find a typical preference quota sheet, which explains how the system works. If you need a quota number, you can get one only if your immigration petition has already been approved. Although its effect comes later, the quota system must be kept in mind from the beginning, because the projected waiting time for any category and for any individual may indeed be a factor in how you or your attorney approach the case. Permanent residence will be covered in detail in part 3 of this book.

Naturalization

Naturalization is the ultimate goal for many of those who dream of coming to America. The process is mechanically so easy that no elaboration here is required. The essential facts will be covered in part 5 of this book.

I should say at this stage that United States immigration laws may well change in the future. For the purposes of this book, however, we will confine ourselves to the current laws.

2

YOUR ATTORNEY

During the last ten years, the number of lawyers in the United States who specialize in immigration matters has increased tremendously. There is at least one immigration lawyer in nearly every large city and hundreds of them in such places as Los Angeles, New York, San Francisco, Houston, Dallas, Miami, and Chicago. Many of these attorneys have highly specialized practices, concentrating on a particular kind of alien. Many deal primarily with matters concerning the immigration services, as opposed to those arising before a consulate or embassy abroad.

This increase in the number of immigration lawyers can be attributed to several factors. A primary reason is that more people than ever before want to get into America. There are millions of foreigners throughout the world besieging American embassies and consulates, especially during the summer months, requesting U.S. visas. When these people need help, they often seek the advice of lawyers.

The immigration process used to be much simpler. I remember

when it was possible to go through the entire process, from labor certification to Green Card issuance, in less than two months. Now, for some immigrants, the same procedure can take years. Partly that's because quotas that were once open are now either closed or severely backlogged. Moreover, the laws have become much tougher and more complex.

As the number of lawyers specializing in immigration law has increased, there has also been a change in their reputation. Let me be perfectly blunt. In the legal profession it's no secret that, until recently, immigration attorneys were often looked down upon by other lawyers. Their practices were frequently criticized, sometimes even investigated.

A sharp improvement is evident today. The caliber of lawyers attracted to this kind of practice has risen dramatically. Not only have their personal ethics and morality improved, but their educational background is now better as well. To a large extent, this change is a response to the nature of new immigration and to a toughening of the laws. Lawyers now need to apply stricter standards to themselves than they did before, and they do. This rise in quality has also meant a rise in legal fees.

Since your attorney may be an integral part of what you can and can't accomplish, I think it's important to tell you something about what you can expect to encounter when you bring your immigration problem to a lawyer.

Your lawyer is not infallible. Often that's not clear to immigrants who come from countries where an attorney can act as an intermediary between a citizen and the government, and to some extent, at least, may give the impression that he can guarantee a result. Sometimes that result is based on bribery, and at other times on realities that may exist in another country but not in the United States.

So let's be absolutely clear about it. Your lawyer can't guarantee that any application you file will be approved. He can make predictions based on his years of experience in similar cases, and he may even be able to tell you what your chances of success are; but if he guarantees the success of a particular application—worse, if he puts it in writing—you can be sure he is either a fool or dishonest.

Your lawyer can and will make mistakes occasionally. It would be foolish to expect anything else. You have a right to expect one thing from him, however—honesty. He should tell you what's happening *as* it's happening, when you ask him. If he doesn't, you have a legitimate right to complain.

Many lawyers have a large clientele, and some charge lower legal fees than others based on the hope of relatively little interaction between them and the client. If you go to such an office, you can't expect a great deal of conversation. You can and should ask the attorney you employ, in advance, whether or not he's in a position to answer frequent questions, and perhaps even to hold your hand, figuratively speaking, if you think it's necessary. An honest lawyer will tell you frankly whether or not this fits in with his practice. If it doesn't, he can offer you his services with the agreement that you'll be billed for the extra time you take, or on any other basis that is mutually agreeable.

The majority of immigration lawyers in this country tend to quote fixed fees for particular categories of services. Most attorneys in America charge by the hour, so when one gives you a price for a particular service, he is to some extent gambling. If the matter goes smoothly, and the attorney spends less time than he anticipated, he comes out ahead. But if the case takes more time than he thought it would, he can lose.

When an attorney or a law firm has thousands of clients, the gamble undoubtedly balances out in the end. In general, you'll find that the attorney will make far more money by charging on a fixed-fee basis rather than by the hour. It's the practice of almost all lawyers, however, even those who charge fixed fees, to limit the stated fee to the normal work performed in the course of an application. This means that if the application is denied and an appeal is required, the client will be billed extra.

A client can also expect to pay for all disbursements, meaning all out-of-pocket costs, such as the expense of phone calls, document reproduction, travel, messengers, couriers, and so on. When attorneys quote a fee for a particular service, they should be quick to point out that the figure is usually a minimum and not necessarily a maximum. Many immigrants come from places where attorneys charge on a different basis than is done in America. Consequently, it's important for foreigners who employ American lawyers to ask questions about their fee practices.

Some attorneys use retainer agreements, as they're called, which specify a fee for a particular service. While such agreements are not in common use among American lawyers, they *are* sometimes used by those who practice immigration law. My firm usually doesn't use retainer agreements. I explain to a client that essentially he's paying me by the hour, with a floor on what can be paid, but not necessarily a ceiling. We do say to all our clients, however, that in the great majority of cases the floor is, in fact, what will be paid eventually.

When you're dealing with an attorney, or with a firm of lawyers, remember that some firms specialize in a particular kind of immigration law. Try to find out what that specialty is, because if the firm's clients have problems different from yours, you may be disappointed.

You must be open with your attorney and tell him what you expect for the money you pay him. You're entitled to ask if he's prepared to respond to your various requirements. But don't forget that, regardless of the deal you make with him, if you call your lawyer every day, perhaps twice a day, and take a great deal of his time, you must be prepared to pay him for the time he spends.

Often in my practice, I've heard clients tell me that their friends had similar cases that went better, or went differently, or went faster. Sometimes these stories may be true, but I've found that most of the time what the client repeats to me as the experiences of his friends isn't exactly correct. A friend may tell you what has happened to him, but he will neglect to add that his case was based on an entirely different set of facts.

If you do hire a professional to assist you, you'll have to depend on his good will and honesty to a certain extent. If you believe everything your friends tell you and mistrust your professional adviser, you are probably doing yourself a disservice—unless, of course, you have reason to suspect that your lawyer has not been honest with you, or that he's incompetent.

A lawyer is not always needed. One of the purposes of this book is to teach you how to get what you want without any help, and that's often possible. Sometimes, however, it may be possible but inadvisable, and sometimes it may even be foolish. In the chapters that follow, I'll be careful to point out when it's possible to avoid using a lawyer, and when not.

PART II

NONIMMIGRANT VISAS

3

NONIMMIGRANT VISAS: GENERAL INFORMATION AND BACKGROUND

Most people who come to the United States need a temporary or nonimmigrant visa (the terms are interchangeable), no matter what their ultimate aim may be. In fact, unless you're an American citizen or a permanent resident, or unless you're one of a small number of exceptions, it's impossible to get into this country without such a visa. Appendix 4 is a table identifying and describing all these visas. I'll discuss each one individually in chapter 4.

It's common knowledge that only a relatively small number of people can become residents of the United States in any one year, but many believe mistakenly that the same restriction applies to everyone wanting to enter the country. It isn't so. There is no limit to the number of temporary visas that can be issued.

Definite rules and regulations set forth the kinds of such visas that can be issued. Fourteen major categories are listed, and within most of them there are several subdivisions that must be considered almost as individual visa categories. The criteria applied to issuing them are established in immigration law, but unfortunately these laws are not free of the confusion and inconsistency so characteristic of immigration in general.

Immigration law presumes that in the absence of positive evidence that you don't intend to remain in the United States permanently, it will be assumed that your intention is *not* to leave. This can be a very damaging presumption, because if a consular official is convinced you intend to stay permanently, he cannot and will not give you a nonimmigrant visa, sometimes without any explanation.

Years ago, when I first encountered this presumption, I was extremely surprised, because, like everyone else, I had been educated to believe that the American legal system, based on English law, presumes everyone to be innocent unless proven guilty. Immigration law seems to start from the opposite point of view, and I have come to believe that this presumption of guilt is one of the basic causes of the difficulties aliens encounter when they have to deal with the State Department and the various branches of the Immigration Service.

When most people think of a temporary visa, they have in mind a tourist visa, the common B-2, which tourists use to visit the United States. In fact, however, there are temporary visas that can be issued for a wide variety of purposes, such as for study or investment. Applicants are often surprised to learn that there are people who stay in the United States legally for many years on a temporary visa.

Let's take a closer look at this subject. Temporary visas are issued by the Department of State, acting through its embassies and consulates all over the world. Physically, the temporary visa is no more than a stamp placed in a passport or other travel document, giving you the right to enter the United States. The visa will be valid for a stated period, or indefinitely, meaning for the life of the passport. Sometimes the stamp, or visa, gives the holder of the passport the right to enter the United States one or more times. Applicants who are lucky get permission for multiple entries—that means for as many entries as the applicant wishes to make during the visa's period of validity. Some consuls restrict the visa to only one entry during its lifetime.

The visa granted doesn't automatically guarantee that the holder will be entitled to enter the United States. Entry is a two-part process. First, the alien must apply for and obtain a temporary visa, and then he will be examined by an immigration inspector at the point where he enters the United States.

It often comes as a surprise to aliens that some are turned away at the border. This may occur for a variety of reasons. Sometimes the immigration inspector doesn't believe the visa holder will be using it for its designated purpose. He has the authority to search your personal effects, and he may find something he thinks is incriminating—for example, a letter accepting employment, advertisements for jobs clipped from newspapers, or personal letters indicating another purpose for entering. If you refuse to submit to this search, the inspector has the right to refuse entry.

Acting on nothing more than his instinct, an inspector may conclude that a particular alien is about to work in the United States without permission, or is not likely to leave after the period of his allowed entry expires. Later in this chapter I'll explain how to deal with such a contingency.

When an alien—other than most Canadians or Mexicans—is admitted, he is usually given a white rectangular card known as Form I-94 (you'll find it reproduced in appendix 5). This form is an arrival-departure record, containing on its face the date of entry into the United States, the visa status under which the alien is admitted, and the period of time he is allowed to remain. Sometimes nonimmigrant status isn't designated, but in most cases it is. This I-94 is a valuable document that is necessary for most subsequent immigration procedures. Do not lose it.

It's important for the alien not to exceed the period of stay allotted to him. Nevertheless, it's well known that millions of those who legally enter the country stay longer than they're permitted. These people are known as overstays and become illegal aliens from the moment this label attaches to them. As I noted earlier, the number of illegals is anywhere from six to twelve million.

Many immigration procedures, such as change of status from one nonimmigrant category to another, require that the alien be legally in the United States at the time the status change application is made. Aliens who want to stay in America temporarily have a wide variety of options. Consequently, intelligent use of the appropriate visa is the best guarantee of staying within the law and accomplishing whatever future goals you may have, such as permanent residence.

Surprisingly, among the several categories of temporary visas, many permit work or study in one form or another. These visas usually require prior application to the Immigration Service or another organization by the prospective employer or school. When this permission is necessary, it usually must be applied for initially in the United States before the ultimate visa can be granted by the State Department. All this I'll discuss fully in chapter 4.

It's also important to understand that no matter which temporary visa you use to enter the United States initially, you can usually change from one to another after you're here. The procedure that makes this possible is known as an application to change nonimmigrant status. You accomplish this by applying to the Immigration Service in the city nearest to where you're living. This kind of changing isn't universally approved within the Immigration Service, and it's wise to remember that it isn't possible to use the device for every visa category. Just the same, it's an important maneuver to keep in mind.

APPLYING FOR A VISA WHEN NO APPLICATIONS IN AMERICA ARE REQUIRED AS A FIRST STEP

If the visa you're applying for doesn't require prior applications in the United States, either to the Immigration Service or to an educational or some other institution, the first step is to go to the American embassy or consulate nearest your home and obtain an application form known as Form 156 (see appendix 6). In the beginning, this application was designed for the visitor's visa, B-2, but now it's used for almost all nonimmigrant visas.

Fill out the form carefully, paying special attention to describing the purpose of your visit. A single passport-size photo, either in color or in black and white, must be attached. Take this form with your passport (which must be valid for at least an additional six months) and either mail the package or present it in person to the embassy or consulate nearest your home.

It's difficult to predict whether or not an interview for your temporary visa will be required. Often, when the application is made by mail, you'll simply get your visa in due course by return mail, but it's also possible that a consular official may request you to come down for an appointment. The same is true when you make the application for your visa in person: you may either be questioned when your turn comes or simply get your visa automatically.

If you're asked questions about your application, these will usually concern your purpose in coming to the United States. The consular official will try to make sure that you have enough money to accomplish your stated purpose and that you'll leave the United States when you're required to do so. Often the consul requires you to furnish proof that you have a job or a home to return to outside of America.

In countries where there's been a great deal of fraud in nonimmigrant visas, it's common to cross-examine aliens, and in such circumstances, it may be difficult to convince a consular official to grant a visa. In more routine circumstances, an interview may not even be required.

When an application for a temporary visa has to be made by an applicant who is not close to his home, it can usually be done at any American consulate or embassy where the alien happens to be. This process, called an out-of-district application, may take more time, however. The American officials may want information about the applicant from the embassy or consulate nearest his home, involving days of delay. An interview may also be required at the embassy or consulate where the application is being made, and after that, the visa will be either granted or denied. In some instances the consul may suspect that you've been turned down somewhere else, and that you've been looking for an easier port of entry—a practice known as "visa shopping"—with the idea of finding a sympathetic official. Recently, this has been particularly common among Iranians.

Most aliens will be familiar with the way visas are issued in their own countries. People in Israel or Brazil, for instance, know how difficult it is to get temporary American visas when they apply from their countries, unless the applicant happens to be a businessman with a record known to the American authorities. On the other hand, visas are much easier to obtain if you're English, French, or a national of any of most Western European countries.

In general, it can be said that for most people it isn't very difficult to get a temporary visa if no prior application or document is required from either the Immigration Service or some other organization in the United States. When this additional documentation is requested, however, the procedure is somewhat different and a little more complicated.

HOW TO APPLY FOR A VISA WHEN AMERICAN DOCUMENTS ARE REQUIRED

Certain visa categories, such as the H and L visas needed for temporary work or training in the United States, require prior application and a grant of permission from the Immigration Service. In the case of H-2, additional permission is required from the Labor Department. For J, F, and M visas, valid for study in the United States, documents are issued directly by educational institutions that have been accredited by the Immigration Service. Only these institutions are allowed to issue the relevant documents. As for the K visa, issued to alien fiancées and fiancés, application is made by the American citizen who wants to marry the alien, at the Immigration Service office nearest to his or her home.

Theoretically, whatever needs to be done in America to obtain the initial permission should be done by the person, institution, or organization requiring your entry. When the job, study, or proposed marriage in the United States is the legitimate reason for seeking entry, most of the work is usually done by whoever wants you: the person or institution will usually take care of any legal work required and push for the prompt issuing of documents you need to get your visa. Occasionally the situation is reversed, and it is the alien who is seeking to get in, with no particular help or enthusiasm from his contacts in America. In such a case, the alien is often required to do all the work and all the pushing, which probably means retaining a lawyer and paying his fees to see that everything that must be done is, in fact, done, and on time.

For example, I've seen many clients who come to the United States to visit schools where they might study in the future. If everything is taken care of while they're here, things usually go well. But when matters are left to friends or relatives in the United States after the alien goes home, he often finds later that nothing has been done. I remember one case in particular, a young man who came to America hoping his uncle would hire him. This presumably obliging relative assured him that all the paperwork would be taken care of promptly, but after the alien left, his letters weren't answered and his calls were not returned. Weeks later, he came back to the United States to arrange the paperwork, and, finding his uncle completely unhelpful, he had to look for another method of entry.

It's important, consequently, for every alien in this situation to assess correctly the sincerity of those who say they want to help. If that assessment is made shrewdly, without taking anything for granted, there will be fewer surprises and disappointments.

When approval in America is needed for particular visas, the procedure differs somewhat from case to case. Once the needed application is filed in the United States and the appropriate documents are granted, these papers are sent either directly to the consular official to whom the application for a visa is being made or to the applicant.

Remember, at the time you appear before the consul, your entire case will be reexamined by the consular official to make sure you have all the necessary qualifications for the particular visa you're there to pick up. The fact that the Immigration Service has already approved your application is no absolute guarantee that the consul will issue the required visa, so you should be familiar with your application and be ready to answer any relevant questions that may come up.

In most cases, the prior grant from the United States guarantees that the visa applicant will have little difficulty when he applies at the consulate. But this isn't invariably true. In Turkey, for example, consuls have been exposed to so much fraud that even when applications for work are granted by the Immigration Service, the consul may take special care to examine all the declarations made on the immigration forms filed in the United States. If even a minor inconsistency is found, rejection is often the result.

In Canada, the situation is very different. Canadians—whether citizens of Canada or Canadian-landed immigrants—are treated in an almost preferential manner in regard to temporary visas. They can present Form I-171C (Notice of Approval of Nonimmigrant Visa Petition; see appendix 14) directly to the immigration official at the airport, without first going to the local United States consul.

Some of these people may not need a visa at all. If you're one of them, you may simply carry the approval notice with you every time you enter the United States, and that will usually be enough to get you in.

This brings up an important point. From the beginning I've warned about the importance of consistency and the need for accuracy. Let me remind you again: don't put into a document what you can't prove. If you're required to prove something later on and can't do it, you may find yourself in needless trouble. Another means of avoiding trouble is to keep copies of *every* paper you fill out. That applies not only to all of your own documents, but also to the basic nonimmigrant visa application that you file for any ordinary visa. Like the others, this form becomes a part of your permanent record.

I recently saw a client from France who came into the United States on a temporary permit, an L visa, which requires, among other things, that the holder show that he is working for a foreign company in an executive or managerial capacity or that he at least has some specialized knowledge important to the company in the United States. In fact, this man was a senior executive, but his papers were filled out without much understanding of the law and without a great deal of care. His employers, who had prepared the papers themselves, discussed his great expertise in foreign sales but neglected to mention that he was an executive. The temporary visa was granted. Sometime later, the man wanted to get a Green Card, and he wanted it in a rush. But the sloppiness of his employer now served as a trap for him, because the Green Card would have been available to him quickly only if his employer had indicated that he was already an executive or manager before he had been transferred to the United States.

When I prepare an immigration case, I try to look at the future, not only at the present. I've learned to make sure that every form has been filled out with the ultimate goal in mind, and I try to resist a temptation to cut corners in order to attain a temporary goal more quickly.

Often people who eventually emigrate to the United States begin their contact with the immigration process out of no more than a simple desire to visit America. Quite often, they change their minds later and want to stay on a permanent basis. And that's why it's so necessary to fill out every form with great care and discretion, remembering that the document you complete innocently now may be compared with forms completed years later by an official who's looking for contradictions of facts. It's essential, therefore, to be truthful, needless to say. But you must also be wise enough to understand that bureaucracies deal badly with *too much* information. For example, if you make a statement about your business, say as little as you can and be prepared to prove later whatever you set down. Don't say or write anything more than the forms specifically demand.

I'm bringing up this issue now because, later in the book, I'll frequently be making the point that immigration is not a simple process. I often think of it as a game, but not a frivolous one by any means. There are winners and losers. If I've won more often than I've lost, it's because I've been cautious. When I file the first application in what I know may be the long process leading to residence and citizenship in the United States, I make sure that I can support every statement my clients make, and I expect my clients to cooperate with me and proceed with the same honesty, care, and accuracy that I devote to their affairs. It's absolutely essential for you to do the same in whatever dealings you have with a lawyer.

The various nonimmigrant visa categories are intended to define and regulate the purposes for which persons can enter the United States temporarily. When your visa is finally issued and stamped on your passport or whatever other travel document is recognized, you'll be permitted to present yourself for entry into the United States.

Sometimes aliens who apply for temporary visas ask that the permit (visa) issued to them not be stamped into their passports. Most people are unaware that it's possible to have visas stamped onto special pieces of paper that can be carried along with a passport and presented to immigration authorities at border points along the American borders.

Since a visa is often so hard to get, why should anyone make such a request? Iran provides a good example. After the revolution in that country, many Iranians were afraid that the passports issued to them by the Shah's government would be revoked by the Khomeini regime that succeeded it. Many of them took steps to acquire additional passports from places like Costa Rica and then requested that visas issued to them by American consular officials be placed on separate pieces of paper, so they would be free to use the passport of their choice. This practice of requesting a visa on a separate document should be used by those who know that it may be difficult for them to get visas because of their nationality or other special circumstances, and who therefore want to avoid the trauma of going through an embassy every time their passports expire. It should also be used when the presence of an American visa in a passport will cause difficulties in traveling to other countries. Occasionally a government may issue two passports to the same person, but that is not invariably true. Having an American visa on a separate piece of paper can solve many problems.

There's an interesting footnote to this practice. Visas dependent on the particular nationality of an alien applicant—E visas, for instance—are invalid automatically when that nationality is no longer in effect.

"Nationality" means that the alien is a citizen of a particular country and is able to demonstrate that fact to an American consular official. ("Citizenship" and "nationality" are used interchangeably in this book.) You may believe that simply because you were born in a specific country, you are entitled to claim the nationality of that country. But that is not invariably true, either in the United States or in other countries throughout the world. There are many exceptions to the rule that nationality is conferred automatically on those who are born in a particular country.

Sometimes your nationality may be in doubt simply because for some reason you're not able to get a passport from the country of which you are a national; that was true for many Iranians. In cases where an American consular official is in doubt, he may refuse to issue a visa if it depends on a particular nationality that can't be proven.

The mere fact that an alien is carrying a piece of paper that has

a visa stamp on it may not guarantee that he is, in fact, entitled
to it. Many aliens sophisticated enough to know the procedure,
however, assume correctly that most immigration officers at border points will take for granted the validity of the visa once it's
presented and won't bother to check on the *bona fides* of the alien's
nationality.

Before an alien enters this country, the U.S. government has no
jurisdiction over him, but once he's in the United States a subtle
change in his status takes place. From the point of entry onward,
he finds himself under the jurisdiction of the Immigration Service.
This is an important point to understand.

As I mentioned earlier, there are some conditions under which
an immigration official may question an alien's entitlement to a
visa already granted by a consular official abroad. In that case, in
some circumstances, the alien may simply be sent back on the next
plane. Here are some things to remember if you find yourself in
this kind of difficulty:

If the immigration official insists that you go back, you in turn
can insist on seeing a judge.

If the official is unsure about whether you're entitled to your
visa, he may send you to another immigration official at the airport
or at the closest Immigration Service office. This is called deferred
inspection; I'll talk about it more specifically in chapter 5.

If the official insists that you're not entitled to enter and sends
you to a judge, what follows is known as an exclusion hearing. In
that case, you haven't legally entered, of course, and you are
usually under suspicion, but only rarely will you be held in jail
until the hearing takes place. Procedures and rules governing exclusion hearings and deferred inspection will all be covered in
detail in chapter 5.

Many people mistakenly believe that they will automatically be
entitled to remain in the United States for the duration of the visa
stamped into their passports. Unfortunately, that isn't true. The
length of time your visa is valid, as shown on your passport, is only
an indication of the period during which you may attempt to enter
under a given temporary status. After the visa expires, you must
get a new one. If you're issued a two-year visa, for example, it

doesn't mean that when you enter the United States you can remain for two years. The permissible length of time you may stay is determined by a border official of the INS who enters the date on your Form I-94.

Under a new regulation, in effect since January 1983, nearly all tourists are automatically given a six-month period to remain in the United States, even if they ask for less time. By adopting this regulation, the INS hopes to cut down on the number of people applying for extensions.

Another change introduced recently was the physical alteration of Form I-94 to make it compatible with computers. For many years nearly all aliens had assumed that neither the Immigration Service nor the State Department had any accurate way of knowing how honest an alien was about his record of entries and departures into and out of the United States. And that was true to some extent, although many aliens or their families have had the experience of being asked by immigration officers to leave sometime after their permitted stay had expired. Now the U.S. government has, for some time, been putting into operation a computer system that is designed to control automatically all information concerning every alien who enters or departs from the country. Obviously, that means lying will be much more difficult.

Until recently, many aliens came into the United States and stayed several weeks or months longer than they should have. They did so without any concern because it was easy for them simply not to hand in the I-94 form as they left. Nor were they afraid that, upon application for reentry, they would be challenged regarding the length of their last stay. Eventually, however, every such alien will have reason to worry on this score, because it's probable that a border post computer will readily determine whether or not a reentering alien had previously overstayed his allotted time. The ramifications of such a computer system are clear. This new procedure may force a more honest compliance with the law, thereby closing a much-used loophole.

NONIMMIGRANT VISA CATEGORIES

Now let's take a closer look at each nonimmigrant visa category, one at a time. I'll discuss some in greater detail than others, depending on the method of application for and the degree of difficulty in obtaining each visa.

To begin, here are the kinds of visas that are available:

> *Governmental visas, for those employed in the United States by a foreign government, an international organization, or a government-related agency:* A, G, and NATO (NATO visas are not discussed in this book).
>
> *Visas permitting work-related activities in the United States for companies in foreign countries:* B-1 and, in certain circumstances, E-1, E-2, and L.
>
> *Visas granting permission to study:* J, F, and M.
>
> *Visas granting permission to work in the United States for affiliates of foreign companies:* L and, in certain circumstances, E-1 and E-2.

Visas granting permission to work in the United States for companies in which one has invested: E-2 and, in certain circumstances, L-1.

Visas where work permission is possible on special application even though the underlying visa may not allow it: J, F, and M.

Visas granting work permission in the United States for American companies: H-1, H-2, H-3, L-1, and, in certain circumstances, E-1 and E-2.

Visas that do not permit work of any kind in the United States: B-2, C, and D.

Visas permitting performers to work in the United States: H-1, H-2.

From this list, you can see that visas may be used in many ways and that a variety of purposes (some of them overlapping) can be accomplished if you have a clear understanding of each category.

Let's discuss each of them in detail.

A. DIPLOMATIC VISAS

ELIGIBILITY

A-1: The A-1 is for ambassadors, public ministers, career diplomats, and consular officials accredited by foreign governments that have been recognized by the United States who have been accepted by the President or the Secretary of State. The A-1 also includes members of the alien's immediate family.

A-2: The A-2 is granted on the basis of reciprocity. It includes other (less important) officials and employees accredited by foreign governments that are recognized by the United States who are accepted by the Secretary of State. Members of immediate families are also included.

A-3: Again on the basis of reciprocity, A-3 includes attendants, servants, personal employees, and immediate family members who work for the officials and employees who have a nonimmigrant status under the terms of A-1 and A-2.

DURATION AND RENEWABILITY

A-1 and A-2 are valid for the duration of the official assignment; A-3 is valid for one year, but it may be renewed annually.

HOW TO APPLY

In general, those who are eligible for A visas will not have any difficulty in finding out how to get them. Applicants will be told what to do by their own governments, and in most cases no personal contact between the A-visa holder and an American consular official will be necessary. It's doubtful that a lawyer will ever be needed.

DESCRIPTION

Holders of A visas are generally entitled to claim the benefits of diplomatic immunity. Full diplomatic immunity is available for higher-ranking officials. For lesser officials, such as clerical staff and service personnel, the level of diplomatic immunity may be somewhat lower. Work in the United States by spouses and children of aliens holding A visas will not affect their status, but the INS will not grant or authorize specific work permission.

There are a number of foreign governments that are not legally recognized by the United States. Officials of such countries who are traveling in and out of America on official missions cannot do so on A visas. They must enter under visa categories B, C, or G.

B. TEMPORARY VISITOR VISAS

B-1

ELIGIBILITY

This type of visa is issued to visitors who come to the United States temporarily for business purposes, including those coming for business meetings, conferences, and similar purposes, for short periods of time. It is also sometimes granted to aliens coming to America for training as employees of a foreign corporation, but not for training in a United States company. An alien widely known as outstanding in his field, coming here to provide expert consulting services as an employee of a foreign-based corporation, may also be granted the B-1 visa. If the goal is employment in the United States, such persons (trainees and experts) may be entitled to an H-3 or H-1 visa; these will be described later. Spouses and children of B-1 visa holders are given a B-2, or tourist, visa.

The essential consideration in granting a B-1 visa is whether the applicant is to get a salary or other compensation from an American source, other than a simple expense account. Working in the United States for an American company, or getting into the paid labor market here in any other way, is a violation of this visa.

If the business or work involved is temporary and done for a foreign company, and if the remuneration comes from outside the United States—for example, if a salesman comes over to take orders or to make a market study—entry is permissible. Those who have B-1 status are free to consult with business associates, lawyers, or accountants, and to take part in business or professional conventions. The B-1 visa also permits businessmen to come here for the purpose of negotiating contracts, or to look for investment opportunities. Both businessmen and investors may come to make purchases for export, or to buy personal or real property.

DURATION AND RENEWABILITY

The B-1 visa, as granted by an American consul, may be valid indefinitely or for a limited period of time, depending on the practice of the consul in the country where he is stationed or on the circumstances of the individual applicant. I have seen B-1 visas valid for as little as three years, and for one entry. I've also seen visas valid for multiple entry indefinitely, for the life of the passport. When you use this visa to enter the United States, you will usually discover that if you ask an immigration official, he'll allow you to stay up to six months. In some circumstances, you may be given up to one year. An advantage of the B-1 visa is that once you're in the United States and want to extend the period of your stay, you can usually do so for six months at a time, provided, however, your I-94 is still valid.

Renewals and extensions usually require a letter from your foreign employer, explaining the circumstances requiring you to stay longer. Normally, it's wise to include statements in such a letter that all your expenses are being covered from out of this country and that you're earning no salary in the United States.

HOW TO APPLY

Application for the B-1 visa is usually made at the American embassy or consulate where you live. This process was described earlier, in chapter 3. If you're not in your own country, you can and should apply at any embassy or consulate nearest to where you have to be. As I've said, this may result in some delay, because a consul may want to satisfy himself that you are not shopping around for an embassy or consulate that will trust you. It's well known that in some countries American consuls are extremely strict in granting visas. People from such countries who go to another one where the consul is known to be more lenient will often find themselves scrutinized more closely than usual.

A consul looks for several things. He will want to satisfy himself that the alien has no intention to work in the United States. He'll want to be sure that the alien has a residence abroad to which he'll return. He may look for such proof as a permanent job abroad, a family tie, or a property relationship that will compel the alien to go back.

When application is made for this visa, the normal nonimmigration visa form should be used and a letter submitted from someone, such as a foreign employer, describing the purpose of the visit. If the applicant is self-employed, a letter from himself or a representative abroad—a lawyer, perhaps—will be enough.

Normally I don't recommend that the applicant provide information about property or family ties unless I know the consul will be looking specifically for this information. (Also, those aliens whose countrymen are known to have had difficulties in general when applying for visas would be wise to come provided with more complete documentation.)

DESCRIPTION

Consuls do not want to issue B-1 visas if the services described seem to be required for more than a year. Also, the letter from your employer that you will submit when you apply, in addition to explaining the purpose of your trip, should document that you will have adequate money for travel, for carrying out your purposes, whatever they are, and for living costs in America.

Spouse and children may accompany the B-1 holder, but if so, be especially careful to document the temporary nature of your visit and the ties at home that guarantee your return.

To obtain an extension of your B-1 visa, you must submit to the local immigration office where you're temporarily living a document called Form I-539 (see appendix 7), entitled Application to Extend Time of Temporary Stay. Filing must be done no more than thirty days and no fewer than ten days before your authorized stay expires. Most aliens file within one day of expiration, however, and get away with it. The application must be accompanied by a letter from your foreign employer explaining why you need an extension, as well as Form I-94 for you and your family, and a fee of $5.00. If the extension isn't granted, there is no provision for appeal. Nevertheless, through your lawyer you can seek a review of your case by filing a motion to reopen and reconsider.

B-2

ELIGIBILITY

This is the most common visa, given to those who want to come to America for purposes of pleasure—travel, visiting friends, or tourism in general. B-2 holders are forbidden to engage in any kind of employment whatsoever, even on behalf of a foreign company.

DURATION AND RENEWABILITY

A B-2 visa may be valid for any period of time determined by the consul. The same thing holds true for the number of entries permitted. If a consul doesn't trust the alien to leave quickly, he may grant only one or a small number of entries. In most instances, however, entries are multiple. As far as the length of stay is concerned, there is really no definite time. Most people get six months or less, and according to rules recently established, six months will become standard for almost all people who enter the United States on a B-2 visa.

Extensions are possible and are routinely granted in many cases.

The procedure is the same as described above for the B-1 visa. Use Form I-539 and add to it your valid I-94 and a filing fee of $5.00. Usually it will be enough to make a simple statement on Form I-539 indicating your desire to tour for a longer period, or to visit friends, or to see a doctor, or for whatever other valid reason you may have. If you're not legally in the United States according to your Form I-94 at the time you apply for an extension, your application will not be granted. The same applies when you try to change your status.

HOW TO APPLY

The application procedure for the B-2 visa is almost identical to the one used when an application is made for a B-1. Therefore, many of the admonitions and caveats I mentioned earlier should be taken seriously here as well—for instance, the risk of "visa shopping." There are, however, some basic differences.

The consul will not, in the case of the B-2 visa, be looking for proof that you are entering the United States on behalf of a foreign business. The consul will be looking, rather, for proof that you actually have the intention of leaving after the purpose of your visit is concluded. The applicant should therefore be prepared to show, if possible, that he has a job, a home, and responsibilities outside the United States. And documentation should be available if necessary.

The normal nonimmigrant visa form is usually the only document that is needed unless the consul believes there is a risk you may not return. In such cases, he will ask for appropriate additional proof of your intention to return to your own country. It is important to remember that in most cases nothing more than a standard visa application and a passport is required. However, in those countries where there are problems, most applicants are already aware that additional proof should be presented.

Sometimes the consul may be willing to grant a B-2 visa if he is not concerned that the applicant will stay illegally in the United States but has some concern about his ability to pay for his expenses while he is traveling. In such a case, the consul may nevertheless grant the visa if the applicant can produce an Affidavit of

Support (Form I-134; see appendix 8) from a U.S. resident who pledges to maintain the visitor for the entire duration of his stay in the United States. But the affidavit in itself is rarely sufficient to convince the consul to grant a B-2 visa unless the applicant can also provide proof of a compelling reason that will assure his eventual return to his own country.

DESCRIPTION

Holders of B-2 visas should be careful not to do anything in the United States that seems to contradict their status. Work is the major contradiction. If you're caught, you will probably be asked to leave.

People who are here on B-2 visas can change their status to B-1 if it can be demonstrated that they have a business reason to remain in the United States. They can accomplish a change of status by going abroad and applying for the B-1 or other visa at a consulate or embassy of the United States. They can also change to most other temporary visa categories within the United States if they can fulfill the necessary requirements and demonstrate their eligibility. Change of status can be accomplished in the United States by filing Form I-506 (see appendix 9), and with it a valid I-94 form, plus a $15.00 filing fee. If you're changing to a B-1 visa, it's necessary to file Form I-506 with the same kind of information and documentation you would have provided to the consul abroad. That means, for example, a letter from an employer or other person indicating the business purpose of your visit. Special care must be taken when changing to a B-1 visa to indicate clearly that there is no intention to accept a salary in the United States, and that all payments for expenses and salary will be coming from abroad.

In some cities in the United States your application will be processed while you wait in the office. In other places, the application form must be filed by mail, and answers may take some time. INS practice differs from city to city, so you'll do best to check either with the INS or a lawyer or another adviser.

Applicants' needs differ, also. Let me give you an example. A young alien from Turkey, who knows that American consuls there are reluctant to grant temporary visas to the United States to young people, may consider himself lucky to have received even his first visa. So if he then wants to extend his stay in the United States—and perhaps to change status from a visa that merely allows him to visit to one that will also allow him to work—he may not wish to take the risk of going back to Turkey for the new visa, since his chances of getting it are not likely to be good. He may wisely decide to apply for a change of status in the United States —but he should be very sure that he hasn't exceeded the time of his allotted stay before he applies.

Someone from France, however, knows that he can apply without difficulty for any visa category for which he has demonstrated eligibility, and he may not think twice about leaving the country.

I've sometimes advised clients who were out of status to leave the United States and attempt a reentry. I've done this in many cases simply because it was necessary to make sure the alien was legally here before any other temporary visa application was made.

This procedure does incur some risk, and so it should be attempted only after getting some careful professional advice. These rules for extensions and changes of status apply with equal force to B-1 visa holders and to most other nonimmigrants.

C. TRANSIT ALIENS

ELIGIBILITY

C-1: For aliens who are in immediate or continuous transit through the United States.

C-2: For aliens who are qualified and in transit from their own countries to the United Nations Headquarters District in New York.

C-3: For aliens in transit to and from foreign consulates, on a reciprocal basis.

DURATION AND RENEWABILITY

The maximum is twenty-nine days, but it's possible, although very difficult, to get an extension.

HOW TO APPLY

Application for this visa is made by filing a nonimmigrant visa form in the same way as for a B-2 visa. I won't elaborate, because the C visa isn't often used and is of little concern to most aliens.

DESCRIPTION

Transit aliens have to prove they hold a ticket or have some guarantee of transportation to their destination. They're also required to provide proof that they have enough money for living costs. They must also state the purpose of their journey and prove that they have permission to enter another country after the transit is completed. Transit aliens from certain countries can be granted transit privileges at some ports of entry for a short period, even without a C visa. This practice is chancy, however, and should not be counted on.

You can't change status in the United States from the C visa to any other nonimmigrant category, or to permanent residence.

D. CREWMEN

ELIGIBILITY

This is a visa given to airline and ship crews who come and go from the United States as part of their jobs.

I won't say much about the D visa, because it has no relevance for most aliens. People who use it to come here cannot change their status to any other category of nonimmigrant visa or to permanent residence.

E. TREATY TRADERS AND TREATY INVESTORS

Both the E-1 and E-2 visa categories result from treaties, usually treaties of friendship and commerce, between the United States and other countries. In recent years, E visas have been used far more often than in the past, frequently by wealthy foreigners as an alternative to permanent residence in the United States. For this and a variety of other reasons, E visas have assumed a special importance. If no appropriate signed treaty between the United States and your country exists, however, you are not eligible for this kind of visa.

E-1

ELIGIBILITY

E-1 is a visa designed for companies or individuals who are carrying on, or want to develop, substantial trade between the United States and a country with which we maintain an appropriate treaty.

The countries, that maintain such treaties are:

Argentina	Japan
Austria	Korea
Belgium	Latvia
Bolivia	Liberia
Brunei (Borneo)	Luxembourg
China	Netherlands
Colombia	Nicaragua
Costa Rica	Norway
Denmark	Oman
Estonia	Pakistan
Ethiopia	Paraguay
Finland	Philippines
France	Spain
Germany	Switzerland
Greece	Thailand
Honduras	Togo
Iran	Turkey
Ireland	United Kingdom
Israel	Vietnam
Italy	Yugoslavia

This visa is good for individuals as well as corporations, as I've indicated. If individuals want to apply, they must be carrying on or be responsible for substantial trade with the United States.

What is "substantial"? Normally, 51 percent of the trade conducted by the individual must be between the United States and the country of his nationality.

Employees of firms in foreign countries carrying on business with the United States are also eligible. But such employees can qualify only if they have the same nationality as the firm. The firm itself must carry on 51 percent or more of its trade with the United States.

The nationality of the foreign corporation is determined by the majority ownership of shares of stock in the company. If owners of the company abroad are living in the United States, they must also be holding treaty-trader status. If part of the stock is held by permanent residents in America, that does not count toward the 51 percent of stock ownership necessary to determine the nationality of the company.

The treaty is available to supervisors, executives, and individuals with special skills needed in the United States for the efficient operation of the enterprise. Such firms as airlines, banks, importers, exporters, and companies specializing in tourism usually qualify. In general, firms employing accountants, lawyers, insurance agents, computer consultants, and other people in the service sector have not been found eligible for E-1 visas. This visa is also granted to the spouse and minor children (regardless of their nationality) of the holder.

DURATION AND RENEWABILITY

Usually this visa is issued for a period of four years, with the alien admitted to the United States for one- to four-year periods, renewable annually. Extensions are virtually indefinite. To renew your E-1 status in the United States, you must submit a letter from your company, indicating that the same conditions still exist for visa issuance, plus Form I-94, Form I-539, Form I-126, and a $5.00 filing fee. All this should be sent to the INS office that has jurisdiction over your place of residence.

HOW TO APPLY

In most cases, application is made at an embassy or consulate of the United States where the alien or the company who employs him is located. The ordinary nonimmigrant visa form is used, along with a photograph and proof of eligibility for the E-1 visa. Some lawyers and companies applying for the visa use Form I-126 (see appendix 10). This form is used to qualify an alien for the E visa when the application is being made in the United States, based on a change of nonimmigrant status.

My own experience is that not all consulates actually require the use of that form when the application is made abroad initially. In most cases, a statement of fact concerning the alien's trade and the nationality of the various components of the company will be enough. Sometimes a consul will ask for more information.

When an application is made in the United States on the basis of change of status, the usual documents in such cases—the I-506 and I-94 forms—are used. All the normal rules for change of status apply, but it will probably also be necessary to use Form I-126, referred to above. This form is somewhat incomplete, however, and it should be supplemented by required documents, which I'll explain below.

DESCRIPTION

Many attorneys who aren't aware of the E visa's increasingly widespread use have had little experience with it except in the United States, which means that they usually apply for it on the basis of a status change after the alien is already here. They're often surprised to learn that, in general, applications for E visas are granted more readily when they're applied for abroad. This is true, I believe, because of a general lack of familiarity with the E visa on the part of the INS itself in the United States.

There's one criterion for getting an E visa that needs to be mentioned specifically, and that is the one implied by the word "substantial." The law is that trade between the United States and the alien's country of nationality must be substantial enough to qualify, but it's difficult to put a monetary value on what is necessary to meet the test. I can only say this: if there's a clear showing that the revenues generated by the trade are enough to support the treaty-trader and his family, in most cases he will find himself eligible.

E-2

ELIGIBILITY

An E-2 visa is valid for aliens who want to enter the United States solely to develop and direct the operation of an enterprise in which they have invested a substantial amount of capital, or their employees. To qualify, the alien must be a national of a country that has a treaty with the United States. If the applicant is an employee, he must have the same nationality as the company. Here it's important to remember that not all countries that have treaties qualifying aliens for E-1 visas also have them for E-2. This visa is also granted to the spouse and minor children of the alien, regardless of their nationality.

The countries that maintain treaties with the United States under which E-2 visas may be applied for are:

Argentina	Luxembourg
Austria	Netherlands
Belgium	Nicaragua
China	Oman
Colombia	Pakistan
Costa Rica	Paraguay
Ethiopia	Philippines
France	Spain
Germany	Switzerland
Honduras	Thailand
Iran	Togo
Italy	United Kingdom
Japan	Vietnam
Korea	Yugoslavia
Liberia	

DURATION AND RENEWABILITY

Exactly the same as for E-1.

HOW TO APPLY

Exactly the same as for E-1.

DESCRIPTION

In the past few years there has been a widespread increase in the use of the E-2 visa by wealthy foreigners coming into the United States. As a result, the American government has issued guidelines that make the criteria for issuing the visa much more clear. Several points about this procedure should be made at the outset.

An applicant must demonstrate that he, or the company that employs him, is actively in the process of making an investment in the United States, or that he or the company has already invested here. In practical terms, this usually means that the alien or his company must be in control of the funds necessary to make the investment, and must be quite close to the start of actual business operations. Many consulates and embassies insist that the visa should not be granted unless the investment has already been made. And it must also be substantial. There's been a good deal of confusion about what "substantial" means. It has been widely believed that $40,000 was the necessary investment, but that's no longer the case. What it comes down to finally is the necessity to convince a consul that your investment is substantial in terms of the kind of business you're in.

There's no fuzziness about one thing: the enterprise must be a true operating commercial business. That means it can't be a passive organization, or a portfolio investment in stocks and bonds. Investment in undeveloped land won't qualify either, but investment in a real estate development project, where something is being built, will qualify you. In general, you should consider that any business that involves an ongoing commercial organization is satisfactory.

You will have to show that the investment is going to provide more than marginal support for you and your family—that is, it must do more than simply return enough income to provide a living. You should try to show that you will be expanding job opportunities in the United States through your investment and that there's a possibility the business will grow into something larger. A demonstration that you have assets to live on other than those being invested will also be helpful.

In addition, you must show that, as the alien applying for the visa, you are in a position to develop and direct the enterprise. That means you must be in substantial control of it. It doesn't always mean, however, that you have to own more than 51 percent of the business in the United States. Nevertheless, control amounting to less than that figure would be acceptable only if no one person controls more.

You'll also have to show that you intend to leave the United States after the E-2 visa expires. Usually, a consul will approve an E-2 visa unless he has a specific reason for thinking the alien won't leave. Your country of nationality may be a factor here. The same applies for the E-1 visa.

If the alien isn't making the investment on his own but is coming to the United States on behalf of a firm abroad that has made such an investment, then the alien must have the same nationality as the firm. Further, the alien must be a manager or an executive or a highly trained specialized individual in that company or of the new company in the United States.

Nationality of the corporation is determined by who owns more than 51 percent of the stock. If you're Dutch, and the company for which you're working is Dutch, 51 percent of that company had better be owned by people having Dutch nationality, none of whom can be residents of the United States even if they also are of Dutch nationality. This is also true for the American company in which the investment is being made—that is, 51 percent of it must be owned by people or companies having the nationality of the treaty country that is relevant to the case. (If you're making an investment as an individual, however, only your nationality is a factor.) In order to be eligible for the E-2 visa, all the above criteria have to be met. If an applicant fails to meet any one of them, he's ineligible.

There has been widespread abuse of this visa during the past few years, particularly by the nationals of certain countries who declared they were going to make investments in the United States and never did. In some of these cases, investments were made in passive enterprises, and in others, outright lies were told. As a result, both the INS and the State Department are examining applications for E visas far more carefully than they did in the past.

I should add that people with E visas (either E-1 or E-2), if they have previously employed a servant, can bring into the United States a servant who has either worked for them abroad in a household capacity for more than a year or who has had one year's prior experience as a servant. Such a person would enter under a B-1 visa.

F. STUDENTS

ELIGIBILITY

F-1: This is another commonly used visa, granted to bona-fide students who have no intention of abandoning their own countries, but who are qualified to pursue a full course of study and want to enter the United States temporarily for that purpose, and for no other, at an established institution or some other recognized place of study. F visas cannot be used by students who wish to study in trade or vocational schools; M visas are used in these cases.

F-2: This is a visa granted to the spouse and/or child of a student. It does not permit the holder to take a job for pay, and this permission can't be obtained.

DURATION AND RENEWABILITY

These visas are often issued for one year, with yearly renewals until the course is completed. In many cases, however, student visas are granted for longer periods and, in some instances, for the anticipated period of study (referred to as duration of studies), which may be as long as four or five years or more. It's often difficult to predict what a consul will decide to do about this in any given case.

Application for the student visa should be made whenever possible at a consulate or embassy abroad. To apply, the alien will have to secure from a place of study in the United States a document known as Form I-20A (see appendix II), called a Certificate of Eligibility for Nonimmigrant Student Status. This form can only be issued by schools that have been accredited by the INS to accept foreign students. It sets forth the period of study that you intend to pursue and the amount of money you'll need to complete it. The form should be accompanied by proof that you have enough financial means to complete the course of study, and it must also be accompanied by the ordinary nonimmigrant visa form and a photograph. In most cases, an applicant will have little difficulty in obtaining the visa as long as he or she has filed the required Form I-20A.

Application for this visa, as for most of the others, can also be made, for those already in the United States, on the basis of a change of status application. The procedure is practically the same as far as documentation is concerned. Form I-20A is filed, along with Form I-506 (Application for Change of Nonimmigrant Status) and a valid I-94 form. All this is sent with the proper fee to the INS office nearest the place of study. In most cases, however, these applications will be denied, since the authorities suspect many aliens of entering the United States on other nonimmigrant visas, intending from the outset to study. The INS greatly prefers that application be made abroad.

Of all the documents, Form I-20A is the most important one you need in order to study in America. It's completed by the institution you'll be attending, but some information has to be filled in by the applicant, who also has to sign it. It's important that the applicant know how long he or she needs to remain in the United States in order to complete the course of study.

This may seem like a small point, but in fact it's another example of how important it is to be consistent. If you indicate in your visa application that you want to stay in the United States for five years, and the I-20A indicates that the study program lasts for only three years, the consul may begin to question your honesty and may deny your visa.

There are several important lessons to be learned from this. You should examine the forms prepared by your school very carefully, so that you know the school hasn't made a mistake. You should then make sure that the documents are consistent with whatever claims you're making on your visa form and also in the information that has to be filled out at the end of Form I-20A. For example, it's important to be sure that the amount of money you say you have is sufficient to cover all the expenses that the I-20A form indicates you'll incur.

The amount of money needed for study in the United States is usually indicated clearly on the Certificate of Eligibility. A letter from a bank, or an affidavit from someone who is willing to support you, is required. The consul who interviews you, or who reviews your papers, will want to be sure you have enough money to support yourself while you're in this country. If an affidavit of support is filed, the consul will want to be sure that the person supporting you has an adequate reason to do so, and that this individual also has enough funds.

It's understood by the government that students may have to work if their personal circumstances change after they've begun their studies. If that's your situation, you must file Form I-538 (see appendix 12) for permission to accept or continue part-time employment, practical training, or on-campus employment. If the application is denied, there's no appeal, but you can seek a review by filing a motion to reopen and reconsider. If your I-20A form carries a statement from your school that you've been offered on-campus employment that won't displace an American resident, you will not need to submit Form I-538. If you're seeking permission for part-time employment because of economic necessity, you must prove that the necessity was not foreseen, and an authorized official of the school has to certify that the employment won't interfere with your studies. Such permissions are granted only for twelve-month periods per application.

If you seek employment permission to get practical training, the school has to certify that the work is recommended for that purpose, and that it isn't available in the student's own country. Since 1977, permission has been granted in these cases for only six months at the most and, with renewals, the total must not exceed twelve months. I'll be talking more about this in a later chapter, but don't forget that practical training is intended to prepare you for a career abroad, not for a permanent job with your American employer.

There were more than 250,000 students from foreign countries studying in the United States at last count. Consequently, the subject of student visas is an important one. Since that's so, I've devoted a separate section, in part 4 of this book, to the issues that concern foreign students in the United States. Most of the further information a student may need will be found in that chapter.

G. EMPLOYEES OF INTERNATIONAL ORGANIZATIONS

ELIGIBILITY

G-1: Given to a principal resident representative to an international organization from a foreign country recognized by the United States. Members of immediate families are included.

G-2: Given to other accredited representatives to such organizations from foreign countries. Also includes immediate families.

G-3: Given to aliens otherwise qualified for G-1 or G-2, but whose government is not recognized by the United States or is not a member of an international organization. Members of immediate families are included.

G-4: Given to officers or employees of the international organizations themselves and their immediate families.

G-5: Given to attendants, servants, and personal employees of the above representatives and the members of their immediate families.

DURATION AND RENEWABILITY

The G-1, G-2, G-3, or G-4 visa is granted for the duration of the assignment, while the G-5 visa is for one year, renewable annually. Spouses and children of aliens with G visas may work, but again, they can't get specific INS permission to do so.

HOW TO APPLY

It won't be hard to find out how to get a G visa if you're eligible. Governments usually tell applicants what to do. G visa holders and American consular officials won't have any contact with each other in most cases. It's doubtful that you'll need a lawyer.

DESCRIPTION

Because G visas are normally taken care of by the organization employing the applicant, it isn't necessary to discuss them any further.

H. ALIENS OF DISTINGUISHED MERIT AND ABILITY, TEMPORARY WORKERS, AND TRAINEES

H visas are among the most important temporary visas that permit work and training in the United States. An understanding of them is essential to an understanding of visa strategy when your ultimate goal is to acquire residence.

H-1

ELIGIBILITY

H-1 is a visa given to temporary workers of distinguished merit and ability who have no intention of abandoning their own countries. These people must be considered as aliens coming to America to perform services of an exceptional nature. Obviously, this means prominent people, or those who have a high level of education in their field. In this category are athletes, mechanics, engineers, professional entertainers, professors, and accountants, among others. Doctors may use this visa only if they are coming here purely for study or research, or if they've been licensed to practice here some time ago.

DURATION AND RENEWABILITY

The H-1 visa is valid for a maximum of two years. It can be extended for as long as the alien's services are necessary, but there must be no intention to remain permanently. In practice, five years is the usual maximum for extensions, which can be obtained annually. This visa is only valid for employment by the sponsoring employer. Sometimes a single application can be used for a group of employees, all of whom fit the same job description and who will be hired at one time.

HOW TO APPLY

To get this visa, your sponsoring employer must first file a petition for your entry. This is Form I-129B (see appendix 13), called a Petition to Classify Nonimmigrant as Temporary Worker or Trainee. A letter from the company has to accompany this petition, along with other documents intended to prove that the alien is, in fact, a person of distinguished merit and ability, and that the services to be performed require such a person.

You'll need plenty of documentation. This may include professional certifications, affidavits, degrees, diplomas, examples of writing, reviews, or similar evidence. If you include school records, diplomas, letters showing previous experience, and similar documents, be sure to include period of attendance, courses of study, and related facts. If you get former employees or recognized experts to submit affidavits attesting to your ability, be sure that they certify in detail your expertise or abilities and explain how they got their information. Copies of any written contracts between you and the petitioner must be submitted, or else a summary of any verbal contract or agreement.

These requirements aren't as difficult in practice as they may appear to be. For instance, foreign lawyers who want to come to the United States and work for a company or a law firm here on a short-term basis can usually get an approval merely on a showing that they're professionals. It isn't necessary for such a lawyer to indicate any substantial expertise. But if that same lawyer tries to get a job as a legal counsel, he'll find in most cases that his application will be denied.

That is an example of how the practice is often different from what the law says it should be. Documentation requirements are often described in a more complex way than what is needed in practice. Documentation requirements can be enforced, however, and when an immigration officer wants to deny a case, he can very easily rely on the rule book and indicate that he won't let you in unless you fulfill the documentation requirements to the letter.

Don't forget that Form I-129B must be filed in the United States at the INS office nearest your place of employment. All documentation has to be filed in duplicate, and any documents that aren't originals must be certified.

When your application is approved, the INS issues Form I-171C (see appendix 14), which will be sent to the consulate designated on Form I-129B. You should send another copy to your lawyer or his representative. Another copy goes to the employer. It is important that you be given a copy of Form I-129B by your employer or attorney for your own use.

If you're applying for the visa abroad, the H-1 approval notice issued by the Immigration Service is usually the only document you'll need, in addition to your passport, nonimmigrant visa form, and a photograph. Take this package of documents to the consulate and request the visa. If for some reason you're applying to a consulate not designated on Form I-129B, be sure to have a duplicate copy of the entire application that was filed with the INS. In most cases, you won't have a copy of the approval, and so you'll have to wait until you're informed by your lawyer, employer, or by the consul himself that approval has been granted and that you're able to apply for your visa. Sometimes the approval itself is not enough, and the consul abroad will insist on having the immigration file, which is usually sent by the United States authorities.

As in the other visas I've discussed, application for an H-1 can also be made in the United States by changing status, but it's important to understand that this can be accomplished only if you're legally here. That means your I-94 must still be valid. If it is, then you must file Form I-129B and Form I-506, Application for Change of Nonimmigrant Status (see appendix 9). Keep in mind, however, that you shouldn't apply for change of status too soon after your initial entry or the INS may decide that it was your intention to work when you first entered. It's best to wait a couple of months before you apply for the H-1, even if you have to file an application to extend whatever visa you're already on before you file for H-1.

DESCRIPTION

H-1 applications usually include two broad categories. One consists of people considered outstanding compared with others in the same field, such as scientists, artists, or entertainers. The other category includes professionals, defined as those pursuing an occupation in which a bachelor's degree is a minimum requirement for entry. Entertainers constitute a very important category of potential H-1 aliens; they'll be covered separately in part 4 of this book.

H-2

ELIGIBILITY

This is for aliens who don't intend to abandon their own countries but come here to work or perform other temporary services for which eligible people in the United States can't be found. Temporary labor certification is required as the first step. The applicant needn't be of any special prominence, and there are no educational requirements. Seasonal farm workers are typical of applicants in this category, but it also includes large numbers of people performing skilled, unskilled, or semiskilled work on short contracts, as well as foreign entertainers who want to perform in the United States.

DURATION AND RENEWABILITY

The period specified on the petition usually represents the period of validity, but it must not exceed a year or be any longer than the period of validity of the labor certification. Three years is the maximum time you're permitted to stay on an H-2 visa with extensions, but to be granted that much is extremely difficult. Every extension requires a new temporary labor certification by the Department of Labor, which will examine thoroughly not only the job requirements, but the current employment situation in the United States as well.

HOW TO APPLY

The application procedure is the same as for H-1—with a single exception. In order to apply for the H-2, it's first essential to get a temporary labor certification from the Department of Labor.

The employer must file Form ETA-750 (see appendix 15) with the Department of Labor, asking for the certification. This attests, in effect, that no qualified people are available in the United States for such employment and that employing the alien won't adversely affect the wages and/or working conditions of American workers similarly employed. This application procedure is an abbreviated version of the process required for permanent labor certification. I urge any alien who needs temporary labor certification to get a lawyer, because the process is involved and the Labor Department's rules are constantly changing. To complicate matters, the rules are also different from place to place in the United States. Consequently, it would be foolish to rely on people who aren't experts in the procedure.

DESCRIPTION

One of the important differences between H-1 and H-2 is that the H-2 applicant doesn't have to show that the worker or alien is of special prominence or has any special education. It's a visa that can also be used to bring in aliens in large numbers.

Another primary difference between the H-1 and H-2 visas lies in the varying interpretations of the word "temporary." To qualify for an H-2 visa, the offered position must be temporary; a seasonal farm worker would be a good example. For an H-1 visa, however, the position can be ongoing, even though the alien's employment must be temporary. For example, an alien might come here for one year to act as an accountant, and although his service here lasts only for that year, the job itself continues.

Recent changes in the Department of Labor regulations concerning H-2 visa applications have made such visas even more difficult to obtain than before. These rules, which took effect May 6, 1983, require, among other things, that the application be filed a minimum of forty-five days prior to the time the alien's services are required, that in certain cases the employer advertise for the position, and that the employer make inquiries to the appropriate unions, placement agencies, and other recruitment sources. As well as making the obtaining of H-2 visas more difficult and time-consuming, the new rules will make the H-1 visa by comparison even more desirable.

It is especially important to remember that it is often very hard to renew an H-2 visa. That's because the very meaning of H-2 is temporary employment. Once it looks as though the employment might be permanent, the INS and the Labor Department become most reluctant to agree to any further grants of permission.

H-3:

ELIGIBILITY

The H-3 visa is designed for aliens who come here temporarily as trainees—that is, nonimmigrant aliens who want to enter the country at the invitation of an individual, organization, firm, or some other institution to get instruction in a particular field, such as agriculture, commerce, communication, finance, government, transportation, or the professions. Physicians coming here for graduate medical education or training are specifically excluded.

DURATION AND RENEWABILITY

Same as for H-1, with the maximum determined by the amount of time that the training could reasonably take, which in general would not be more than two years. It's very difficult to renew an H-3 visa, because it is generally assumed that after a short period of training, no more time will be necessary.

HOW TO APPLY

The application procedure is the same as that for the H-1 visa. No temporary labor certification is necessary.

DESCRIPTION

An H-3 visa can be granted only if it can be demonstrated that an individual or organization in the United States wants to train an alien in a particular field. It's important to demonstrate an actual training program, and if such a program isn't already in effect, it is often difficult to convince the INS to grant an H-3 visa.

An accompanying statement must describe the kind of training that is offered, the position for which the alien is to be trained, and why this training can't be obtained outside the United States. He can be paid either in America or in his own country. The petition must also include a detailed description of the training program —including classroom teaching, observing others, specialized courses, and on-the-job experience—as well as the percentage of time that will be spent in each category. An alien trainee can't get an H-3 visa if the work he does is productive. If the employment is incidental to the training, however, and doesn't replace any American worker, there should be no problem.

A hopeful H-3 applicant may assume he can get into the United States as a trainee through any company willing to offer to take him into a training program, but that isn't the case. In my first years as a lawyer, when I worked for a large firm, a young man was sent to me by a small trading company on West Broadway in New York. The company wanted to bring the young man in as a trainee. At that stage of my practice, I knew very little about immigration law and nothing about training programs. I researched all the regulations meticulously and came up with a description of a training program that made perfect sense and that, in fact, was quite accurate. But the application was never approved.

That was one of my first lessons in understanding that you can't really rely on what the regulations and laws say. What I discovered was that, while training programs set up by large corporations, which have been in force for some time, will work for an H-3 visa, ad hoc programs set up by small companies will not.

I. REPRESENTATIVE OF FOREIGN INFORMATION MEDIA

ELIGIBILITY

An I visa is simply one granted on the basis of reciprocity to representatives of the foreign press, radio, television, film, or any other kind of foreign information medium who come here to pursue their work. It includes spouses and unmarried children under twenty-one.

DURATION AND RENEWABILITY

The visa is usually valid for extended periods. Admission is authorized for a year at a time, with annual renewals. Those who hold this visa can't change from one information medium to another, or change employers, without permission from the INS.

HOW TO APPLY

Most people with I visas get them from consulates and embassies abroad. Application is made with the regular nonimmigrant visa form, a photograph, and a letter from the medium represented, demonstrating to the consul who reviews the application that the alien is indeed eligible for this visa.

It's also possible to apply for the I visa through a change of status in the United States, but the procedure is relatively rare and needs no discussion here.

DESCRIPTION

Most people who are in the United States under this visa are well informed and familiar with the rules concerning immigration. Consequently, it would be superfluous to give them any special advice.

J. EXCHANGE VISITORS

ELIGIBILITY

The J-1 visa is given to aliens who are bona-fide students, scholars, trainees, teachers, professors, research assistants, or leaders in a field of specialized knowledge or skill who come here temporarily to take part in exchange programs designated by the Secretary of State for purposes of teaching, instructing or lecturing, studying, observing, conducting research, consulting, demonstrating special skills, or getting training. Nonimmigrant aliens are classified as exchange visitors if they are in an approved exchange visitor program, if they have enough money to cover their expenses or if money will be provided for them, and if they have enough proficiency in English to undertake the program. The grant of a J-1 visa is only possible when the alien has obtained a form known as IAP-66, Certificate of Eligibility for Exchange Visitor Status (see appendix 16). This form is granted by the institution sponsoring the alien. The J-2 visa is for the spouse or a minor child of an exchange visitor.

DURATION AND RENEWABILITY

The period of validity is whatever period is specified on Form IAP-66, but it must not exceed one year. Extensions are granted up to the limits prescribed by the particular program, as approved by the State Department.

HOW TO APPLY

Application for a J visa is made in exactly the same way as for a student visa, except that Form IAP-66 is used instead of Form I-120A. This form is filed with the American consulate, along with the regular nonimmigrant visa form and the usual evidence of support.

Exchange visitors must present Form IAP-66 to an immigration officer when they enter the United States and whenever they re-enter this country after a trip outside. Extensions must be applied for no earlier than thirty days and no later than fifteen days before the authorized stay expires. Make your application for an extension to the district director of the Immigration and Naturalization Service who has administrative jurisdiction over your place of temporary residence. This application must be endorsed by the sponsor, showing the time and terms for the extended stay. If you want an extension beyond the program time limitation, your application will have to be supported strongly by the sponsor, who must show evidence of exceptional circumstances. If you have immediate family members with you, attach a statement to your Form IAP-66 showing the name and relationship, the place and date of birth, and the nationality of each member.

DESCRIPTION

Most J-1 visas carry an onerous condition—the two-year foreign residence requirement. What this means is that after your J-1 visa period is over, you must leave the United States for two years. You are not permitted to change to another visa or to apply for permanent residence until this two-year period has expired. The rule doesn't apply to all J visa holders, however. It does apply to those who have been in a program financed either by the American government or the alien's own (including travel grants), and to those who have occupational skills listed by the Secretary of State on a "skills list" as being necessary in their own country.

If you fall into one of these categories, you'll still have the possibility of a waiver if you can meet any one of the following four requirements:

1. If an American government agency makes a formal request for you and the State Department recommends it.

2. If you are able to show that leaving this country will be an exceptional hardship for your spouse or child—that is, if either one is an American citizen or a permanent resident alien.

3. If you can't return to your last country of residence of nationality because you would be persecuted if you did.

4. If you can get a "no objection" letter from your government, declaring that it has no objection if you don't repatriate for the two-year period, and if you're favorably recommended by the State Department after it confers with the agency sponsoring your program.

Such waivers are not often granted, however, The letters themselves are relatively easy to get, and years ago such a letter was the key element in proving to the United States government that you should not be required to return. Recent experience, however, shows that waiver letters don't help very much, and that regardless of what the law says, it's very difficult indeed to get around a two-year foreign residence requirement if it applies to the training program of which you're a part.

The two-year foreign residence requirement is a problem for many people—a problem many aliens aren't aware of until it's too late. Consequently, the J visa should be used with the understanding that in all likelihood the alien and his or her family will have to return to their country of origin before they reenter the United States as specified above.

If you're here on a J visa, you can accept employment and be paid for it if your program contains that authorization, or if authorization is granted later. A spouse can get permission to work only if it's financially necessary for his or her own support or to support minor children.

K. FIANCÉE OR FIANCÉ

ELIGIBILITY

This is a visa given only to a fiancée or fiancé of an American citizen who wants to come here only to enter into a valid marriage within ninety days after entry. Minor children, if any, can also come in on this visa. Holders can work within the ninety-day period. If the marriage does not take place within that time, however, the alien must either leave or change status.

The K visa doesn't come up that much, and so it isn't necessary to say more about it. But it *is* a useful device to be taken advantage of when it's called for.

L. INTRACOMPANY TRANSFEREES

ELIGIBILITY

The L-1 visa is given to aliens who have been employed continuously for a year by a foreign firm, corporation, or other legal entity, and who want to come to the United States temporarily to continue working for a related company in the United States as a manager, an executive, or as one who has specialized knowledge. This situation must exist immediately before the alien applies for admission to the United States.

There are three requirements to meet for the L-1: (1) the petitioning company in the United States must be related to the company abroad as its branch office, subsidiary, or affiliate—meaning that one company has significant control of the other (contract relationships are not enough); (2) you must have been employed continuously by the foreign company for a year before the petition is filed, not including time in America on temporary assignment or as a trainee of the foreign firm; and (3) you must be coming here to serve as an executive or manager, or to use your specialized knowledge. Such specialized knowledge might even mean that possessed by an executive secretary who has particular expertise in significant procedures.

DURATION AND RENEWABILITY

An application for the L-1 visa can be made for a period of up to three years. If the initial application is for a shorter period, renewals are not difficult to obtain. If the maximum period of three years is applied for, however, it is difficult to renew the visa.

HOW TO APPLY

The application procedure is the same as that described for H-1. The United States employer files a petition on Form I-129B (see appendix 13) at an INS office closest to the place of employment in the United States. Along with this form must be a letter from the petitioner, with any necessary supporting documents, explaining the relationship of the companies and giving a description of the alien's job abroad and the job he'll have in America. The employer must provide proof of both the U.S. and foreign companies' existence, and state whether specialized knowledge is involved, describing the nature of that knowledge and its importance. All this must be supplied in detail, and all the forms and documents must be submitted in duplicate. There is a $15.00 filing fee. It isn't necessary to maintain a residence abroad, as in the H categories, but you must still make it clear that you intend to come here only temporarily. There is an L-2 visa for a spouse and minor children.

DESCRIPTION

The L visa was created for large international companies that have branches around the world and that either have an existing branch in the United States or want to open one here. Typical examples of people who regularly enter this country under the L visa are senior executives of multinational corporations, and international banks.

The L-1 has proved to be an important stepping stone toward the goal of permanent residence. In fact, it's one of the few visas that can almost guarantee a subsequent automatic change of status. After you've been in the United States on an L status, it's very easy in certain circumstances to become a resident without having to prove much more. The L status permits a labor certification waiver, which means that there is no need to prove a scarcity of United States workers qualified for the job. No prior application to the Labor Department is necessary.

It's important to keep in mind that the foreign company must have been in active existence for a year before the application for L status is made, and every individual requesting this visa must have worked for the parent company for at least a year before the date of the application.

Applicants for the L visa must be executives or at the managerial level, or must have specialized knowledge that the business in the United States requires for its smooth operation. For *all* personnel, it's generally required that they occupy positions in the United States similar to those they occupied abroad. There are exceptions to this rule, however, particularly when the level of employment is upgraded in the United States. Managerial and executive personnel are required to prove that they will be undertaking the normal duties that accompany such jobs—such as supervision or business management.

Some firms have business practices that are complicated, perhaps even unique. When that's the case, it isn't unreasonable to expect that these companies will want to transfer personnel who will help to guarantee the smooth and effective operation of the company in the United States. For instance, I've been successful in getting L visas for secretaries who had specific knowledge about the accounting systems of multinational companies.

I should qualify here a statement I made earlier, that the L visa can be used as an almost automatic stepping stone to a Green Card. This occurs only in the case of managers or executives. Employees with specialized knowledge don't qualify, even if they're upgraded to managerial or executive positions after they come to work here.

In cases where new subsidiary or affiliate offices are to be established in the United States, when an application is made for the L visa, proof must be submitted to the local Immigration Service office that the business is close to being launched. It's helpful to bring proof of a lease or plans for expansion. I've found it unnecessary to show the presence of an American bank account, however. Often the INS assumes that the viability of the parent company abroad is enough to guarantee the American operations.

I should add that the existence of a formal entity abroad isn't necessary. Companies need not have a corporate organization. I've been successful in applications for L visas where the business was operated out of someone's house. Regardless of the nature of the foreign organization itself, it is important to document its existence and activities. Items such as balance sheets, financial statements, and official registration should be shown where possible.

There's disagreement from time to time about what kind of relationship between a parent company and the American-based corporation will qualify. There's no question that ownership by a foreign company of 51 percent or more of an American company qualifies that company as a subsidiary of the foreign parent. This is equally true if the stock ownership of both the foreign company and the American company is essentially the same but the number of shares held by the stockholders is somewhat different. The establishment of a branch office is ideal. For example, foreign airlines often operate in the United States without bothering to incorporate their branch or branches. These companies are simply licensed to do business in this country.

Affiliation relationships are sometimes vague. For instance, firms owned as separate franchises, but governed by franchise rules and under extensive supervision by a central organization, are often considered to be affiliates.

Surprisingly, after the L visa has been granted, it's no longer necessary for the foreign corporation to remain in existence. In fact, the corporation needs to maintain its identity only up to the date of filing. Recently, I've had the case of an alien who was granted an L visa after the parent company was dissolved. The date of application was several weeks before the date of the parent company's dissolution. After the American corporation was a year old, application was made to change the L visa into permanent residence under a procedure I'll explain later. Although the INS turned down the initial application, an appeal was taken, and it was held that the existence of the parent company needed only to be up to the date of filing for the L visa. The client prevailed, much to the surprise of many.

An L visa may often be preferred even if other visas are also possible. For example, an investor in the United States can sometimes get permission to stay in this country for up to four years under an E visa. But, as we've seen, he may have to prove a great deal of business activity here before consuls in some countries will issue an E visa. If, however, that same foreign investor is able to set up an American company that is a branch of a firm he already owns abroad, he may be able to get an L visa without showing any investment or activity in the United States whatsoever. In addition, this same alien gets the additional bonus of having laid down a stepping stone toward residence, if he or she should want it.

For this reason, I often recommend to clients who can get E visas, or other visas that may seem to be more convenient, to try for the L visa instead. The same logic also applies if an E visa is unavailable because of a lack of an essential treaty between the alien's country and the United States.

In times of stress and potential political upheavals of an unpredictable nature, it's comforting to know that there is one visa that almost automatically leads to the Green Card. For instance, I've recommended the L visa especially to clients from Hong Kong who are concerned about the fate of this Crown Colony when British rule ends and the People's Republic of China becomes its next ruler.

As we've seen, the L visa can be issued for a period of up to three years; but the actual period stated on the passport for any individual applicant may be based on reciprocity agreements between this country and the alien's. For example, in the case of South Africa, which gives Americans visas for only one year, the United States in turn gives an L visa for only one year to a South African (even though the Immigration Service will allow three years). Reciprocity for each country can be checked with any United States consul abroad.

In the case of my South African clients, it's interesting to note that although the duration listed on their L visas is only one year, they're often granted three years on their I-94 when they enter. In effect, it means that if they choose not to leave the United States after they've entered, they can stay for three years even though their visas are good for one.

The Immigration Service recently made changes in the rules that apply to the L visa. The changes were to help large corporations who bring many people each year to the United States as intracompany transferees. Under the new rules, companies that bring ten or more executives or managers to the United States in any one year will be able to bring additional executives or managers into this country without any further application to the Immigration Service. This new rule has been referred to as the "blanket L-1" rule.

After ten or more L-1 applications have been approved for any one company in a single year by the Immigration Service, the Service will provide, upon the request of the company, a document indicating that the blanket L-1 is now in effect. This document is provided to the consul along with the other necessary documentation. The blanket L-1 is valid for three years and extendable for an additional three years if a steady stream of intracompany transferees continues.

Executives and managers who come to this country after the company qualifies for the blanket L-1 still have to have documentation proving the required prior employment, and this proof still has to be brought to the American consulate outside of the United States where the application is being made. The principal benefit is that the consul, upon presentation of the documents and proof of eligibility under the blanket L-1, will be able to issue the next L-1 on the spot.

Intracompany transferees who wish to enter the United States under the specialized knowledge category of the L-1 are not eligible for a blanket L-1 approval.

M. STUDENTS

The M visa is a separate category for foreign students who want to study in the United States at vocational or similar schools. The INS created this category to distinguish these programs from the more traditional academic studies.

In almost all respects, the M visa is identical to the F visa, with one exception: it's more difficult to extend its duration or to change from program to program. In all other respects, however, the two visas are so similar that further description is unnecessary.

These are all the nonimmigrant visas that the law makes available. The next chapter deals with special nonimmigrant procedures.

SPECIAL NONIMMIGRANT PROCEDURES

With a few exceptions, the list of various nonimmigrant visas set forth in the previous chapter is complete. Reading each category should be enough to tell you which one is relevant to your case and, if more than one is available to you, how to choose among them.

In general, I think every alien should use the visa that provides him with the most options for the future. It's the advice I've given to my clients since I began practicing immigration law, and I continue to swear by it. Some aren't lucky enough to have a choice, of course, and they must resort to whatever visa they can get. Others should study carefully the options available to them.

Many aliens don't know that they can switch from one temporary visa to another while they're in the United States. Let me explain how it's done.

CHANGE OF STATUS FROM ONE NONIMMIGRANT CATEGORY TO ANOTHER

If you're in the United States with a currently valid nonimmigrant visa—that is, the time limit listed on your Form I-94 has not yet been reached—you're eligible to change your status to another nonimmigrant category. This is done by filing Form I-506 (see appendix 9), Application for Change of Nonimmigrant Status, along with Form I-94 to prove your valid entry and status in the United States. You'll also have to provide a $10.00 filing fee and whatever documentation is needed to establish your eligibility for the new visa category.

When you're applying to change status, check the requirements for the visa you want to change to and collect all the forms and documents to be filed along with Form I-94 and Form I-506. Chapter 4 tells you in detail what items and fees should accompany each form.

Whether your application is granted depends on the category you're changing from and the one you're changing to. Timing is crucial. For example, if you enter the United States as a tourist with a B-2 visa, then three days later apply for an H-1 visa, the chances are that you'll be rejected. The usual ground for such a rejection is called "preconceived intent." This means the Immigration Service will assume that at the time you entered as a tourist, your real intention was to be employed in the United States. Thus you've violated your tourist status, and your request for a status change will probably be denied.

There is obvious validity in this reasoning. It *does* take some time to establish contacts and get a job offer, and if you're looking for employment after only one or two days in America, obviously your intention was not to be a tourist.

With careful planning you can avoid being turned down. If you enter as a tourist and decide later to become employed, regardless of when you changed your mind, it's better to wait for a period of time before filing any papers. This greatly increases your chances of success in getting a worker's visa, so it's worth the wait.

Timing is particularly important in changing from a tourist to a student visa.

There's no guarantee that *any* request for changing your visa category will be approved. Consequently, it's wise to obtain the correct documentation and plan your strategy. Those are the key words: planning and strategy. Remember, too, that you must be careful not to overstay the time allotted on your Form I-94. Many aliens find themselves in a dilemma on this point. They've been granted only a short period of time to stay in the United States, and if they want to change their status they will find themselves in a Catch-22 situation. If they change too quickly, their application will be turned down because of preconceived intent, but if they wait too long, they'll be here illegally and so will have little chance of success.

A useful strategy is to file an application to extend the time of your temporary stay, a procedure I'll explain shortly. This will ensure that you're here legally, at least until the new period granted expires or until your application to extend has been decided on. Then, after a suitable period of time, you can file an application to change status. Such an application can be filed even before you've heard the result of your application to extend. By following this procedure, you won't be here illegally when you make your application to change status.

It's useful to keep in mind that after you've filed any application with the Immigration Service, your status will be temporarily in limbo until that application has been either rejected or approved. If it's denied, you're usually given a brief period of time to arrange your departure or to appeal. If it's approved, however, your status becomes whatever it was you applied for.

When it's approved, your change of status is endorsed on Form I-94. Remember, though, that this isn't a visa. It's only an authorization by the INS for you to stay in the United States, and within a particular category. If you want to go abroad, you'll have to get a visa in the new category before you reenter the United States in your new status.

Keep in mind that when you *do* go abroad, and request that your new status and new visa be entered in your passport, you may have to start at the beginning with the consul, who has the right to review any application as though for the first time, regardless of what action was taken by the Immigration Service.

It's also important to remember that when you're applying for a working visa, you must *not* work until the visa is granted. If you do, you'll be unable to apply later on for a permanent residence without first leaving the country. Many people solve this problem by working on a "payment deferred" basis. This is risky. Nonetheless, a good many aliens have discovered that it works.

EXTENSIONS OF STAY

Regardless of whatever your nonimmigrant visa classification may be, you or anyone else holding such a visa can usually apply for an extension of stay in the United States. The length of time you'll be given or the number of extensions you may be granted depends on the kind of nonimmigrant visa you possess. For instance, a tourist visa usually cannot be extended beyond a one-year period. An H-I visa, however, can be extended a year at a time for a maximum of five years. An L visa may be given for an initial period of up to three years, and after that extensions are quite difficult to get. Again, see chapter 4 for details.

To apply for an extension, it's necessary to complete and file Form I-539 (see appendix 7), Application to Extend Time of Temporary Stay, with documentation to indicate the need for the additional period of stay in the United States. You must also submit a valid I-94 form, along with a $5.00 filing fee. With tourist visas, it is usually not necessary to prove your need for additional time; you only have to state why it is requested. But in the case of a B-I visa, for instance, you would need a letter from your employer explaining the need for your extended presence in the United States.

If the actual visa in your passport expires during the time of your extension, or at any other time while you're in the United States, you have a choice of two procedures. Whichever procedure you choose, remember you can stay here as long as the I-94 says you can, even if your visa has expired. And you can even apply to extend your stay after your visa has expired.

REVALIDATION

Many aliens and lawyers don't realize that it's possible to have a new visa entered into one's passport without leaving the country. It's an exception to the general rule that visas can only be entered into passports abroad. Here's the exception: for visa categories A, E, G, I, and L, aliens who haven't exceeded their stay as set forth on Form I-94 can apply to the Office of Diplomatic Liaison in Washington, D.C., where new visas will, in most cases, be stamped into their passports.

It's extremely important to remember, however, that this won't take place unless your passport is valid for an additional six months. Also, you must not have exceeded the length of your allowable stay as set forth on Form I-94.

Here are the requirements for revalidation:

1. Complete the Nonimmigrant Visa Application (Form 156; see appendix 6), the same form you used when you applied for your visa abroad. Be careful in filling it out that you don't contradict anything you stated earlier; this underlines the importance of keeping copies of all previously filed documentation.

2. Include a letter explaining the need for the new visa and the inconvenience of having to go abroad to a consul to have it issued.

3. Fill out Form I-94, to show that you're not an overstay.

4. Attach a passport-size photograph to your visa form.

5. A filing fee is sometimes necessary, depending on reciprocity with certain foreign countries. These fees vary greatly, and so every alien should check with the Office of Diplomatic Liaison before making application.

6. Give proof of the granting by the INS of your underlying visa, when approval by the Immigration Service is required.

After you've assembled all the necessary documents, send them to the Office of Diplomatic Liaison, also known as the Issuance and Accreditation Branch, Visa Office, Department of State, Washington, D.C. It's wise to check with the State Department to find out how long you may have to wait for a response. That's important, because if your I-94 expires during the waiting period, you'll be out of luck.

APPLYING ABROAD FOR A NEW VISA

This is the other choice you have if your underlying visa expires. You can leave the United States and apply abroad for a new one. The procedure is almost the same as the one required when you applied in the first place.

If you're an alien whose temporary visa expires while you're here, and if your visa requires an application to the Immigration Service, or to a school or university (either Form IAP-66 or Form I-120A), remember to make an application for fresh documentation before you leave the United States. That's necessary because once your initial immigration or other approval has expired, and the period of validity of your visa expires, your application abroad is for all practical purposes a new one.

If you travel abroad after your visa expires, and you have not revalidated the visa in the United States, you'll need a new visa to reenter. In that case, you'll have to go through the same process as you did to get the original visa. For H and L aliens, when the time initially granted by the Immigration Service has expired, you will have to refile for the initial immigration approval. After you get this approval from Immigration, submit the application to an American consular post for action. You're really starting all over again.

TRAVELING TO CANADA OR MEXICO

Aliens often want to know how their visa status is affected if they're in America and want to travel to one or both of our two neighbors, Mexico and Canada. There are special rules for such trips.

If you stay in one of those countries less than thirty days, it isn't legally considered a departure from or a reentry into the United States, so it isn't necessary to have a valid visa. But remember, it *is* necessary to have a valid I-94 form, which demonstrates that you have a valid status beyond the date of reentry. If you've filed an application for adjustment of status, your departure from the United States may sometimes be ruled as an abandonment of the adjustment application. A final word of caution: whatever your circumstances, consult an attorney before you leave the United States, because these technical rules can trap the individual who ignores them.

PRECAUTIONS AS YOU ENTER

Earlier, I indicated that any alien entering the United States with a nonimmigrant visa has essentially to go through two admission procedures. First is the actual issuing of his visa by the consular official abroad. As we've already seen, that in itself may require several steps to be taken initially in America. Then, after the nonimmigrant visa is issued, the alien must convince an immigration official at a United States border point that he should be admitted—and sometimes he won't be successful.

Why? There are a good many reasons, some you may never have considered. For instance, it may sound foolish to you, but sloppy dress and uncombed hair can provoke a negative response on the part of a conservative immigration official. You should be aware that many of these officials will judge you by how you look. I've often had to advise my clients to dress discreetly when they come into the country. It may not be reasonable or right, but if some immigration official thinks you look like a junkie or a hippie, he may prevent your entry.

Another thing—be sure not to carry documents with you that contradict the purpose of your entry as it is implied by your visa status. If the visa permits you only to tour in the United States, don't carry such documents as résumés and letters to potential employers. It is quite possible you will be searched.

Please understand, I'm not encouraging you to be deceitful. I know that many people come here to visit and lay the groundwork for future employment. That's entirely legal if the alien intends to leave the country before applying for such employment. But the Immigration Service officer who examines you doesn't know you're going to leave. In fact, he may assume incorrectly that you'll abuse the purpose of your visa, and to him, that's a serious offense.

I've always advised my clients to send over by mail any documents they think might complicate their case at the border, so that they'll arrive separately.

Use your own good sense. If you're waiting in line at an entry point, and you see a particularly disgruntled official who's giving the people ahead of you a hard time, quietly slip into another line. He may have just heard a particularly atrocious lie, or he's encountered a nasty applicant, and he's ready to view everyone with suspicion.

Be polite, too, no matter what the official says to you. Don't forget that he has almost dictatorial power over you. He can send you back home, harass you if he feels like it, make you feel uncomfortable, or embarrass you. He may do all these things, for justified or unjustified reasons. Sometimes aliens provoke this kind of abuse by their attitudes. If you're traveling in circumstances that could be described as awkward, for any reason, be particularly careful and sensitive to the mood that seems to be prevailing at the port of entry. The more polite you are and the more patient you are, the less likely you are to be treated badly.

During the Iranian crisis, people from Iran were almost always singled out for special treatment when they entered the United States. That was understandable, considering the hostage situation. But nationals from some countries are routinely given a harder time than those from other nations.

If you're singled out for further examination, your passport and documents will usually be placed in a red folder and you'll be instructed to go to a separate waiting area for an interview. Don't panic. Be calm and patient. If the examiner sees that you're impatient, it may well have a bad effect on him. As for the interview itself, it's nothing to be frightened of—really no different from what everyone else gets, except that the examiners take more time to question you.

If, in spite of all your ingenuity and planning, you still get an immigration inspector who doesn't think you should be admitted, he will advise you of this and tell you that you'll be sent back on the next plane. (That can happen even if you're carrying a Green Card. The official may not believe you're still a resident, especially if you have stayed out of the country a long time.)

When such a crisis occurs, you can always insist on seeing a judge for an exclusion hearing. The immigration inspector may tell you it isn't possible and inform you that he'll put you in jail overnight. Be firm in that case. Insist that you know the law and that you're entitled to a hearing before a judge, because that *is* the law. Usually the inspector, who knows the law well enough himself, will permit you to see one, and if that isn't possible until next day, you are likely to spend the night in a hotel, not in a jail. The inspector has another alternative. He can set up a deferred inspection and admit you to the United States on parole, with a specific date set to appear before an inspector at the Immigration Service center closest to the city of your destination.

Being paroled into the country puts you in a fairly advantageous position, because for many purposes you do have an immigration status, which is not the case if you're sent to a judge. I will discuss parole later.

Be sure to follow explicitly the instructions on your parole form and appear at the Immigration Service on the date that document specifies. If you don't, you will automatically be considered an illegal alien, and the consequences could be extremely damaging.

Another possibility exists. The inspector may simply decide he doesn't have enough information or the time to deal with the issue of your eligibility, and in that case, he'll decide to schedule you for another inspection, by an examiner who will really be no different from the one you saw at the airport. This procedure is called a deferred inspection.

If you're scheduled for an exclusion hearing, I earnestly recommend that you get a lawyer to represent you, because the government will have its own attorney, representing the INS, and he will be your opponent. He will usually try to convince you to withdraw your application to enter. If he succeeds, he and the judge will often let you stay for a while, perhaps for a couple of days, so that you can visit people or set your affairs in order.

If you think your case for entry is a poor one, and consequently that you don't have much chance of winning, it may be a good idea to agree to leave. If you go into court to argue your case and you lose, you will then be excluded from the United States, and that fact goes into your permanent record. Every time you fill out an immigration form after that, you'll have to set down the fact that you were once excluded, and people who have been excluded find it very difficult to get visas.

Listen to your lawyer. He'll advise you on your chances of success in an exclusion hearing, and he will probably tell you, as I do now, that once such a hearing is scheduled, the chances are that you won't get in. It will be a perilous procedure for you, and you'll certainly need a lawyer's help.

You have much less to worry about, however, if the immigration inspector schedules you for a deferred inspection. It isn't always necessary to have a lawyer in that case, but I would recommend one unless you're prepared for whatever may happen and have a reasonable understanding of the law.

At a deferred inspection you'll be asked to appear at the Immigration Service at a stated time. Sometimes it happens that you appear only to be told that your file hasn't arrived from the airport, in which case you'll be given another date. The inspection itself, you will find, is no different from the one you were given at the airport, except that this time the inspector isn't as rushed. If you explain the purpose of your visit carefully, and if you can convince the inspector that you won't exceed the time you've been given to stay, and that you entered for a correct purpose, there is an excellent chance you'll be admitted.

On the other hand, if you leave the inspector with the same feeling the original official had at the airport, you may well be scheduled for an exclusion hearing, which this time will probably take place the same day, and possibly on the spot. If it does, the procedure will be the same as I've outlined above.

I remember a client of mine, a young man carrying an E visa, who was stopped by an immigration officer at Kennedy Airport in New York. He had shaggy hair, wore sloppy clothing, and was very young. The visa he had is normally granted to wealthy foreign investors. Unfortunately, my client was annoyed by the attitude of the immigration inspector, which was justifiable to some extent. This official had never before seen a holder of an E visa dressed in that way, or one so young; consequently, he scheduled the young man for deferred inspection.

I arrived with my client at the time appointed for the inspection and explained the situation to the supervisor. He was quite understanding, remarking that it was unusual for such a young man to have so large a business. We were able to demonstrate, however, that the investment was real, and that my client did indeed own the company he had cited on his application, and that it was active. The young man was then admitted without any difficulty, but the experience sobered him. When he entered the United States afterward, he dressed like a middle-aged businessman.

I have sometimes been called in by clients to help with exclusion hearings, and I have usually advised them to withdraw their applications to enter, especially in cases where I knew they would have great difficulty in convincing the Immigration Service that they were really coming only to visit. A case referred to me by a large law firm some years ago is particularly relevant. It involved a man whose nephew had wanted to enter the United States ostensibly to tour the country. At the entry port, however, the inspector decided to search the young man because he was unable to produce a round-trip ticket or to provide a clear answer when asked how long he intended to stay. The search turned up a letter clearly indicating that he intended to work here.

I had to advise the law firm retaining me that the chances of overcoming their client's problem were remote. My advice was to withdraw the application. There were good reasons underlying my advice, aside from the unlikelihood of convincing the Immigration Service that the young man had not lied to them.

Withdrawal of an entry has a distinct advantage, since the individual is neither deported nor excluded—and as I mentioned earlier, exclusion and deportation have serious effects on later applications. Nothing happens upon withdrawal except the cancellation of the person's visa. Nevertheless, this cancellation must be declared when applying for a nonimmigrant visa at a later date. Unfortunately, many people lie about cancellation of their visa, because they know that, usually, they'll be able to get away with the lie. Sometimes they *don't* get away with it, however, and if that happens, the consequences are severe.

By now, I'm sure you understand that the process of entering the United States can be unpredictable. Don't be discouraged. Difficulties occur in a relatively small number of cases, and the process is usually quite smooth. Most people, in fact, get in with no trouble at all.

I've learned several important things about entering America. One is that you must be definite when you enter. You should be able to give an examining officer a clear idea of what you intend to do in the United States and exactly when you intend to leave. As I said earlier, don't volunteer any more than is absolutely necessary, but make sure you have answers prepa ed for questions you can expect to be asked. After reading this book, you should be aware of what it is your visa allows you to do, and then it shouldn't be too difficult to answer the few questions you'll be asked at the entry point.

VISA WAIVER

There are some circumstances in which you can enter the United States without a visa. I'll address some of those circumstances later on, in the section on refugees and humanitarian parole, but here I want to discuss briefly the exception that is known as the visa waiver.

Not long ago, a prominent businessman from a country then in a state of revolution called me from Zurich and told me he was about to enter the United States on a business trip. I knew he didn't have a valid visa in his passport, so I questioned him about his intention to enter. He told me there was no time to get a visa, and because of the strained relations between his country and ours, he doubted that he could get one in any case. He reminded me of his prominence in the business world, and that he was so well known to the State Department his file there was "six inches thick."

During our telephone conversation, I tried to convince him that he should apply for a visa before he came in, because I knew that, even though he might be successful in entering without one, he would certainly be delayed for hours at the airport. He was unconvinced, however, and I wasn't surprised two days later when an immigration official called me at seven o'clock in the morning from the airport. My client had arrived without a visa.

I requested a visa waiver, which is simply a request by the Immigration Service directly to the State Department that an alien be admitted with no documents. This is a rare procedure, but it worked in this case because my client was, indeed, an internationally famous businessman who had rendered valuable services to our government in the past. But the procedure wasn't simple. Famous or not, the businessman was detained at the airport for four hours while telephone calls were made to and from Washington. The Immigration Service at the airport had to request a visa waiver from the State Department, the request going through an officer of the Central Immigration Office in Washington, which is in charge of all border admissions. The chief of that office called the State Department, which in turn called its desk in charge of the country my client came from. In the end, a file was created, examined, and ultimately reviewed, and it was determined that the alien in question should be allowed to enter.

Visa waiver is a procedure to be used only as a last resort, and only in an emergency, or where an obvious error has occurred. I don't recommend it.

APPEALS

When you apply to the Immigration Service for such visas as H or L and your application is denied, you can appeal to a regional commissioner in control of the Service where you've been rejected.

But, once you're here, if your application to extend your stay or to change your status is denied, no such appeal before the regional commissioner is possible. You'll be limited to a review called a motion to reopen and reconsider. That means you apply to the same immigration office that rejected your application and ask the officials to reexamine the circumstances in which you applied.

If it is a consul who is denying your visa, hire a lawyer to fight your case. Even he will have a hard time, however, for the review procedure within the Department of State is not nearly as structured or effective as it is in the Immigration Service.

INELIGIBILITY

Any member of the Communist party will have difficulty in entering the United States. Aliens with certain diseases, such as tuberculosis or a venereal disease, are also not likely to be admitted to this country. In fact, there is a surprising number of reasons for barring the admission of an alien who wishes to enter the United States. Some of these reasons are set forth in appendix 17, and are known as the grounds of excludability. These make it difficult to enter the United States either as an immigrant or on a temporary visa—difficult, but not impossible. In certain circumstances, the otherwise ineligible alien can come in if either the Secretary of State or the Attorney General decides to waive the objections in a particular case.

It is well known that certain foreign entertainers who perform in the United States regularly have had drug convictions that should make them ineligible to enter the United States. Nevertheless, many of these people enter the United States regularly. They do so because they have been given waivers.

The subject of ineligibility and waivers is a technical one, beyond the scope of this book. It's sufficient to say that if you're in this predicament, seek the proper legal advice.

CONCLUSION

I have tried to cover what most applicants will need to know about getting temporary visas. However, certain categories of applicants, such as students, entertainers, doctors, and others, have been singled out for special treatment later in the book because of their importance and because what I have to say is often relevant to both temporary and permanent residence.

PART III

PERMANENT RESIDENCE

6

HOW TO GET YOUR GREEN CARD

For millions of people around the world, the ultimate aim is to establish legal residence in the United States, a goal symbolized by those magic words, the "Green Card." The card itself, as I remarked earlier, is no longer green but white and is roughly the size of a credit card.

Although many aliens are at first interested in coming here only for a short time, I'm sure that the majority of those who read this book will want to know how to get the Green Card, and I'm going to tell you how to accomplish that goal.

The road to permanent residence is littered with obstacles, such as regulations and bureaucrats whose sole purpose, so it seems much of the time, is to slow down the overwhelming tide of humanity trying to get into America. For some applicants, the problems may be few and the waiting minimal; but for others, the dream of residence in the United States may go unfulfilled.

Those are the extremes. Most of you will find yourselves in a vast middle ground, where it's possible for you to use the rules to your advantage if you learn something about them. Some of those who find their attempts blocked may try to get around the obstacles by illegal means. A few of these people will even get away with it. My strategy is different, however, and I'm convinced that it works.

When a client comes to me, I first ask him a simple question: "What do you want?" Once he tells me it is permanent residence, I try to find out as much as I can about his background, his family relationships, his potential relationship with citizens or residents of the United States, and any other information I think will make it possible to accomplish his goal. Then, using my knowledge of the law and the practical information I've acquired over the years, I try to lay out a path of least resistance for him. It isn't always the shortest path, or the cheapest, but for me these considerations are less important than the possibility of success.

About half the immigrants to America enter as a result of their relationships with residents and citizens of this country. The other half consists of workers, both skilled and unskilled, political refugees, beneficiaries of humanitarian parole, investors, and others who may be covered by immigration rules that are sometimes quite obscure.

I shall use the term "permanent residence visas" throughout this section. Don't confuse these with nonimmigrant visas. "Permanent residence" means exactly what it says, and permanent residence visas represent permission to enter our country to live here permanently. The visas issued for permanent residence are available in accordance with an allocation system established by Congress, which exerts careful control over the number of people who can get Green Cards within a year. It also creates categories of applicants, some of whom have a higher priority than others.

The law says that a total of 270,000 visas for permanent residence can be issued in a given year. There are groups of individuals who are exempt from this numerical restriction, however. For these lucky people, the immigration process will, in general, be less complicated than for the others. The rules and regulations governing permanent residence in the United States are known as the Immigration Selection System.

To start sorting everyone out, let's talk first about those immigrants who can come into the United States without permanent residence visas. Many of them may also qualify under the rules allocating the 270,000 visa numbers available every year, but none of them may use a number if they can get in without one. This rule was made to ensure that visa numbers won't be used where they aren't necessary.

IMMIGRANTS NOT SUBJECT TO NUMERICAL RESTRICTIONS

Years ago, when immigration was governed by a quota system based on country of origin, the people I'm talking about were called nonquota immigrants. Now they're known as nonpreference immigrants. They fall into two general categories, immediate relatives and special immigrants.

Immediate Relatives

If you're the husband, wife, minor (under twenty-one) unmarried child, or parent of a United States citizen who is twenty-one years old, you will neither need nor be able to use a visa number to achieve permanent residence in the United States. It's important to understand, however, that only an American citizen who is more than twenty-one years old is able to confer such a benefit on an immigrant. It makes no difference whether the American's citizenship is based on birth or naturalization.

(Later on, when we discuss the preference system, you'll see that a number of categories are reserved for relationships between aliens and American residents and citizens. In general, such relationships have a higher priority than most of the other categories that qualify for permanent residence visas. Don't confuse these categories available under the preference system with the category of immediate relatives, who are nonpreference and considered part of the "nuclear family.")

Immediate relatives don't need visas, but they are strictly limited to the small group I've just mentioned. Let's take them one at a time.

Spouse. If you're married to a citizen of the United States who is over twenty-one, you can immigrate to this country without using a visa number. It makes no difference how old you are or where you live. You must remember, however, that all immigrants can be refused a Green Card if they've committed certain acts or if they fall within certain categories that make them ineligible to become residents. The rules of ineligibility apply to everyone, so I'll discuss them at the end of this chapter.

Unmarried children. Under the law, a child must be under twenty-one and legitimate. To qualify as a child of an American citizen, the child must be unmarried and the parent must be over twenty-one and a citizen of the United States. Don't forget, however, that even a child who qualifies for immigration may still be unable to get a Green Card if he or she falls within the class of individuals who are ineligible for permanent residence.

Parents. An alien who is the father or mother of an American citizen over twenty-one is the last of the categories exempt from the requirement to apply for a visa number. Again, the rules of ineligibility still apply.

Although these immediate relatives are given high priority among immigrants, they aren't exempt from the application procedures. They must make an application either in the United States or outside—or both, depending on where they are and how they want to get in. In other words, they must use the normal application procedures everyone else has to comply with. But their task is easier. All they have to do is to demonstrate that the relationship is real, and they'll get in. Of course, they'll also have to show that someone will support them, or that they can support themselves —in short, they must assure the immigration authorities that they won't become public charges after they come here. That restriction, however, applies to everyone.

Special Immigrants

People in this category set up by the immigration law are also exempt from the need to apply for a visa number. The following aliens qualify:

Returning resident aliens. This category embraces aliens who had the status of United States permanent residents and left the country intending to return and are now coming back from a temporary visit abroad. An alien in this category must demonstrate that he hasn't abandoned his intention to live in the United States and must also show that if he was away for longer than a year, it was for reasons beyond his control or else that he applied for a reentry permit before he left.

From time to time, I've been called on to help people who got their Green Cards years earlier but were afraid to come back in because they had been told by friends that if they stayed outside for a long time, their Green Cards would lapse. In general, that's true. Permanent residents of the United States must not stay away from this country for more than a year. Further, they must manifest an intention to live here continuously or else their Green Cards may be taken away when they attempt to reenter—taken away technically, and perhaps literally, too.

Certain former United States citizens. The law recognizes four different kinds of cases:

1. women expatriates who lost their American citizenship because they married an alien before September 22, 1922;

2. women expatriates who lost their American citizenship because they married an alien who was ineligible for citizenship after September 22, 1922;

3. women expatriates who lost their American citizenship because the spouse lost *his* citizenship; and

4. persons who lost their American citizenship during World War II because they entered or served in the armed forces of certain nations unfriendly to the United States.

Certain ministers. This applies to aliens who are ministers of a religious denomination who have functioned in that capacity for at least two years before their petition for immigration was filed, and who seek to enter this country for the sole purpose of serving a bona-fide religious organization that is of the same denomination and needs the services of these applicants.

Recently, I was called on by a minister of an obscure Middle Eastern denomination to help with an application for his residence. I was concerned that the American government might not recognize his denomination because I felt sure that few public officials would ever have heard of it—and I was right. I filed the application for residence at the American embassy in London, which referred it to the visa office of the State Department in Washington.

The man had been a minister for two years before the time he applied for residence, but he hadn't been able to show that a formal ministerial degree had been conferred on him because, in his sect, such a formality isn't required. We were able to demonstrate, however, that he was accepted by his religious group as a religious leader and teacher. We were also able to prove that there already existed in the United States an organized religious group of his denomination that required his services. Several weeks later, the application was approved.

It's important to understand that the operative word is "services," not employment. My minister client was careful to point out that he didn't work for a living, and that he was not paid for his services, but chose to help people pursue their religious goals. He insisted that I should not describe anything he did as employment.

I make this point because, within the quota system, there is a way to get a Green Card based on a job offer by a religious sect to a minister or teacher. But that employment requires a visa number. A minister of religion who falls within the group of special immigrants, like the one I've just described, does not. I should add that the spouse and minor children of a minister are also covered and are included in his application.

Certain former United States government employees. An employee, or an honorably discharged or retired former employee, of the United States government who has worked for the government for at least fifteen years qualifies here. Such an alien must be recommended for special immigrant status by the senior officer in the American government office where he works. Usually this is an embassy or a consulate somewhere outside the United States. And again, the spouse and minor children of such aliens are also eligible.

None of these special immigrants is exempt from the application procedures controlling the immigration process of all aliens. However, they don't have to demonstrate any relationship beyond that set forth in the categories above. If they're outside the United States, they must file the normal immigrant visa forms. If they're already inside the country, they must make use of the normal change-of-status forms. Instead of trying to qualify for a visa number of preference, however, they will merely set forth the factual situation that backs their claim that they qualify for the special immigrant category. The ineligibility rules I've referred to earlier still apply.

Refugees

In addition to immediate relatives and special immigrants, there are two other categories of foreign immigrants who are able to come into the United States beyond the 270,000 limitation. They are those who qualify for refugee status and those who are granted political asylum. The actual number of those permitted to enter the country each year is determined by an agreement between Congress and the President. Determining who will qualify and who won't is a political matter. The rules concerning refugee status and political asylum are complex. If they concern you especially, read the detailed discussion of them in chapter 10.

IMMIGRANTS SUBJECT TO NUMERICAL RESTRICTIONS

The special categories of aliens I have described above, who don't need visa numbers in order to get Green Cards, are relatively few. Nearly everyone else who wants to come to America permanently falls within the immigration preference system that permits no more than 270,000 aliens to come in permanently every year. There was at one time a separate allocation for residents of the Western and Eastern hemispheres. That's no longer the case.

The 270,000 figure doesn't include the categories who are exempt from numerical restrictions. There is a per-country limitation of 20,000 aliens per year who are allowed permanent residence here, and that ceiling is allocated proportionately to each preference category. There's also a restriction on colonies of 600 aliens per year, which means that someone from Hong Kong, for instance, would have to qualify under that limitation and not under Great Britain's yearly limitation of 20,000.

All visa applicants for permanent residence are considered, for purposes of the per-country limitation, as citizens of their country of birth. This is known as chargeability. The country of citizenship is not important. There are, however, four exceptions to the basic rules of chargeability under which you're not limited by the quota limitation of your country of birth. These exceptions are known as the rules of cross-chargeability, as follows:

1. If your spouse's nationality is different from yours and the quota limitations for your own country of origin have been exceeded, you may be able to apply under the quota rules for your spouse's country of origin. For this rule, it doesn't make any difference which spouse is the principal applicant.

2. Children may always be charged to the place of birth of either of their parents.

3. Aliens who were once American citizens by birth can be charged to the country of their last citizenship or of their last residence if they're not citizens of any other country.

4. If an alien was born in a country where neither of his parents was born, he may be charged to the country of birth of either of his parents if they did not have a residence in the alien's country of birth at the time he was born.

It's important to keep these rules in mind, because even though you may qualify for permanent residence, your place of birth may limit your ability to enter the United States as a permanent resident. Sometimes a wait of many years is required. In the Philippines, for example, under many categories, a wait of ten years or more is not uncommon. If you can show, however, that you fall within the rules of cross-chargeability, you may be able to come in much sooner.

Before we go any further, you should understand the manner by which visa numbers are allocated. This preference system, as it's called, creates rules of eligibility for six categories of immigrants, and they are not divided by nationality. In general, each category is given a certain percentage of the overall 270,000 numbers allowable every year. When a particular category doesn't use all of the numbers allotted to it, those that are unused either pass down to the next preference or they're put into a pool that is available to the lowest category, known as the nonpreference category. Unfortunately, that category has been unavailable for years, because the higher preferences have completely used up their allocations.

Although the preference system is a vast improvement over the national-origin quota system, delays for nationals of certain countries under certain preferences are quite common. During the past several years, for instance, there have even been extensive delays for people applying for residence under the third and sixth preferences, regardless of their citizenship.

The State Department publishes a bulletin each month that sets forth in detail a list of backlogs for particular preferences (see appendix 3). These backlogs are cross-referenced to each country that is affected.

If you're affected by a backlog, you must try to get onto a waiting list as quickly as possible. Your place on that waiting list for a particular visa category is known as the priority date. You may obtain a priority date in several different ways.

If your application is not based on a labor certification, your priority date will be the date when your immigration application was first accepted for processing at an office of the Immigration Service. If your application for a preference is based on a labor certification, your priority date will be the date a local office of the Department of Labor first accepted your labor certification application for processing.

This is how the preference system works:

First preference: Unmarried sons and daughters, over age twenty-one, of United States citizens—20 percent of the overall limitation of 270,000 in any fiscal year.

Second preference: Spouses and unmarried sons and daughters, over age twenty-one, of aliens lawfully admitted for permanent residence—26 percent of overall limitation plus any numbers not required by the first-preference category.

Third preference: Members of the professions or persons of exceptional ability in the sciences and arts—10 percent of overall limitations.

Fourth preference: Married sons and daughters (also over age twenty-one) of United States citizens, and their families—10 percent of overall limitation, plus any numbers not required by the first three preference categories.

Fifth preference: Brothers and sisters, twenty-one years of age or over, of United States citizens—24 percent of overall limitation, plus any numbers not required by the first four preference categories.

Sixth preference: Skilled and unskilled workers in short supply —10 percent of overall limitation.

Nonpreference (other immigrants): The nonpreference portion of the quota includes all immigrants not classified as immediate relations or special immigrants, and immigrants who do not fall within any of the six preference categories. They can only get visas if all the numbers allocated to preferences from one through six (for a total of 270,000 per year) have not been used. Since 1978, however, no nonpreference numbers have been available because the quota has been entirely exhausted each year by the six preference categories. When numbers were available, many foreign investors and retired people entered the United States as nonpreference immigrants. The category was also used by many others such as aunts or nephews of U.S. citizens and other related individuals who did not otherwise qualify for a preference. Unfortunately, this is no longer possible, and the situation is not likely to change in the near future.

If you can show that you have a family relationship to an American citizen or resident that qualifies you under the first, second, fourth, or fifth preference, you'll be in a generally good position. You'll still have to file immigration documents and forms to demonstrate the relationship, but your path should be fairly easy, even though in certain cases the process may take quite a long time.

If no such relationship exists, however, your entry will have to be based on a job offer that qualifies you under the third or sixth preference. Most people who qualify under these two preferences will first have to argue the merits of their case before the Department of Labor. Only after that department grants them labor certification will they be able to take their case before the INS.

An alien may be eligible for a permanent residence visa under more than one of the seven categories listed above. And that is why immigration strategy becomes very important. It's necessary to look carefully at each category and choose the one that will get you here faster.

It's more than likely that if you have a professional degree of some kind, and if you're married to an American resident, you can come into the United States with a Green Card in several different ways. If you happen to be from a country from which an application in a family relationship category would be delayed longer than one in the professional employment category, you would be wise to choose the latter preference, even though it may appear to be more advantageous to choose the former. Remember, you have a choice, and you should exercise it, based on what will work best for you and not on what appears most logical at first examination.

When it comes to permanent residence, as with temporary visas, you can choose one of two entirely different but not necessarily inconsistent paths in order to get in. You may first enter the United States on a temporary basis and then apply for permanent residence while you're here—a process called adjustment of status. Or, if you wish, you can go through the whole procedure while you're still abroad, applying for the Green Card through an embassy or consulate; that method is known as consular processing.

Rules for each of these procedures, and the papers filed for them, are quite different. The choice of route is based on the personal circumstances of each alien, but of course not every alien has a choice. For example, anyone working illegally in the United States after January 1, 1977, is not eligible by law to apply for an adjustment of status to that of permanent resident. That also applies to aliens who entered this country illegally. In the case of these illegals, marriage to an American citizen will help.

If you make your application outside the country, you can usually anticipate a much shorter wait than if you make it at an INS office in the United States, because the INS offices have substantial backlogs and those in large cities are exceptionally slow. Processing outside the country is rapid in most places.

Once you file an application to adjust your status in the United States, you cannot travel abroad until the adjustment has been made, unless you have special permission to do so. This permission is called advance parole. If you travel outside the country without it, you will have abandoned your application to adjust status and will be forced in most cases to wait abroad until processing is completed. Occasionally—in cases where, for example, you left without such permission because of an emergency—the INS official at the airport or at a deferred inspection may choose to ignore a lapse of this kind and take no action to withdraw your application. But don't count on it.

ADVANCE PAROLE

In order to get advance parole, you must go down to the Immigration Service with proof that your travel is required either because of a personal family emergency or because of an urgent business necessity. If it's for business, permission will normally be granted only to the individual who needs to travel. Some immigration offices in the United States grant advance parole quite readily, while others are very strict. The Los Angeles office, for instance, is far more strict than the one in New York. But in whatever place you apply or the reason for your application, you'll need proof, either by letter or telegram, that your trip is required for business reasons or for reasons of personal emergency—medical, for example. If the application is for business reasons, the letter should include your itinerary. You'll also need to bring a round-trip airline ticket and, in most cases, Form G-325A (see appendix 18), two photographs, and a fingerprint record.

To request advance parole, you should present yourself at an Immigration Service office very early in the morning and be prepared to wait until permission is granted. That grant will consist of two immigration forms, one to hand in to the Service when you leave and the other to give to the INS officer when you come back.

Most aliens should not attempt to get advance parole without legal advice.

If it's important for you to travel abroad while you're waiting for a Green Card to come through, you're probably better off making application at an American consulate. Of course, you won't be able to travel in and out of the United States unless you have a valid temporary visa. If the immigration processing is likely to take some time, you may be able to convince the consul who is processing your permanent residence application to give you another temporary visa. That may be done if the consul believes you won't use it to enter the United States and then apply for a change of status while you're here.

Every alien who wants a Green Card—even the person who doesn't need a visa number—must decide which of the two methods to use in applying for it. Many people opt to stay and apply for adjustment of status, because they are afraid to leave the United States; often that fear is legitimate, since nationals of certain countries sometimes find it harder to get out of their homeland once they've gone back. In that case, it may be advisable to stay here until the entire procedure is completed.

If you decide to go through the immigration process entirely in the United States, you'll need to be very careful about illegal employment, and also about the timing of your exits from and reentries into the country. In general, the INS frowns on an alien who makes an application to change his status to permanent residence if he does so too soon after he applied for his latest nonimmigrant visa. Indeed, he may be accused of visa fraud and thus find it impossible to adjust his status here. Your lawyer may advise you to apply for your Green Card abroad if he suspects that not enough time has elapsed since the date of your application for a temporary visa.

If you're living abroad, you should make your application for the immigrant visa at an American consulate or embassy, either in your native country or in the country of your last residence. Sometimes this isn't practical, however, and you may be compelled to make your application in the country where you happen to be, which may not be easy.

If you're already in the United States, you can choose to make your application either in America, through the adjustment-of-status process, or outside the country. Of course, some aliens have valid nonimmigrant visas that permit them entry and exit. In that case, even if you're outside of the country at the time the preference petition is granted, you have the choice of coming back into the United States and making application for adjustment of status after you've reentered.

GREEN CARDS ISSUED OUTSIDE THE UNITED STATES

If you want to get your permanent residence visa outside the United States, apply for your Green Card at an American embassy or consulate that has authority to issue immigrant visas. But remember, not all embassies and consulates have these powers. If your permanent residence is based on the grant of a preference, you'll have to have your immigration file sent to the consulate or embassy where the processing will take place. This can be done either by you or by your attorney. In many cases, it's done automatically by the INS when the preference is granted.

When the consular post gets your approved preference petition, and is satisfied that you're currently eligible for a visa number, you'll be sent something known as "Packet Three," which contains two forms, OF-169 (see appendix 19) and OF-179 (see appendix 20). These are biographical and information forms that must be completed. They're both straightforward and should present no problems.

After the forms are filed with the consulate, you'll be told when to expect an interview. In the meantime, the embassy will clear you with the FBI and other relevant organizations. The interview takes place at the consulate, and all members of your family who are getting Green Cards must come with you. A good part of this process can take place by mail, and sometimes it can even be done when the applicant is in the United States on another basis. In fact, aliens sometimes stay in America illegally or legally while the entire consular proceeding is taking place abroad. That occurs frequently, because there is often a period of waiting even after your preference petition has been approved. The delay is simply the result of backlogs for various preferences and countries, and these change from month to month. You'll find a typical list in appendix 3.

If you are coming in as a special immigrant you won't need to show any documentation that emanates from the INS. In such a case, all you have to do is to take the two forms, OF-169 and OF-179, along with proof of your qualifications, and file them at the embassy or consulate.

Whatever the basis of your immigration application, when you're called for your interview, you'll have to submit another form, Form 230 (see appendix 21). This is a four-page document that must be filed in duplicate. Separate forms are required for each member of the family. The embassy will make arrangements for you to have a medical checkup before the time of the interview. They'll be checking you for various communicable diseases. You will be given a list of doctors eligible to give you the medical checkup.

At the interview, you'll have to bring the following documents:

1. Passport
2. Birth certificate
3. Police certificates
4. Court and prison records, if any
5. Military records, if any
6. Photographs
7. Evidence of support
8. Marriage certificate
9. Letter from the prospective employer

If any of these required documents are in languages other than English, or in the language of the country where the consul happens to be, you'll have to provide translations. Remember, everything you supply should be in duplicate, and if possible make duplicate copies for your own records. You can show the consul the originals at the interview, but don't let him keep them. If you do, you'll probably never see them again.

At the interview all members of the family over fourteen years of age will be fingerprinted.

Permanent residence visas are generally issued on the day of the final interview, or immediately thereafter. Sometimes a consul may request that you furnish all the required information in advance of the interview, so that the records can be reviewed carefully.

When you apply abroad, police certificates are required to demonstrate good conduct in every country where you or your family were residents for more than six months after the age of sixteen.

If employment is the basis for your immigration application, you must provide a job letter that conforms to the job offer as set forth in your earlier application. The letter must state that you're already working, if you're permitted to do so, or that the job is still waiting for you. If your application isn't based on a job, then you can either submit proof that your job is waiting for you or provide an affidavit of support to prove that you won't become a public charge.

When you finally get your immigrant visa, it may surprise you. It will be a thick, unimpressive-looking bunch of documents stapled together in a curious manner. It isn't your Green Card, of course. Not yet. You and all the members of your family must enter the United States with the visa within four months of receiving it, and you must hand it in to the immigration inspector when you enter. At that point, a temporary Green Card stamp will be stamped into your passport. You should get your Green Card in the mail within six months thereafter.

I say you *should* receive it within six months. In my experience, however, more than a quarter of all Green Cards arrive late—or never. If the Green Card does not arrive soon after the six-month period has elapsed, you should call your attorney or whoever else you can call upon to make inquiries. I have often had to file additional applications for my clients, with new fingerprints, in an effort to rectify such a situation.

ADJUSTMENT OF STATUS

If you decide to make the application to get your Green Card in the United States, an entirely different set of forms is required. You can make this application only if you qualify for a preference category that is current—that is, available to you. You can check on that beforehand by looking at the Preference Chart contained in the *Visa Office Bulletin*. You'll find a sample of the chart in appendix 3.

If your application is based on an immediate-relative petition, or if you're a special immigrant and therefore don't need a visa number, you can apply at any time. In general, you should apply at the immigration office closest to where you're living. That office will usually have the complete file on your visa eligibility. If illegal work or illegal entry has made you ineligible to make application for adjustment of status, don't bother doing it. You will probably be caught, and if you lie you may be in even more serious trouble.

The following forms are required for an adjustment of status:

     1. Form I-485, Application for Status as Permanent Resident (see appendix 22)
     2. Form ER-531, to indicate address for Green Card mailing (see appendix 23)
     3. Form G-325A, Biographic Information (see appendix 18)
     4. Fingerprint chart (see appendix 24)
     5. Two passport-size color photographs
     6. A valid passport, with Form I-94 (see appendix 5)
     7. Medical interview data

The spouse and children of the applicant must provide the same documentation, with the exception that children under fourteen do not have to supply either Form G–325A (Biographic Information) or fingerprints. They're also exempt from the medical x-ray (as are pregnant women), but not from the medical examination itself.

Again, if employment is the basis of your application, you'll have to do as those applying from outside the country are required to do, as I've described earlier in this chapter. You will need a job letter conforming to the job offer in your earlier application, stating that you're already working, or that a job is waiting for you.

At some INS offices in America, the entire package of documentation, along with an application fee of $25.00, can be filed by you or your lawyer in advance, either in person or by mail. You must then wait for an interview to be scheduled, and shortly before the date of your interview, you'll be called in for a medical examination, since that exam must be fairly recent.

In most INS offices, however, a limited number of applications are reviewed on a walk-in basis. This usually means that the applicant has to get up very early in the morning and wait in line with complete documentation. If you're one of the lucky ones, you'll be called by number or name for an interview and to have your application reviewed that day. Unless a visa number is required, you may even get a temporary Green Card in one day. But if a visa number is required, the INS must get it for you, and that can take from thirty to ninety days.

One of the advantages of filing papers in advance is that at the time of your interview, if the INS has done its job, the visa clearance procedures will have been completed and a visa number will already be waiting in your file; if everything is in order, you may get a temporary Green Card on the spot.

In the past, the Green Card was actually presented at the interview, but that is no longer the case. Now, in every instance, at the end of the interview, if all is in order, a stamp is affixed to your passport or on a separate piece of paper that says that you have been made a resident and that you can travel in and out of the United States for a period of either six months or a year, at which time the actual card will be issued to you.

You should get your Green Card in the mail within the period indicated on the temporary stamp; but too often, unfortunately, it doesn't come within the required time, and new applications must then be made. Fortunately, however, these delays have no real effect, since you're considered a permanent resident (with all rights) from the date of your temporary stamp.

INELIGIBILITY

At the end of the previous chapter, I explained that there is a list of several categories of aliens who, while they may in other respects be eligible, will be denied entry into the United States. This applies to immigrants as well as to those who want to enter on temporary visas.

In appendix 17 you'll find a general list of the more important grounds for exclusion—reasons why an alien may be ineligible to enter the United States—but in general, this subject is too technical to cover in detail here. Some of the categories are obvious— for instance, if one is a member of the Communist party or has been convicted of a serious crime. Probably it's enough to be aware of the difficulties and their possible solutions.

If you're ineligible for any reason, however, it doesn't mean you're necessarily barred from residence permanently. You can apply for a waiver of ineligibility. The waiver form (Form I-601; see appendix 25) should be filled in by an attorney. In fact, if you've decided that you're ineligible, you should promptly consult a lawyer who's an expert in immigration law.

The circumstances in which a waiver may be granted must be studied carefully before an application is made. In nearly every case, these applications are referred to the Attorney General of the United States, who makes the final decision. As you might suspect, it helps if you have some good connections to the United States —an American spouse or child, for instance—but such relationships aren't necessarily conclusive.

DEPORTATION

If you've exceeded your permitted stay in this country, or have otherwise violated the immigration law, and if that violation comes to the attention of the INS, you'll have to account for your behavior, and you may be asked to leave. This procedure is known as deportation. I don't intend to say much more about it except to warn you that if you find yourself in a situation where that procedure is a possibility, the best thing to do is to consult a lawyer who's an expert in the field. Deportation can have serious consequences, not only over the short term, but for the future as well.

KEEPING YOUR GREEN CARD

In certain circumstances your Green Card can be taken away from you. This is admittedly a rare occurrence, and the INS can reclaim it only with the greatest difficulty. Nevertheless, it can happen.

Many aliens get Green Cards not because they want to live in the United States, but because they want to have what amounts to insurance to fall back on should they be forced to leave their own country. They want to be sure that they will have a place to go to, and the United States is the place of first choice for many people. Consequently, many people who have Green Cards don't live here, and that can be dangerous. To retain your right to keep your card, you are not allowed to be absent from the country for more than a year. And there's still another rule: an alien must manifest an intention to live continuously in the United States. If your residence is really somewhere else, and it becomes clear to the INS as you come and go from the country that you're not actually living here permanently, you may be stopped at some point as you attempt to enter and asked to explain where you do in fact live and how you can justify your claim to your Green Card. Get a lawyer at once. He'll be in a better position than you to deal with this problem.

It's also possible for the INS to take away your Green Card if you are suspected of having committed fraud in the course of an application procedure. That's one of the reasons why I've urged you at various points in this book to be very careful about what you say and do whenever you file any applications.

REENTRY PERMITS

Any alien who is a permanent resident of the United States who intends to remain outside the country for more than a year is well advised to request a travel document known as a reentry permit. This document, which looks much like a passport, is issued by the American government. You apply for it by filing Form I-131 (see appendix 26) at an INS office in this country. You must apply for it thirty days before your departure from the United States. An alien holding it is permitted to stay outside the United States for up to two years.

These, then, are the rules controlling the application procedures for permanent residence in the United States. They're not, however, the most important rules you need to know. In the following chapters, I'll tell you how to go about qualifying yourself for residence in a variety of other cases. Again, I won't try to cover *every* case, only those that apply to the vast majority of potential applicants.

FAMILY REUNIFICATION: IMMEDIATE RELATIVES AND FIRST-, SECOND-, FOURTH-, AND FIFTH-PREFERENCE ALIENS

Most of the rules concerning visas and immigration are extremely tough. But there's an important exception: the area of family reunification, which is a stated objective written into the Immigration and Nationality Act.

Certain categories of relationships are seen as so essential that visa numbers aren't needed. These I have already mentioned in the previous chapter. But there are other categories of family relationships, also discussed in chapter 6, that are almost as important, although those who are included in these categories are subject to numerical restrictions. Let's review them again briefly:

First preference: Unmarried sons and daughters, over the age of twenty-one, of American citizens.

Second preference: Spouses and unmarried sons and daughters of aliens lawfully admitted for permanent residence. Again, the children must be over twenty-one.

Fourth preference: Married sons and daughters, over age twenty-one, of American citizens, and their families.

Fifth preference: Brothers and sisters, over age twenty-one, of American citizens. The American citizen who is petitioning for his sibling must himself be over age twenty-one.

In previous chapters I've discussed how to go about getting your Green Card after your preference has been approved, and how those aliens not requiring visa numbers, which includes immediate-relative immigrants, can make application for permanent residence. Now I'll tell you how to go about qualifying for one of the preferences listed above, so that you can position yourself to make whatever application is relevant in your case.

The concept of "family" is much broader in many other parts of the world than it is in the United States, broad enough in some nations to include aunts, uncles, and even distant cousins. Because of these different conceptions, the American government is careful to define "family" as including, for immigration purposes, father, mother, children, and siblings. These are the only family members included in the preferences listed above and in the more restricted category of immediate relatives.

The importance attached to family reunification is a great benefit for most immigrants. The majority of people who immigrate to this country come in as a result of such ties. The United States, is, after all, a nation of immigrants. This is a familiar fact of history, but we fail to see the irony in setting up immigration laws that are essentially exclusionary in a nation whose citizens are so proud of their origins in other countries. It may be an uneasy conscience, expressing itself on the legislative level, that has resulted in making the concept of family reunification basic to our immigration laws. It's so important a concept that it merits being treated here in a separate chapter.

All immigrants who want to come into the United States on the basis of a family relationship, whether they qualify as immediate relatives (not requiring visa numbers) or fall into one of the five preferences I've just listed, must file Form I-130, Petition to Classify Status of Alien Relative for Issuance of Immigrant Visa (see appendix 27). It's a simple form in which the United States citizen or resident relative is designated as the petitioner—that is, the person filing and initiating the application—and the alien who wants to come into the country as the beneficiary, the person for whom the application is being made.

This form can be filed, along with its supporting documents, either at an American embassy or a consulate abroad, or at an Immigration Service office in the United States. Don't forget that in most cases the application will be processed much more quickly if you file it outside the United States.

Let me discuss the procedures in more detail.

FILING FORM I-130 IN THE UNITED STATES

Form I-130 and its supporting documents can be filed at an INS office nearest to the home of the American resident or citizen petitioner. In some cities, these offices have a huge backlog, but in others the congestion isn't quite as bad.

One of the principal advantages of making application in the United States is that the beneficiary doesn't have to be present when the application is made. The filing can be done either by mail or in person by the petitioner. If the beneficiary is already in the United States at the time the petition is filed, then the documentation and forms for adjustment of the beneficiary's status can be filed at the same time. Remember, though, that the filing for adjustment can only be done if the relationship qualifies the applicant for a preference that is open and available for the country of which the alien is a national or if the alien qualifies as an immediate relative for whom a visa number and preference are not required.

If the relationship you're depending on is a marriage, remember that the INS, especially in the largest American cities, has been exposed to a good deal of fraud. In New York, for example, the Service has encountered certain American citizens who have been married as many as twenty times, all to different aliens who obtained Green Cards as a result of the marriage. This kind of fraud has made the INS officials in New York and other big cities highly suspicious, and they're likely to scrutinize such claims closely.

Oddly enough, there isn't anything illegal about getting married for a Green Card as long as the marriage is a viable one. The INS defines "viable" as meaning that the two people are actually living together, sharing the same apartment. At an immigration interview, husbands and wives may even be taken into separate rooms and questioned individually about their marriage, after which their answers will be compared to see if they're consistent. The INS is well aware that thousands of marriages every year are based on the need for a Green Card and so it investigates any suspicious arrangements closely for fraud. Lawyers are usually reluctant to get involved if they suspect a marriage of convenience that won't withstand close inspection by the INS.

Once the I-130 application is filed, either with or without the adjustment of status papers, the immigration case will probably move along quite smoothly. Nevertheless, don't expect prompt action everywhere; it depends on the INS office where it is being processed whether your petition is approved slowly or quickly.

FILING FORM I-130 OUTSIDE AMERICA

At the outset, let me say that to file Form I-130 abroad both the beneficiary and the American resident or citizen petitioner must be present at the consulate or embassy at the time of the filing. Don't forget to bring all the required documents with you.

This ruling requiring the presence of both beneficiary and resident is one of the chief difficulties when the filing takes place outside the United States. If the beneficiary is a Canadian or a Mexican, of course, there's no problem. In such cases, the petitioner can often simply drive across the border and make the application. But when distant travel is required, it's unfortunately true that many people can't afford the air fare that would make such a filing possible. Yet this method of application is probably the better way to file.

There are two reasons why I think it's better, if you can, to file the I-130 application outside the United States. One is speed. The application can be approved on the spot if the beneficiary and petitioner are present at the consulate or embassy, armed with all the necessary forms. Then the official reviewing the documents can approve the case without delay, often immediately. The other reason is that rarely, if ever, will a consular official at an embassy attempt to judge the merits of an application based on a marriage. In nearly every case, no detailed interview is required.

DOCUMENTATION REQUIRED FOR PROOF OF RELATIONSHIP

Whether filed in the United States or abroad, the I-130 form and its supporting documents, plus a $15.00 filing fee, are required for immediate relatives as well as for those applying on the basis of one of the preferences. In either case, you will have to prove your relationship to the petitioner.

Here are the details about the documentation you'll have to provide along with the form and the filing fee:

1. If your application is based on a relationship to an American citizen who was born in the United States, that citizen will have to provide his original birth certificate or a copy with a raised seal. A baptismal record may be used if a birth certificate is not available. If neither one is available, you can provide affidavits from two citizens of the United States who have personal knowledge of the circumstances surrounding the birth of the American citizen. If *none* of the above is available, it's best to consult a lawyer. Naturalized citizens can present their naturalization certificates. Remember, it's a federal offense to duplicate a naturalization certificate; the original must be presented.

If the petitioner claims to be an American citizen through his parents or his spouse, he must present proof of their citizenship. Sometimes, in the case of a claim of citizenship through parents, additional information is also required.

If the relationship claimed is with an American resident, the resident must submit proof of his status. Usually the presentation of his Green Card will be enough.

2. If your application is based on a marriage, you must present proof of your marriage, as well as of the legal termination of any previous marriages. This is true for both parties.

3. If the application is based on a child's relationship to its mother, the child must present a birth certificate showing the full

name of the mother. If the claim is based on a relationship to a father or a stepparent, a marriage certificate for the parents as well as proof of legal termination of previous marriages must be shown, and the birth certificate of the child must be provided as well. If the child has been adopted by the petitioning parents, the adoption must have occurred before the child reached fourteen years of age, and the child must have resided with the parent at least two years before the filing.

4. If the relationship is with a brother or sister who is an American citizen, you'll have to present the birth certificates of both the American citizen and the beneficiary. The certificates must show a common mother. If the brother-sister relationship is through a common father with different mothers, the marriage certificate of the petitioner's parents and of the beneficiary's parents, and proof of the legal termination of the parents' previous marriages, if any, must be shown.

5. If the beneficiary is the mother of an American citizen over the age of twenty-one, the American citizen petitioner must show his or her birth certificate, indicating the name of the mother. If the father or the stepparent is the beneficiary, then the petitioner must present his or her birth certificate, along with the marriage certificate of his or her parents and stepparents, and the evidence of legal termination of any previous marriage.

6. Marriage certificates must accompany the petition if either the petitioner or the beneficiary is a married woman. This is to explain any change in family name. If, however, a mother-child relationship exists between the petitioner and beneficiary, the marriage certificate of the mother will not have to be submitted if the mother's current married name appears on the birth certificate of the child.

7. A certified copy of an adoption decree must be presented along with the petition if the petitioner and beneficiary are related to each other by adoption. But remember that adoptions are only valid relationships if they take place before the time the child reaches the age of fourteen. I-130 applications can be filed on behalf of an adopted child only two years after the date of adoption.

GENERAL CONSIDERATIONS

Family relationships are usually approved routinely, and you probably won't have much to worry about. There are some exceptions, however.

When it comes to nationals from Far Eastern countries and other parts of Asia, consuls and immigration officials are likely to be very strict in assessing the real nature of family relationships. There are several reasons. For one, a great deal of fraud has been discovered in recent years. Record keeping is usually quite different in the Far East than it is in the West, which makes the process of verifying the facts surrounding a family relationship much more difficult. As a result, in certain countries special additional visa forms are required. This should be checked with the consulate in advance. Bear in mind the fact that although some nations do not consider polygamy a crime, the United States does.

For most of the world's countries, the quotas that fall into the category of family reunification are open. There are some traditional exceptions, such as mainland China, India, Korea, Mexico, Hong Kong, and the Philippines. You will find the full list in appendix 3. If there's any difficulty in proving a relationship, it's safest to employ a lawyer. In most cases, however, this won't be necessary.

Right here I need to say a word about a delicate subject— illegitimacy. In some countries it does not have the negative connotation that it does here, but please remember that it will be an American official who will be reviewing your immigration files. Although standards in this area have been somewhat relaxed recently, illegitimacy still causes serious difficulties in the immigration process. The rules in these cases are very detailed and beyond the scope of this book. A lawyer should be consulted.

Whatever documents you submit in support of Form I-130 must all be written either in English or in the language of the country where the consular official happens to be. Otherwise, certified translations must be provided. If the application is submitted in the United States, the documents must be either in English or with certified translations attached to the original document or certified copy.

There are so many benefits to be derived from making your immigration application on the basis of family reunification that I urge you to study the possibility carefully, to see if you qualify. If you do, your residence in the United States should be accomplished without much difficulty.

WORK-RELATED IMMIGRATION: THIRD- AND SIXTH-PREFERENCE ALIENS AND LABOR CERTIFICATION

If your goal of American residence can't be achieved through family reunification, and you are not an immediate relative, you'll probably need an offer of employment instead. In this case, only the third or sixth preference will be open to you. I'll define these two categories once more below.

Third preference: Aliens who are members of the professions or who, because of their exceptional ability in either the sciences or the arts, will provide a substantial benefit to the national economy, cultural interests, or welfare of the United States, and whose services in the professions, sciences, or arts are sought by an employer in the United States. Third preference is given 10 percent of the overall numerical limitation of 270,000.

Sixth preference: Aliens who will perform skilled or unskilled labor that is not of a temporary or seasonal nature, and for which a shortage of employable and willing persons exists in the United States. Sixth preference gets 10 percent of the overall numerical limitation.

For whichever preference you qualify, essentially you will be entering the United States as a result of an offer of employment. Because employment is the basis of immigration applications under the third and sixth preference, the prospective American employer must nearly always get permission from the United States Department of Labor to hire the alien. This is where labor certification enters the picture. There is a small group of exceptions to this rule, however, appearing on a list known as Schedule A. These are occupations that are exempt from the requirement that an American employer seek permission from the Labor Department before he requests a preference from the INS on behalf of the alien he wants to bring in. The decision as to whether or not an alien qualifies under Schedule A is usually made by the Immigration Service. Over the past few years, Schedule A has become increasingly important, and I'll discuss this subject fully in chapter 9.

Most aliens don't qualify for Schedule A, however, so their first application will be to the Labor Department, for labor certification. It's important to understand that labor certification, whether it's granted as the result of the normal application process or because of a waiver under Schedule A, does not in itself secure entry; it merely makes the alien eligible to apply for a subsequent immigration benefit. That benefit is either the third or sixth preference. Let's look at the rules and application procedures for those preferences and then at labor certification itself.

In chapter 6, I explained that there are two ways to apply for permanent residence in the United States—from abroad or by adjustment of status for those who are already here and qualify. Most aliens who want to get Green Cards have to qualify for a preference. If third or sixth preference is required, an alien has to recognize that applications in both of these categories are usually backlogged, which means that visa numbers are not immediately available. Consequently, some long-term planning is usually required.

If it's necessary for you to be in the United States while the applications are in process, you must first apply for a temporary visa in order to be here legally; the temporary visa will permit you to remain in the United States and perhaps (depending on the visa) to be employed while you're waiting for approval of residence. If you're content to remain outside the United States while your application is pending, the issue of a temporary visa isn't as important. Of course, many—perhaps most—aliens enter on temporary visas and stay longer than they should. Many file immigration applications while they're illegally here and subsequently even file for adjustment of status (available only if you have never worked without permission). The availability of this procedure to "overstays" is one of the oddities of American immigration law.

Whatever you decide to do, be sure to obtain the services of a lawyer who is an expert in immigration law and qualified to advise you. Your first step after that is to apply to the Labor Department for certification, unless you come under Schedule A rules; the second step is to apply to the INS for a third or sixth preference. Let's assume for the moment that you get your labor certification, and that you are now ready to apply for a preference.

THIRD PREFERENCE

This preference was designed for a limited number of people that the American government has designated for special treatment. The language of the law, as I've noted, defines them as professionals and persons of exceptional ability in the sciences or arts whose expertise will substantially benefit the United States. But what does "professional" mean? The definition is broader than you might think. Naturally, it includes lawyers, doctors, teachers, architects, engineers, and those engaged in similar occupations, but it also covers business executives. The basic requirement is usually a degree from a college or university. You can be considered a professional without such a degree, however, if you can show that you deserve professional status because of your actual experience, your reputation, and the position you hold in your field.

For example, there have been several cases in which I was successful in obtaining a third preference for business executives who lacked any formal education at all. In one instance, the president of a small, privately held corporation in England came to me with a request that I help him obtain permanent residence quickly. Unfortunately, this businessman, although he was a successful executive in a small corporation, had never gone to a university. Even though a university education isn't an automatic stepping stone to third preference, it does help. I was able to assemble a number of affidavits from bankers and local business people, all of which asserted that this man, although not a graduate of business school, was a true professional and had achieved a level of expertise that matched or even surpassed that of persons with professional qualifications in the field. This tactic proved successful.

I should point out quickly, however, that my success could have been affected by which Immigration Service office I approached. I was lucky to have gone to one that was fully informed about the law, which states that you do not need a professional degree if you can show that your accomplishments are equal to the professional standards the degree represents.

Sometimes, however, even a degree from a college or university isn't enough. If your degree is in a specialty not relevant to the job offer, or a university degree is not necessary to fulfill the job requirements, the INS may not consider you a professional. What the Service decides about professional status depends on the documentation you provide and the circumstances of the individual case.

If your application for third preference is based on exceptional ability, you must document a unique or an unusual talent in an occupation that requires that special talent or skill in a specialized field, such as the arts or sciences. In general, the arts are considered to be such areas as poetry, sculpture, architecture, design, music, and related fields. If your application is based on professions in the sciences, you will probably have to show that your endeavors in that science will be pursued in institutions of higher learning in the United States. Exceptional ability must be documented completely, and the INS has developed general guidelines for that documentation as follows. The alien must demonstrate that:

1. He is the subject of published articles or books.
2. He is the author of articles or books.
3. He is a member of an organization or group where excellence is the criterion for membership.
4. He is internationally famous.
5. He is earning a salary commensurate with his claim to be of exceptional ability.
6. He has some evidence of awards, prizes, grants, or similar marks of distinction.

It isn't necessary to qualify in *all* these respects; if the alien qualifies in some, there is a good chance he will be classified for third preference in this category. In the end, decisions are made on a case-by-case basis.

If you apply for third preference based on a claim of exceptional ability, you're really at the mercy of the INS examiner who reviews your application. I have found wide differences all over the United States in the application of these criteria. For example, I've filed applications in New York that were approved routinely, yet I knew they would have been denied on the spot if they had been filed elsewhere. There are some INS offices that consider Nobel Prize winners the only people eligible to be designated as having exceptional ability. That kind of petty-mindedness is rare, of course. Nevertheless, it's important to understand that you should provide as much documentation as possible if you're filing for this category.

An unexpected benefit often results from approval on the basis of exceptional ability. If you qualify, you may also be exempt from the labor certification requirement, because one of the exempt categories under Schedule A includes aliens who have exceptional ability in the sciences or arts.

Third preference has one practical advantage over sixth, and that is speed. Even though both preferences are customarily back-logged, delay for the third preference is usually much shorter for most countries.

SIXTH PREFERENCE

If you have an approved labor certification or an exemption under Schedule A, and you don't qualify for a third preference, you'll be classified as a sixth-preference immigrant. As I've said, the chief drawback here is the larger backlog. There are few other practical differences. There was a time, not long ago, when both third and sixth preferences were current—that is, up to date and available—but that is no longer the case, and the situation is likely to grow worse.

HOW TO FILE

The basic form necessary for both third and sixth preferences is the same—Form I-140 (see appendix 28). At the top of the form, you must indicate your choice of either third or sixth preference. Once you've done that, the information provided is identical for both, with just one exception at the end. A sixth-preference application must be signed by the employer (who is the petitioner). If you're eligible under the third preference, the application may be signed either by the employer-petitioner, or by the alien-beneficiary.

Your I-140 application must be filed with a $50.00 fee at the INS office nearest to the place of employment in the United States. It must be accompanied either by a labor certification or by proof that an exemption is available.

Even if labor certification is not required, you'll have to provide proof of a job offer in the United States and a statement of your qualifications for the job. The document used for this purpose is Form ETA-750 (see appendix 15), which has two parts, one to prove that a job offer is available and the other to show that the applicant is qualified for the job. This is the same application that is filed in applying for labor certification, although in this case no certification is required.

In Form ETA-750A you'll have to provide proof that you have the experience and special skills required for the job. A professional must provide proof of his or her professional standing and degrees. If the claim to that standing is based on experience, it must be documented with affidavits.

In principle, *all* your experience must be documented by affidavits, but in practice I've found that most INS offices in the United States rarely require them. Be sure to remember, however, that if you're claiming exceptional ability, you will have to document your case very carefully indeed.

The application, with supporting documents, can be filed either by mail or in person. In big cities, where the INS offices usually have a shortage of employees and an excess of applications, the review of your application may sometimes take as long as a year. But in cities where there isn't this kind of pressure, review may be accomplished in as little as thirty days.

Your employer and attorney will both get copies of the notice of approval. If you're waiting outside the United States, this notice will be sent to the embassy or consulate designated on your Form I-140, and the consulate will take over the processing from that point. If you are in the United States, and you file Form I-140 and its supporting documents at a time when the quota is open for the preference under which you're filing, then you can make the application for adjustment of status at the same time, if you wish.

This may often occur in cases where the application was based on an approved labor certification. The reason is that when you file for certification, your name is placed on the preference waiting list according to the date you first filed. Since the certification process itself usually takes anywhere from three to nine months —and in some places as much as a year and a half—by the time labor certification is approved there's a good chance you will have also cleared the preference waiting list, even on the more lengthy sixth-preference list. You can then file for adjustment of status at the same time. But be sure you do not work without authorization until your application for adjustment of status has been filed. Once the application has been made, you will get work permission, and any employment with your petitioner will then be legal.

Now let's talk about labor certification itself. First, an admonition: don't attempt to file for labor certification without the help of an attorney. It's a perilous process. I know there will be a temptation to do it alone, especially when your lawyer tells you how much his assistance will cost you. The temptation increases after you approach your local Labor Department official, who will gladly give you brochures explaining the whole process in detail. Although you won't get the impression from reading the brochures that the procedure is easy, you may be led to believe that it's possible to proceed without an expert.

But don't do it. If you follow the procedure exactly as outlined in the brochures you're given, your chances of failure are enormous—not because the brochures are misleading but, rather, because labor certifications are often filed to help friends and not because there is a legitimate shortage of Americans to fill a particular job.

LABOR CERTIFICATION

Any senior official at the Labor Department will tell you that lawyers win labor certification approvals in most cases. Lawyers have not only mastered the rules and regulations, they have also learned from experience that actual practices are often quite different from the law. That is in part why I don't advise anyone to attempt the process without expert help. The rules and regulations are complex enough in themselves, but their application varies widely from place to place throughout the United States. I shall, however, tell you enough about certification in the following pages to guide you if you nevertheless persist in attempting it without help. But I hope that what you read will convince you, instead, to seek competent advice before you go ahead.

In order to obtain a labor certification, the American employer must demonstrate that there is a shortage of qualified and available workers for the specific job, and also that employing the alien applicant won't adversely affect the wages and working conditions prevailing for the particular position in the United States. The only exception made is for teachers. In that case, it must be demonstrated that the alien is the best-qualified applicant for the job, and that this was determined in the course of a competitive recruitment and selection process.

If your job falls under Schedule A—the group of jobs precertified by the Labor Department—your application won't be made to that department but directly to the INS.

If your job falls within a list known as Schedule B, however, your problems will multiply. Schedule B (see appendix 29) is a list of forty-nine occupations for which the labor supply is excessive and thus certification is unobtainable unless a waiver has been granted. What these occupations have in common are unskilled work, long and irregular hours, poor working conditions, low wages, and few or no educational and experience requirements.

For some employees, in certain locations, an employer can request a waiver from the prohibition against these Schedule B jobs. This waiver must show not only that the alien fulfills all the requirements for individual labor certification, but also that a job order for the particular position had been filed with the local unemployment service for the past thirty days and no qualified American worker could be found for it.

APPLICATION PROCEDURE

First of all, the employer should carefully examine Forms ETA-750, Parts A and B (see appendix 15), since the exact wording of the job offer on that form is often critical to the application process. But there are crucial points to consider before the offer is drafted.

Since the requirements for the qualifications of the alien are listed in Part B of Form ETA-750, the logical assumption would be that the employer should try to prepare the job description in such a way that only the applicant he is trying to bring in would be able to fill the requirements. If he does that, however, the Labor Department will probably deny the application, in the belief that the employer is attempting to tailor the job to the alien and is deliberately creating a job that is not available to an American worker.

On the other hand, if the employer makes the requirements

extremely general, he runs the risk that the department may come up with many qualified American workers when the job is posted at the unemployment office, as required. It's necessary, then, to find a middle ground, and here only experience can be your guide.

The employer must also show that he has made efforts to find an American worker for the position by placing advertisements in periodicals and/or newspapers, by posting job notices at the place of business, by registering the position with placement agencies, and, in some instances, by other kinds of recruitment customary for the position.

Initially, the application for labor certification begins with filing Form ETA-750 at a local job service office in the city where the job is to be performed. In some cities, clippings of newspaper advertisements for the position must be included at the time of filing. In others, the Labor Department first reviews Form ETA-750 and then requests that the position be advertised. The employer should consult the Labor Department office nearest his place of business for specific instructions.

The advertisement must include all the details of the job offered as described in Part A of Form ETA-750. If the ad is placed in a newspaper of general circulation, it must run for three consecutive days. The requirements for publication in a professional, trade, or ethnic journal are less rigid; normally, one advertisement is enough.

In principle, the prior-recruitment requirement assures the Department of Labor that any American workers who want to apply for the job can do so. In fact, the Labor Department often recognizes, or at least suspects, that the job isn't really open to American workers. Just the same, if the advertisements comply with the regulations, and the employer follows all the certification steps carefully, the waiver is likely to be granted.

Sometimes it's possible to shorten or dispense entirely with advertisement procedures. That can be done if the employer can show that an effort was made in good faith in the preceding six months to find a qualified American worker, without result. This is easier to do in an area acknowledged to suffer from a lack of qualified individuals.

Upon reviewing the certification application, the local office of the Labor Department may ask for more detailed information about the nature of the job or it may say that the rate of pay being offered is too low. I've found that if the employer complies, within reason and in detail, with everything the department requests, he'll probably be successful. Of course, there are circumstances that may prevent the employer from following the department's directives—if, for instance, the local office suggests a rate of pay that is unacceptable to the employer. In those cases where I cannot comply with what the department requests, I try to reason with the officials, and if my arguments are sound, I often prevail.

Once the application has been accepted by the local office, and the position has been advertised (if required), the local office will place a job order in the local job bank computer, to run for thirty days. Unless the employer has been released from further advertising, in most cases he, too, will have to advertise once more during this thirty-day period. Specific requirements for this second advertisement procedure vary from place to place, so it's best to check with the department's local office. Sometimes, in special circumstances, this second recruitment period can be either reduced or eliminated entirely.

After its review, the department's local office will make and forward a recommendation, along with all the forms and documentation, to the regional certifying office that supervises that particular local office. The length of time this review will take and how thorough it will be differs from place to place. The employer and the lawyer (if a lawyer is involved) will then be given either a certification or a denial, or, sometimes, a "Notice of Findings." This notice will request changes or additional information and, if it is not complied with in a manner satisfactory to the regional office, it can lead to a denial of the application.

If certification is granted, Form ETA-750 is returned to the employer with a special stamp on it, together with all the forms and documentation originally filed with the department. This package, known as the labor certification, becomes the basis of the application for either third or sixth preference.

When the application is not immediately granted, the employer will get a notice of findings from the certifying officer, explaining what further clarification is needed. The employer then has a thirty-five-day period in which to rebut the department's findings or comply with its demands. The certifying officer then makes a final determination. If this proves to be negative, the employer still has an additional thirty-five days during which he may request a judicial review. Obviously, he'd be foolish even to think of embarking on such a procedure without the help of a lawyer.

If the application is finally denied, a new one cannot be made by the same employer for the same job for at least six months, unless the application was denied only because of a disagreement over the prevailing wage. In the latter case, the employer is free to refile immediately, stating the salary. Obviously, it would be foolish to refile using the same wage that was originally offered and rejected, unless the job description has been changed in such a way as to justify the original salary.

A labor certification, once granted, is valid indefinitely, or for as long as the position is available to the alien. Consequently, it's extremely valuable. In principle, it can be used as late as ten or more years after it was originally granted. But if a great deal of time has elapsed between the original grant and the time the alien beneficiary finally enters the United States as a permanent resident, the INS will usually check all aspects of the employment very carefully with the prospective employer.

The opportunities here for fraud are very great, and they're frequently seized upon, usually by the alien, but sometimes by the employer who offers the job. In either case both parties, but especially the alien, are in trouble if they're caught. In fact, people seldom are caught, even if both the INS and the Labor Department suspect that an employer has no real intention of employing the particular alien whose certification application he has submitted.

Earlier, in discussing temporary visas, I observed that, in principle, applications for temporary work in the United States that require prior approval by the INS should be initiated by the employer, who is petitioning for the right to employ an alien as beneficiary. But in fact, this isn't always the case. It's often the alien beneficiary who approaches an employer and asks for help in getting a temporary visa. The employer may not even be very enthusiastic about the idea, and may believe that if he consents he will be doing the alien a big favor. This also seems to be true in many applications for labor certification. Often it's the alien who hires the lawyer and encourages both the attorney and the employer to push his application through.

Ideally, the process is supposed to work differently, with the alien and the petitioner pressing with an equal degree of enthusiasm for approval of the application, but that is an ideal rarely achieved. The important thing to remember is that no matter how your application is initiated, and regardless of whose enthusiasm provides the impetus for it, be careful not to place yourself inadvertently in a situation where you can be accused of fraud. When I discussed marriage, I told you that there is nothing illegal about getting married for a Green Card as long as the marriage is viable. The government has no right to insist that people marry only for love; some may marry for money and others for a Green Card. To some extent, the same is true when you apply for a labor certification. In my opinion, it isn't wrong for an employer to give someone a job so as to help him get a Green Card, provided the job is actually offered in good faith and the prospective employer intends to hire the alien when the time comes for him to do so. But if either alien or employer has no intention to follow through on the job offer, and the absence of intention can be proved, both can find themselves in deep trouble.

I feel very strongly about this matter. I tell my alien clients that, although it isn't my place to police their ultimate intentions or inquire into their private motives, they must understand that when they file for a labor certification, they must intend to accept the job that is being offered. Similarly, I tell the employer that he must intend to follow through with employment when the time comes. I explain to both that if fraud can be proved, the penalties are likely to be severe, and I advise them that if a job offer is withdrawn, or if the alien changes his mind about accepting the position, the government must be immediately informed.

Temporary Labor Certification

In chapter 4, I mentioned that an applicant for the H-2 visa—which gives an alien permission to live and work in the United States for less than one year—must first get a temporary labor certification.

The application procedure for temporary labor certification is a streamlined version of that required for permanent certification. The major difference, however, is that, in most places, the applications for temporary certification are dealt with far more quickly.

In some cities, there is no requirement to demonstrate previous advertising, but this is rapidly changing. It used to be possible to persuade a local office of the Labor Department to act on an application within days, after which it was sent to the regional certifying officer, who usually handled it promptly. But this is no longer true in most places. Now advertising is usually required.

As I've said before, practices are often different from place to place in the United States, and you should check with the office in control of your area before making any application. One of the essential elements in making such an application is to demonstrate clearly that the job is temporary, which means less than a year.

Most applications made on behalf of an entertainer move more quickly than those for persons in other occupations eligible for the H-2 visa. The Labor Department knows that entertainers are often hired and booked on short notice, so both INS and Labor Department officials are trained to deal with entertainers in a special way.

If I seem to have painted a rather negative picture of the labor certification process, it's only because I'm anxious to discourage anyone from making the application on his own. In defense of the government, I should add that there's good reason why the process is made so difficult. It is of primary importance for the government to protect the jobs of American workers, and the Labor Department knows or suspects that many applications are made for jobs that aren't really open to Americans, so it attempts to screen out fraudulent or undeserving applications. I have found, however, that if an application is truly meritorious, and if special circumstances can be demonstrated, the Labor Department will move very quickly indeed.

For many people trying to get into the United States, labor certification is the cornerstone of the application process, and they often believe that once certification is granted, their permanent residence is virtually assured. This is usually the case. Even so, it's wise not to forget the importance of being able to prove that you have the experience claimed in applying for labor certification. This proof must be produced when you file for a preference with the Immigration Service. If there's a discrepancy between your documented experience and the experience required for the job, your certification may be revoked. Nor is this just a remote possibility; it happens in many cases.

And what if certification is denied? Well, it isn't the end of the world. Because the application is filed by the employer rather than the employee, there's no limit to the number of such requests that can be made on behalf of the same alien. This means that if the alien is resourceful enough, he can line up an infinite number of employers and request that they simultaneously make application on his behalf. Of course, such a procedure would be time-consuming and expensive, so rarely is more than one certification at a time filed on behalf of a single alien.

But it does happen. Not long ago, I was called upon by an alien to process simultaneously two requests on his behalf from employers in different parts of the United States. He was rich, and desperate to get into this country in a hurry. Not wanting to risk denial of certification, he filed two applications. In the end, both applications were approved, even though only one was needed. Yet to my client this procedure did not seem like a waste of time and money, because he placed a high value on his peace of mind.

Before the nonpreference portion of the quota closed in 1978, labor certification was usually the principal immigration requirement for residence. It was not necessary to file additional applications for third or sixth preference. Unfortunately, since 1978 this hasn't been the case. Today even certain privileged groups such as rich, retired people and investors must seek labor certification or exemption from it in order to enter the country as permanent residents.

EXEMPTION
FROM LABOR
CERTIFICATION:
SCHEDULE A

Not everyone who needs a labor certification has to apply for one in the usual way. There is a small group of people who are exempt from the normal labor certification application procedure—people who are granted labor certification almost automatically. These people fall into occupational groups for which the United States Employment Service has predetermined that there is a shortage of United States workers and that their employment will not adversely affect the wages and working conditions of American workers similarly employed. The listing of this group of occupations is known as Schedule A.

The Department of Labor created Schedule A because it was believed that foreigners in the occupations listed would present no threat to the American job market and that their entry into the United States would benefit the United States economically, culturally, or intellectually and should be encouraged.

If you're covered by Schedule A, there's no need to apply to the Department of Labor for a labor certification in the manner described in the previous chapter. Your eligibility for a Schedule A labor certification will usually be made by the Immigration Service at the time you apply for either third or sixth preference. In most other respects, however, the certification, when it's granted to you, serves the same purpose as the one granted to any other alien.

You will still need to fill out both parts of Form ETA-750, which is filed along with the other documents and immigration forms necessary to qualify you for a preference. If you are also simultaneously making an application to become a permanent resident while you're in the United States, then all the papers necessary for adjustment of status will have to be filed as well.

Since it's the Immigration Service rather than the Labor Department that is determining your eligibility under Schedule A, you must not only prove your eligibility for the waiver when you file your application but also provide proof of your previous experience at the same time. All the necessary documents must be presented at once.

Remember, however, that Schedule A is not carved in stone; it can and does change from time to time. Therefore it's important to consult either with the Department of Labor, or with the Immigration Service, or with a consulate or embassy abroad, before taking for granted that you're eligible for a labor certification exemption.

Now let's discuss the four categories listed currently on Schedule A.

GROUP I

Group I covers occupations that are considered by the Department of Labor to be in short supply. At this time there is an insufficient number of qualified American physical therapists and professional nurses to meet the needs of our country, and in certain geographical areas there is a shortage of American doctors. Group I, therefore, consists of the following three occupations:

1. Aliens who will be employed in the United States as physical therapists and who can present proof that they possess all the qualifications necessary to take the corresponding licensing exam in the state where they propose to practice.

2. Professional nurses from foreign countries who can document that they have passed the Commission on Graduates of Foreign Nursing Schools (CGFNS) examination, or who hold a full and unrestricted license to practice in the state of intended employment. The CGFNS is located at 3624 Market Street, Philadelphia, PA 19104. Any requests for information about the CGFNS examination should be directed to that address.

3. Foreign doctors who will be employed in the United States as physicians if it can be determined that there is an insufficient number of physicians in the particular specialty of the foreign doctor in the geographic area where the doctor will practice.

Foreign doctors, even if they're listed on Schedule A, are not exempt from the special testing requirements I'll discuss in chapter 13, unless, of course, they are eligible under Group II, which covers aliens of exceptional merit and ability in the sciences and arts. Most foreign doctors, however, are not internationally famous, and few qualify under Group II.

Canadian doctors are usually exempt from the special testing requirements because they are eligible to take parts 1 and 2 of the National Board of Medical Examiners' Examination (NBMEE).

A foreign doctor who holds a valid specialty certificate and was also permanently licensed and practicing in the United States on or before January 9, 1977, is exempt from all special testing requirements. But the doctor will not be eligible for labor certification waiver unless his or her specialty is needed in the geographic area where he or she will practice.

GROUP II

Group II covers aliens of exceptional ability in the sciences or arts who have been practicing their science or art during the year immediately before their application for exemption and who intend to continue to practice the same science or art in the United States. College and university teachers of exceptional ability in either the sciences or the arts can qualify under Group II for Schedule A certification. Unfortunately, this privilege is not available to entertainers or performing artists.

For purposes of this Schedule A certification only, science or art is considered any field of knowledge or skill in which study usually leads to a college or university degree. It's interesting, consequently, to note that formal education at a college or university isn't absolutely necessary in order to qualify for Group II certification. You can prove you're outstanding in other ways.

You must document your claim extensively, and that means through letters testifying to widespread acclaim and international recognition by recognized experts in your field, as well as documentation demonstrating that your work in the field during the past year required exceptional ability. Letters, articles, and awards are all helpful.

In most offices of the Immigration Service throughout the United States, your claim to exceptional ability will be examined very carefully, so it's important to prepare your application for exemption meticulously, providing as much detail as possible. Presentation may be as important as substance in this case, and repetition isn't necessarily to be frowned upon.

Nevertheless, the judgment by the immigration official reviewing the application is largely subjective, and applications that would be denied in one place may be quickly approved in another.

If you think you are eligible to be considered an alien of exceptional merit and ability, seek the advice of a lawyer. The money you pay him will be well spent, because if he believes you fulfill the criteria, your application will be prepared in a professional manner that will increase your chances of success.

If your lawyer doesn't think you qualify, you'll save a lot of time and energy and will probably be better off filing in the normal way for a labor certification.

GROUP III

Religious workers who come to the United States to work in the same kind of capacity in which they've worked for the previous two years constitute Group III. Proof of previous employment can be provided by officials of the alien's religious organization. It's important to itemize the alien's duties, the length of his term, and the duration of his work at his U.S. assignment. The religious work performed must account for more than 50 percent of the alien's working time.

In certain circumstances, religious workers may be considered special immigrants and are therefore exempt not only from the labor certification process, but also from the obligation to apply for an immigrant visa number. A special immigrant usually enters the country to serve a particular religious order, but not to be employed. Group III is meant to cover the circumstances of an actual job offer in the United States. Nevertheless, there is a great deal of overlapping.

Most religious organizations are well skilled in the immigration process. Consequently, aliens eligible to enter the United States as religious workers do not usually require the assistance of an attorney.

GROUP IV

Group IV comprises foreign intracompany transferees who were continuously employed by international corporations or organizations as managers or executives outside the United States for at least one year before entry, and who intend to emigrate permanently to the United States to work for the same international corporation or organization in managerial or executive positions.

The first category in Group IV covers aliens who have already been admitted to the United States with L visas. The second category covers aliens who are outside the United States and currently working for an international corporation or organization that has a branch subsidiary or affiliate in the United States.

In most respects, the criteria for eligibility under Group IV are almost identical with the criteria for the L visa. There are, however, several important differences.

The United States company, as a branch, affiliate, or subsidiary of the foreign corporation, can only act as an employer of a Group IV alien if it has been doing business in the United States for at least a year before the submission of the application for exemption under Schedule A. This means a regular, systematic, and continuing course of business conduct, with an emphasis on offering and providing goods and services.

Another important difference between Group IV and the L visa is that only managers or executives qualify for Group IV eligibility. As we have seen, an L visa can be granted in certain circumstances to especially skilled individuals who are neither executives nor managers.

Several years ago, there was no need to show that the American company had a one-year history of business activities in the United States. As a result, many attorneys obtained Group IV waivers on behalf of their clients by the mere establishment of an American shell company. Eventually, the Immigration Service discovered this loophole and closed it.

Any application made under Schedule A, Group IV, is carefully scrutinized, and the Immigration Service takes special pains to satisfy itself that the business is, in fact, really in operation. Group IV is often utilized by international companies for employees they wish to transfer to the United States, or to effect the permanent transfer to the United States of an employee who is already there under an L visa. An employee already working in the United States for an international company under an E or H visa can also apply for Group IV certification if the circumstances of the previous overseas employment and the relationship between the foreign and American companies meet the test for Schedule A, Group IV, eligibility.

It's important to show that the employee was employed by the foreign company abroad for at least a year as an executive or a manager before the submission of the petition for Schedule A, Group IV. If the employee is already in the United States on an L, H, or E visa, he must also prove that he was admitted to the United States to be employed as an executive or manager by his company.

If a U.S. branch, affiliate, or subsidiary of a foreign company has conducted business in the United States for a year before it applies for transfers for any of its foreign managers or executives, the company has the option of moving its high-level staff to the United States either under an L visa, which can be granted for a period of up to three years, or, if permanent residence is the ultimate aim, by filing applications for residence immediately under Schedule A, Group IV. Of course, such an application for permanent residence must be made in conjunction with an application for a preference, which can be made only if the appropriate third- or sixth-preference portion of the quota is open for the alien on whose behalf the exemption is being sought.

I've had many clients ask me to get them into the United States as intracompany transferees, and recently I have had to explain to them that both the third and sixth portions of the quotas are backlogged, and so it isn't possible to get them in immediately. Those who want to skip the step of the L visa have no option but to make an initial application to the Immigration Service for either a third or sixth preference. This step establishes a priority date. The filing must demonstrate that the alien who is the beneficiary of the job offer is qualified under Section A, Group IV. Then he must wait until the priority date clears the preference backlog. At that time, he can make an application for adjustment of status, but only if he is already in the United States in circumstances that qualify him for a Group IV waiver. If the alien is abroad, then in all probability the L visa will accomplish his goal much more directly, because in most big American cities there's a substantial delay in the review of basic preference applications.

The principal benefit of first making an application for an L visa is that it can usually be secured very quickly—much more quickly than a Group IV waiver. In New York it's possible to have an L visa approved within one month. Once such a visa is approved by the Immigration Service in the United States, an embassy or consulate abroad can issue it on the spot. Later on, an application for permanent residence can be made in a leisurely fashion.

Although there is a great similarity between the criteria for the L visa and for the labor certification waiver, the Immigration Service will tell you that the documentary requirement for the waiver is greater than it is for the L visa. In practice, however, I've found that this is not the case.

The criteria governing the relationship between the foreign company and its United States affiliate, subsidiary, or branch are identical with those already covered under the L visa.

SOME PROS AND CONS

One of the principal advantages of Schedule A certification is that you can avoid the long and arduous task of making application for a labor certification in the normal way. If you think there's any doubt about your eligibility, however, think twice before filing, because if it's determined that you're ineligible for the waiver you applied for, you will then have to start the regular labor certification process from the beginning. Weigh your choices carefully, depending on your particular situation. Such a waste of time may not be important to you, but if time is of the essence, you may be better off making your application directly through the Labor Department.

Many aliens who apply for labor certification waivers are already in the United States, and their applications for waiver will bring them to the immediate attention of the Immigration Service. If their applications are denied, the Service may well ask them to leave the country, pending the outcome of their normal labor certification application. So from a strategic point of view, think twice before you make your decision.

Despite the technicalities and the various difficulties I've asked you to keep in mind, Schedule A, Group IV, remains one of the most valuable loopholes available under the immigration laws. It has clearly been abused, but it has nevertheless been a valuable tool for thousands of people who have come here. As long as you're sure you can negotiate the potential difficulties, it should be seriously considered.

POLITICAL REFUGE, ASYLUM, AND HUMANITARIAN PAROLE

By reputation and tradition, America has always been known as a haven for people suffering from persecution abroad. Our first settlers were fleeing religious intolerance in England, and those who came after them were victims of oppressive religious or political attitudes. It was only later that immigrants came as a result of severe economic conditions in other parts of the world.

For nearly three centuries the door stood wide open to refugees, but in recent years it has begun to close. Not completely, of course, but it isn't as easy now as it once was to get into America as a refugee. The intent of existing regulations is to provide a method for real victims to come here. Now the decision about whether you qualify or not is often a political one, and the number of those admitted is strictly controlled.

During the past decade, the troubled state of the world has made refugees a major concern for American immigration authorities, and for many other branches of government as well. Even the President has become deeply involved in these issues.

We have had waves of refugees from all over the world—Asians, Central Americans, and many from behind the Iron Curtain. Some Americans fear that the tide threatens to overwhelm us. From the time of the Iranian revolution until the end of 1982, more than twenty-five thousand applications for political asylum were filed by Iranians in the United States. With deteriorating social and political conditions around the world, pressures continue to mount.

Fortunately, refugees have long been a concern in this country of many religious, social, and ethnic organizations. There are a good many groups devoted to helping victims of persecution relocate in the United States, including agencies of the United Nations.

Although lawyers aren't usually as useful to these refugees as they are to other kinds of immigrants, they can nevertheless make admission procedures easier by assisting the applicant in working his way through the bureaucracy. Lawyers have been of considerable help to Iranian and Cuban victims of persecution.

One thing a lawyer can do for you, if you think you need one, is to help you write your application in a way that will be logical and convincing to the immigration authorities. He can also be useful in obtaining the evidence you need to support your claim for asylum or refugee status. In some cases (during the recent plight of the Haitian boat people, for example), constitutional issues have been raised, and competent legal help has proved to be essential, as the Haitians in American detention quickly learned.

In this chapter, I'll discuss three separate ways a victim of persecution can obtain refuge in the United States. He or she can apply for: (1) political refugee status; (2) asylum; or (3) humanitarian parole.

In a broad sense, the three categories are very similar. In theory, if you are a victim of persecution because of race, religion, nationality, membership in a particular social group, or political opinion, any one of these three options should be available to you. In real life, however, your ability to navigate successfully your entry into the United States is largely dependent on political considerations here.

In 1980 Congress enacted legislation that addressed itself to these issues. The law was known as the Refugee Act of 1980.

REFUGEES

The President of the United States, in consultation with Congress, determines how many refugees may enter the United States each year, and from which countries. Refugee status, however, is very specifically defined under the law. You are eligible for this status only if you're outside your own country of nationality (or if you have no nationality and you're outside the country in which you last habitually lived), and are unwilling or unable to return to that country because of a well-founded fear of persecution. In certain special circumstances, the President may specify that a particular person who is within the country of his nationality (or, if he has no nationality, within the country in which he habitually resides) is eligible for refugee status. This is rare, however.

Aliens admitted to the United States as refugees are not deducted from the overall numerical limitation of 270,000 immigrants per year, so in a sense they're almost like special immigrants.

Every applicant for refugee status must execute Form I-590, Registration for Classification as Refugee (see appendix 30), which is the basic form for determining whether or not you're eligible. This form must be accompanied by the familiar biographic information form (Form G-325; see appendix 18) and the standard fingerprint chart for each applicant who has reached the age of fourteen. These forms may be submitted only outside the United States, by the alien and his family requesting refugee status, either to the nearest United States Immigration Service office (outside the United States) or to one of the designated consular offices set forth below:

Argentina: Buenos Aires	Djibouti: Djibouti
Botswana: Gaborone	Egypt: Cairo
Brazil: Rio de Janeiro	Germany: Frankfurt
Cameroon: Douala	India: New Delhi

Japan: Somalia: Mogadishu
  Fukuoka   Sudan: Khartoum
  Naha   Swaziland: Mbabane
  Kobe   Taiwan: Taipei
  Osaka   Yugoslavia: Belgrade
  Tokyo   Zaïre: Kinshasa
Kenya: Nairobi   Zambia: Lusaka
Korea: Seoul
Pakistan:
  Islamabad
  Karachi

In most cases, each applicant and every member of the applicant's family will be interviewed by a consular or immigration
official to determine if they qualify. At the time of the interview,
submit all the documents that you think will help you establish
your claim as a victim of persecution—documents such as identification books, military books, passports, birth records, marriage
certificates, newspaper clippings, and similar items. You must also
provide proof of guarantees of either employment or support; these
are normally provided by family members, or international and
religious organizations. You must submit two passport-size photographs for each member of your family. There will be a medical
examination. If your application is approved, you will then be
allowed to enter the United States. Within a year after the date of
your entry, you will be able to apply for permanent residence by
filing the usual adjustment-of-status papers. While you're waiting
for that year to pass, you may work if you wish. If your application
is not approved, appeal is not available.

If the Immigration Service finds that you are qualified to enter
the United States either as an immediate relative or as a special
immigrant, you won't be allowed to enter as a refugee. And if it
appears that you may be eligible for one of the preference classifications, you'll be encouraged to seek that form of entry.

Because only a certain number of people are admitted as refugees each year, and these people are allocated according to nationality criteria established by the President and Congress, it

often happens that there's a waiting list for particular categories of refugees. The date on which Form I-590 is filed establishes the priority of the alien seeking refugee status. The U.S. Attorney General has the right, however, to take individuals out of turn if, for example, he believes that such factors as family reunification or close associations with the United States provide a good reason to do so.

The normal grounds of inadmissibility that apply to almost all aliens entering the United States are, for the most part, suspended in the case of people seeking to enter the United States as refugees.

ASYLUM

The criteria for refugee and asylum status are similar, but there are differences. If you're in the United States, or at a land border of the United States, and believe that you're a victim of persecution according to the same definition applying to those eligible for refugee status, you can make an application for asylum in this country.

This application can be made even if an alien is here illegally, temporarily, or on parole. Asylum may be terminated, however, if the Attorney General determines that the alien is no longer in the kind of jeopardy that created a valid claim in the first place.

An application for asylum is made on Form I-589, Request for Asylum in the United States (see appendix 31). This form is much like the form filed to seek refugee status. Unlike an application for refugee status, however, separate applications do not have to be filed for the applicant's spouse and children. Each application must be accompanied by Form G-325A (biographic data) and the standard fingerprint form for every child over the age of fourteen.

Application for asylum is filed with an office of the Immigration Service, which will review it and usually request an interview with little delay. After the interview, the application is sent to the Department of State for review and for its recommendation. That recommendation, either granting or denying asylum, is almost always followed by the Immigration Service. An alien who is granted asylum can usually apply for permanent residence by the standard adjustment-of-status procedure one year after the grant of asylum.

That's the theory. In practice, however, I know many foreigners who have been in the United States for years after their applications for asylum were filed, and who have heard nothing, either from the Immigration Service or from the Department of State. This is largely a political matter; it isn't accidental. It is sometimes reasoned that by delaying any action on applications from aliens of a certain nationality, perhaps the political situation will change and there will be no further need for granting asylum.

It's also important to keep in mind that only five thousand aliens can enter the United States annually for asylum. Consequently, I wouldn't place a great deal of hope in this procedure, unless the facts and the documents are strongly in your favor.

I have advised many of my clients who believe they may be eligible, but who would probably have to wait for years to get any results, not to rely on asylum as a means of acquiring American residence. I urge them, when it's possible, to file instead for residence under the preference system. Many lawyers who know their clients aren't eligible for asylum nevertheless encourage them to file, because they know the government takes years to deal with the matter. The client is essentially protected from the time the asylum application is filed until the government denies the case, at which time the alien may be asked to leave the country. Recently, the INS has hardened its position on such "frivolous" applications. It will not grant work authorization where an application seems to be groundless.

I've been told that more than one hundred thousand applications for asylum are currently on file, "in boxes" in the State Department. All those people who filed can stay here, and even work in most cases, while the government decides what to do.

The documents that must accompany an application for asylum are the same as for refugee status. It's here that a lawyer can be helpful, primarily in drafting the application and assembling the necessary material to prove that you are, in fact, a victim of persecution.

Many Iranians fleeing the Khomeini regime were able to show that they had been convicted of crimes *in absentia*.

Often these crimes had more to do with the acquisition of wealth than with any wrongdoing. Any friendship or association with the Shah was anathema in the eyes of the Ayatollah Khomeini. Nevertheless, despite the turmoil and hardship that occurred, the Department of State has not been generous in granting asylum to Iranians in the United States, especially to those Iranians who are adherents of the Muslim faith.

There is clearly a bias on the part of both the Immigration Service and the Department of State in favor of people seeking asylum because of religious persecution. For example, those Iranians in the United States who claim and can prove that they are Bahais or Jews are much more likely to be granted asylum than are Muslims.

Unless you believe your case is solid and are willing to wait for years, I think you should apply for residence in other ways, as I have said before. That shouldn't be too hard. As time passes, people develop connections here. Some get married, others find jobs, and still others make investments in the United States. All of these are stepping stones to an application for residence. And don't forget that you already have an advantage over many other aliens. You're here and, in most cases, you're eligible to work.

If you've been offered residence in another country, or have established strong connections in it, there is a strong likelihood that your application will be denied. The issue here is whether or not another country has offered you a home that you've accepted, or could easily accept. If you think you're eligible for refugee status or for asylum in the United States, you should avoid establishing a residence elsewhere before you come to America.

There are those who use asylum as a tool, a delaying tactic, even though they know they're actually ineligible. Because it is an effective stall, immigration authorities often scrutinize such applications with great care. Abuse is particularly easy when a government from which an alien says he's fleeing has collapsed, since nothing can be checked.

It is often hard for the U.S. government to decide who is really being persecuted politically, who is coming here purely for economic benefit, and who is simply considered undesirable by his own government. If you feel you are eligible, however, then applying for asylum is a good method of entering the United States.

HUMANITARIAN PAROLE

If you think there are compelling reasons for your admission to the United States—reasons such as persecution, medical difficulties, or family reunification—but you are not eligible for refugee status, you can request any consulate for permission to enter America on the basis of humanitarian parole. This means that there are urgent humanitarian reasons for your admission to the country without a temporary visa or a Green Card, or that your admission is in the national interest of our country.

After the Iranian revolution, for example, many Iranian Jews and Bahais were admitted to the United States in this way. That happened because the Iranians didn't fit within any of the definitions developed by the President and Congress covering refugee status, but our government nevertheless believed that the religious minorities who were forced to flee from the Khomeini regime were legitimately entitled to enter the United States for humanitarian reasons.

This method of entry has been widely abused, however, and has provoked the anger of many consuls who thought that many undeserving people were taking advantage of it, or using it to get into the United States and then go underground. It's now very difficult to get into the country in this way, and if you've heard it's easy, I caution you that it isn't.

Parole can be applied for in either of two ways, directly to a consul at a consulate or embassy where you happen to be, or to the Central Immigration Office in Washington. If you apply directly to the consulate, your application will be submitted on the usual nonimmigrant visa forms. If you apply in the United States to the Central Immigration Office, a letter will be enough.

In either case, you'll have to provide with the visa form, or by letter if your application is made in Washington, a detailed explanation of why you believe you're eligible.

If you apply abroad, the consul will interview you and examine any documents you have provided that support your claim. If you apply in Washington, claims you've made will normally be taken at face value.

When the consul is involved, he will telex or write to the Immigration Service in Washington and await a response. If the application has been made directly to the Immigration Service in Washington, the Service will instruct the consul either to admit or not admit. The consul may have little discretion in the matter. He may, however, have a prejudicial influence on your application. It is my experience that consuls can often harm, but seldom help, such cases, and I recommend that you apply directly to the Immigration Service in Washington.

Assuming your application for humanitarian parole is granted, you'll probably want to file for asylum the moment you arrive in the United States.

PART IV

SPECIAL CATEGORIES

PERFORMERS, WRITERS, AND ARTISTS

Creative people have been coming to the United States for work-related purposes throughout our nation's history. The motivation for most, perhaps, is their conviction that careers are not firmly established until they "make it" in the United States.

These individuals often find themselves plagued by all kinds of frustrating technicalities and regulations embodied in American immigration rules. Particularly affected are entertainment executives, promoters, and booking agents who employ and work with these individuals. The executives often find themselves frustrated by a lack of understanding of the regulations applicable to the performers they wish to bring in to the United States. A basic knowledge of the applicable rules and regulations and the often unstated purposes behind them should help to ease the way for these performers—a result beneficial both to them and to the cultural climate of the United States.

Often the realization that the individual entertainer or performer hasn't done what is necessary to obtain the proper visa comes at the point of entry. Overworked immigration officials may not have heard of him, even though he may believe he's well known. To the official, he may be just another would-be immigrant.

It isn't always an easy task to obtain the right kind of visa for an entertainer or performer. Delay is the constant enemy. Time means less to the Immigration Service than it does to an agent or manager, to whom it means broken contracts, disrupted shooting schedules for motion pictures, lost rehearsal dates for a theater, or the return of tickets already sold for a particular date in a concert hall.

In fairness, it must be said that very often the difficulties and misunderstandings can be attributed to ignorance—ignorance of how to file applications, of how much time it may take to process them, of what documents may be required, of time-saving alternatives that can be utilized. The agent or manager who's acquired a working knowledge of all these things, or has the good sense to hire someone who has, is in a far better position to serve his client than one who hopes for the best without preparation.

It will often be necessary to deal with the State Department, the Department of Labor, and the Immigration Service, as well as unions. I should note that sometimes these government agencies are quite helpful in accommodating the time schedules of foreign entertainers.

Let me emphasize that whatever pathway of entry you choose, it should be part of a total strategy. If you have no plans to live in America permanently, for instance, you probably won't want to apply for anything more than a temporary work visa, one that's relatively easy to get. But if your career calls for being in the United States a great deal, possibly living here, then you may want to try for permanent residence.

To begin with, here are the choices available:

1. *The B-1 visa.* This is issued by an American consulate or embassy in your home country, and in the case of entertainers, the rules are different from those for other aliens. Entertainers can't come to the United States on B-1 visas for the purpose of performing in the United States. This holds true even if they are perform-

ing without any compensation. A foreign entertainer can, however, use the B-1 visa if he's coming to the United States for meetings, negotiations, or perhaps public relations on behalf of an overseas company. In a few cases, when no compensation is paid, some immigration officials have advised me not to bother with an H visa and to get a B visa instead even for those who intend to perform here temporarily, or others, because of the absurdity of the rules. They even offered to look the other way. That kind of offer is helpful but unusual.

2. *The H visa.* H visas are the only *temporary* visas available to foreigners who want to perform in the United States. H-1 visas are given to performers, or other aliens, of exceptional merit and ability; the H-2 is given to all other performers or other aliens coming here for temporary employment.

The decision on who qualifies for H-1 often seems relatively arbitrary. If the name of the person applying is a household word, there is no problem. (The H-1 visa, I should add, avoids the Labor Department and is filed directly with the Immigration Service.) But for others, various factors are weighed by the Immigration Service. These factors include past experience, the salary being offered for the American position, and the kind of position it is. In the case of rock groups, for example, examining officials will consider the size of the hall where the performance is to take place, the percentage of the gate to be paid, the performer's position on the bill if others are appearing, and similar considerations.

Past experience and renown must be demonstrated by written proof. This can consist of clippings of reviews from magazines or newspapers, or letters of reference from employers or professional colleagues.

Periodically, during times of higher-than-usual unemployment for American performers or entertainers, the Department of Labor comes under pressure from the unions to stop the infiltration into the United States marketplace of foreign performers. The Department of Labor usually gives in to such pressures and denies a much higher percentage of cases, or else changes the regulations to exclude many more performers.

H-2 visa applications are filed first with the Department of

Labor, and temporary labor certification must be granted before the application can move on to the Immigration Service. The Labor Department makes its determination on the basis of such factors as wages to be paid, the availability of qualified American performers for such available positions, and union clearance. You can't, for example, hire a British sound engineer as part of a British musical group's tour without paying him what an American union sound engineer would have to be paid. Recent changes in relevant regulations now hold that before you can successfully obtain an H-2 visa for a British musical group, for example, you must indicate by responses to advertising that a similar American group can't do the job as well. This and other changes in regulations have proved unrealistic, and are being criticized by lawyers, managers, and even by Labor Department employees who must administer these unpopular changes. At this writing, the hope is that pressure from all these sources will encourage the Department of Labor to amend these rules once more.

In certain cases, the entire cast of a British stage production may be turned down in favor of an American cast. This occurred not too long ago in the case of the highly successful London hit *Cats* when it was brought to New York. It was decided that an American cast could do just as well, and pressure from the American theatrical unions, many of whose members were out of work, became the crucial factor in the ruling that *Cats* must have an all-American production in the United States.

Earlier, however, a contrary conclusion had been reached in the case of another huge British stage success, *Nicholas Nickleby*, when it was transferred to Broadway. The conclusion then was that the British character of the production—it was the work of the Royal Shakespeare Company—was crucial and that only British actors could perform the play successfully. Consequently, the members of the entire British cast were granted the appropriate United States visas.

In particular cases where the position to be filled involves a combination of duties—writer, director, sound and light engineer, for instance—clearances must be obtained from all the relevant unions. Wages must be high enough to satisfy the higher of the prevailing wage scales. A finding must also be made in certain cases that an American worker could not do the identical job.

In general, union clearances are an internal matter, checked by the Department of Labor after the application is filed. These clearances are essential to the success of H-2 applications. As far as the H-1 visa is concerned, however, the assumed level of excellence obviates the requirement for the temporary labor certification and its requisite checks and clearances.

H-2 applications require approval of a temporary labor certification and then the filing of this certification with the Immigration Service to obtain issuance of the visa itself. For both H-1 and H-2 applications, the next step after approval is for the alien to appear at a United States consulate and have the actual visa stamped on the passport. Incidentally, this isn't simply a rubber-stamping procedure. The consul or State Department official has the right to make further inquiries, and for various reasons can decide to deny the visa application. Most often, the reason would be suspicion or proof of fraud, misrepresentation discovered on the application, or an arrest record. Waivers may be granted in such cases that will allow the alien to enter in spite of past faults. Among the most frequent waivers are those given despite previous drug convictions. Granting a waiver is usually within the discretion of consular officials.

As I've noted, H visas are obtained through an employer or agent in the United States who acts as petitioner for the alien coming to the United States for a temporary job. For visiting performers, there's a Catch-22 in this process. The rules say that the incoming alien can work only for the petitioner, which certainly complicates matters for a visiting concert pianist, let's say, who is going on tour and will be paid from several different sources. To make a case with the Immigration Service, such a petitioner would have to be shown as the person through whom the money from the tour is paid. The visitor has therefore to be very careful about whom he picks as a petitioner. It needs to be someone with whom he's going to have a continuing relationship while he's on tour—the tour's promoter, or a record company, perhaps.

Just to make it more difficult (or so it seems to some entertainers), the Immigration Service has on occasion been asking the opinion of union officials about alien immigrants in the entertainment business, especially when there is some doubt about the alien's status. Officials say they do so because the unions have "opposing interests," but since the opposing interest is to protect American union members from foreign competition, it's reasonable to doubt whether an unbiased opinion will be given. It's too easy for a union official to say, "Never heard of him," or, "We've got a hundred actresses out of work who could do a better job." Unions don't always cause problems, however. Sometimes it depends on the country of the performer's origin. On occasion there are reciprocal arrangements with foreign unions. Where the United Kingdom is concerned, for instance, unions on both sides of the Atlantic have a policy of "You let in our musicians and we'll do the same for yours." This policy, which ensures equal access of performers to both shores, has been in effect successfully for several years. American union officials keep strict track of the number of foreign performers admitted to the United States, and ensure that an equal number of United States performers are admitted to the United Kingdom. This system has operated smoothly, and only periodically do pressures from union officials produce a tightening up.

About the only time an H-2 visa will be issued without any question is when it's granted to touring groups who have no counterpart here—Chinese acrobats, for instance, or the Grand Kabuki Theatre of Japan, or other well-known regional artists.

Entertainment industry executives are often required to travel internationally. In these times, when multinational companies are so frequently involved in the management of talent, visiting executives or managers find that the simplest approach for them is the temporary visa. Such a company executive can enter either on a B-1, if he is paid abroad, or on an L-1, if there is a United States branch of the foreign company that will employ him here. The L visa, if granted, allows the executive the option to live and work in the United States, traveling in and out of the country as the job may require, and the retention of foreign residence, if that's desired. Otherwise, he will live the same way as permanent residents for a three-year period. If the executive at any time decides that his presence in the United States will be permanent, he can apply for permanent residence based on the intracompany transfer method previously discussed.

Permanent residence, if desired by a performer, may not be easy to acquire. There is a basic difficulty: the need to find a permanent job. The Immigration Service has made it quite clear that a job offer involving only performing, even when the contract may be for several years of work, does not qualify as a "permanent" job. To meet the requirement, you would have to be offered a permanent *nonperforming* job. You might get an opportunity, for instance, to be an acting coach for a repertory company, or to be a consultant for some ongoing entertainment venture, like the Kennedy Center. Immigration says the offer must be for a permanent job, but it does not define "permanent." "Permanent," as discussed in case law, refers to a period left open-ended. Consequently, no specific length of time may be stipulated.

The application procedure is much like that for an H-2 visa. First comes the labor certification, including a finding that American employees of this kind are unavailable or in short supply. Then an application is filed with the Immigration Service for third or sixth preference. This Labor Department procedure is not necessary, however, if the individual qualifies as an intracompany transferee, or as a person of international renown (not, however, as a performer). Those individuals who do not need labor certification can go straight to the second step, which is the application for one of the preference categories.

Up to now I've been discussing people in the performing arts, but there's another category that shouldn't be overlooked, and that is writers. They, unfortunately, have great difficulty, since they are not performers and are often not employed in the usual sense. Those who want to come here for research purposes can usually do so on a variety of temporary visas, such as B-1, H-1 or H-2, or possibly an I visa, if they're legitimately employed in the communications industry.

Most writers, however, who intend to come to the United States for a short period of time, either to do research or to write regardless of where they are being paid, do so on a simple tourist visa. Experience has taught them that an explanation to the consul of their true intention will most probably involve a rejection of their visa application. They have found that by coming into the United States and keeping quiet about what they're doing, they encounter little or no difficulty.

Of course, this assumes that they're not employed. If they are, they usually break the law by working for cash. This procedure is dangerous and unlawful. The simple truth is, however, that writers find it difficult to obtain regular employment, and take what they can get.

When writers want permanent residence, they encounter great difficulty. A contract from a publisher in the United States to write one or more books will not be considered by the Immigration Service as permanent employment for the purposes of an application for residence. Writers are consequently forced to seek other avenues. The normal procedures for residence based on family relationships apply to them without restriction. If they are business people as well, they can get their residence by forming companies that will employ them. This procedure is especially useful when a writer has ongoing work and can contract with publishers through a personal holding company.

If a writer is married to someone who has another form of employment, that nonwriting spouse may provide a less complicated method for seeking residence. If your spouse gets a Green Card, so do you.

Artists in the fine arts have problems that are even greater than those faced by writers in seeking entry into the United States. Many artists struggle their whole lives and are rarely compensated for their work in amounts that allow them the luxury of not having to search for other employment. If artists have independent sources of income, or if they're married to someone who has a job or another way of getting here, then they will have fewer difficulties. But if this is not the case, then even a temporary visa, other than a tourist visa, may be difficult to get.

What I've said doesn't apply to artists in the field of commercial art, where employment is not as hard to organize as it is for artists who are trying to exhibit their work in art galleries. Art directors and graphic artists who are employed by companies have a much easier time entering the United States than do entertainers and writers.

The problems faced by creative people are often greater than those faced by other applicants for visas to and residence in the United States. These problems are not insurmountable, however.

12

DOMESTIC WORKERS

Domestic workers make up one of the largest groups of aliens coming into America, and they arrive here from all over the world. The procedure they follow to residence is almost always that of labor certification. Domestics are so numerous, and therefore so important, that their special problems need to be addressed separately.

While the certification process is substantially the same for these people as it is for others, there are some basic differences. Most important is the requirement that, before they begin the process, these household employees must have a minimum of one year's experience in the same kind of job they will be doing here. Even more important, they must be able to document this prior experience in the form of a letter or affidavit from the former employer.

Domestics are usually less affluent and less skilled than other immigrants, and many are members of racial minorities, so they may have to contend with prejudice, among their other problems. They are perceived by the poor minorities already in the United

States as rivals for jobs, and the government believes many of them will wind up on welfare. Consequently, the whole area of alien domestic help is charged with political and economic considerations.

There's another point of view to be considered, however—the needs of those who require household help, a part of the population that increases every day. With women constituting nearly half the work force, there is a rising number of two-job families. And there are many other households where help is required. It is the consensus among these people that help is almost impossible to get unless aliens are utilized. These groups sponsor immigrants for labor certification whenever it's possible, and try to help get Green Cards for them so they can stay.

This situation has led to a very delicate problem. Countries that provide the bulk of applications for domestic jobs in America often have such a low standard of living that there are few opportunities for the same kind of domestic employment that the alien applicants will be seeking in the United States. Nevertheless, they have to produce proof of a year's experience, and the letter proving it becomes their ticket of entry, the price of admission to America. It's not surprising, then, that our consuls working in the countries of South and Central America have, through experience, learned to doubt the authenticity of many of the letters presented to them.

The question often arises, how do these people ever get visas at all? Many will answer that the visas are often fraudulently issued. This is the answer of cynics and skeptics, and by those who believe that the State Department is often corrupt. The State Department itself has often asked this same question and has, I believe, not been satisfied with what it has found.

Speculation aside, it's a fact that hundreds of thousands of people who work as domestics in the United States enter from places where theoretically it should be next to impossible to get legitimate visas. Of course, many enter illegally; but others manage to obtain visas. Sometimes these are obtained by a plea to the consul that the applicant requires medical attention in the United States. Others may convince the official that they have family members outside of the United States to whom they will return.

Many people who could actually get to the United States in other ways believe that it's easier to enter as a visitor, to stay illegally while an application for domestic work is pending, and then, after the Green Card is issued, find other suitable employment. Such is the case with many women who have little or no qualification for work in this country. Thousands of young women from Europe enter each year, only to find an overcrowded job market; they realize swiftly that employment as a domestic worker is a relatively easy if not necessarily quick avenue to residence.

Part of the anomaly in the immigration law—and I've discussed it from the beginning of this book—is that the law itself is often responsible for generating the dishonesty that it's meant to protect against. The fact is that Americans employ hundreds of thousands of illegal workers in their homes. This should lead to the conclusion that these people are necessary, not merely interlopers who should be treated as illegal aliens. The law makes it difficult for them to regularize their status here, and the resulting frustration leads to the breaking of the law. Even those who enter the United States legally and legitimately, and who entertain an offer of domestic work in a home in the United States, are forced because of the nature of the regulations to be less than forthcoming when they're filling out the applications required for labor certification here.

The Labor Department insists on having hourly schedules of work, along with free time, set down. But what if the domestic is to take care of children belonging to a working mother, the most common kind of job? Plainly, if the children are at home and the mother is at work, the domestic who's taking care of them is going to be on duty all day long, every day, and her free time during the workweek, if any, is going to be in the late evening, plus whatever weekend freedom she is given. Few domestics really work the kind of wages-and-hours schedule the Labor Department requires. Nevertheless, applicants are almost compelled to claim a schedule that bears only a remote resemblance to the actual working situation.

Live-in domestics are in much shorter supply than nine-to-five workers, and their applications have a much greater chance of success. Day-help workers, however, are another story. Our government presumes that there is no shortage of such workers, and they are therefore on Schedule B. For such workers, the presumption must be overcome even before a labor certification application can be filed. Even so, such an application has inherent problems and is quite difficult to work through successfully.

On the other hand, where the position is for a live-in domestic, provided you follow all the rules regarding hours and wages—and, most important, can document the fact that a live-in domestic is a "business necessity"—your chances of success are much greater.

The qualification that the live-in domestic be a "business necessity" is interpreted quite strictly. Consequently, you can't simply state that you prefer a live-in domestic and hope the application will be approved. You must say why it's absolutely necessary that you have such a worker. Commonly stated reasons, usually accepted, include such explanations as: that there are two working parents, with small children at home; that the parents are involved in quite a lot of business entertaining after work hours, when children need to be looked after; or that it is a one-parent family, where the parent is employed, has irregular working hours, or travels frequently. If any or several of these can be documented, the chances of successfully getting labor certification for a live-in domestic are greatly enhanced.

If certification is granted, an application is then made for a preference, almost always the sixth, since domestic labor is unskilled. Adjustment-of-status applications require proof that the applicant did not work in this country before work permission was granted. That isn't often the case, however. If the alien is here and the government doesn't know it, the domestic simply waits until there's a quota number available, and the consul at home schedules an interview for which the alien returns, after which the alien can come back to the United States as a permanent resident. Even if the government does know you're here, the matter of going abroad can sometimes be delayed until the interview.

For some, there's another legal means of entering that not many have heard about, and it may be a valuable thing for you to know. If you've worked as a domestic for a foreign family whose head is the holder of an E or H visa, and if you can prove either that you have domestic experience or that you have worked for a year with this family, consuls will usually give you a B-1 visa to accompany your employer while he's staying in America on his E or H visa. It isn't a foolproof method, and there is also some variation among consuls in the way they treat such applications, but it can be done. This, like any other, is a method subject to abuse. People sometimes write letters falsely declaring they were employed by a family. Many families cooperate in this matter, because they want as much continuity in their domestic help as they can get.

Getting a job through labor certification remains the best way to come here as a domestic, and eventually to get the Green Card. But be careful. What you do has to be carefully defined if you expect to qualify.

Application as a domestic worker for labor certification is a tight line to walk, both for you and your prospective employer, who must follow the regular certification procedure I described earlier. Advertising the position is a necessity and should be done in a way that will eliminate all unwanted or unqualified applicants. Most Americans will not take live-in domestic positions for a simple reason—they don't want to work evenings and weekends in someone else's home. And most advertisements for this kind of position specify weekend work.

Employers must also disclose on the certification form what their income is, the makeup of the family, and the size of the residence. Any qualifications stated will be closely scrutinized by the Department of Labor, however, and must be justified against a fairly strict standard. For instance, I know of an employer who professed a desire for a live-in domestic to take care of her children, one who spoke French and could, in conjunction with her other duties, familiarize her children with the French language. The Department of Labor held that such a requirement was not a business necessity, and so must be dropped. Preferences of this kind will not often be permitted as a job requirement by the Department of Labor.

Fraud is pervasive in the system. What's worse, everyone involved in the process—lawyers, consuls, people in the Labor Department—knows what's going on. Domestics already here are aware of the climate of suspicion that exists. Few are willing to go back home and begin the usually lengthy process of certification, and their fears of doing so are legitimate. Most are afraid the consul will find some suggestion of fraud, whether it exists or not, or that, if delays come up, their employer will decide to drop the whole thing. Others fear that it will be dangerous for them to return—Haitians, for example. That's why so many choose to stay here illegally, hoping that one day they will be given amnesty. Meanwhile, they live in a legal twilight zone.

Those who have been working here illegally know they will ultimately have to pick up their final visa at home. Nevertheless, they try to stay here as long as possible. And there are ways of stalling. Legal help is essential in such a case, since it will be necessary to strike some kind of bargain with the Immigration Service so that you can stay until your application is nearly completed. There are all kinds of stalling devices. A common one is to plead that you must have medical treatment that is only available here. It must be remembered, however, that few domestic workers have any medical insurance whatsoever. In fact, aliens who are here illegally are not entitled to any welfare assistance. If such assistance is actually sought by an alien, this in itself can be the ground for denying residence that may otherwise be forthcoming.

I don't want to sound completely discouraging about getting into America legally as a domestic. It isn't all that bad. Thousands of people get their Green Cards every year without undue difficulty, so the system *does* work, and those on both sides of the immigration fence benefit from it.

It's too bad, however, that the system has made matters so difficult that thousands of applicants are virtually forced into illegality and deception. Compliance with the law as it is has been made extremely hard, because the law is so inconsistent with what reality dictates.

DOCTORS

Doctors were once regarded as a privileged class of immigrant to America. They had an easier time getting into the country than almost anyone else. To gain entrance, they had only to show that they were graduates of an accredited medical school, were duly licensed to practice medicine, could speak English fluently, and possessed an offer of medical employment in the United States. Years ago, many doctors who were able to demonstrate their eligibility got their Green Cards in less than a month, some in less than ten days.

One of the reasons they were treated so well was that the authorities felt more physicians were needed here. Consequently, doctors were placed on the Labor Department's Schedule A, which meant that they did not have to apply for a labor certification before being eligible for immigration to America. Furthermore, because doctors were professionals, they were eligible as third-preference immigrants almost immediately after they applied for the status. In addition, the American Medical Association, one of the world's most powerful professional organizations, had not yet changed its permissive attitude toward foreign doctors.

Then, in 1977, the rules changed abruptly. Doctors were removed from Schedule A and so had to apply for labor certification like anyone else. In addition, they were not even eligible to apply for such certification until they passed an extremely difficult examination known as the VQE, the Visa Qualifying Examination. Recently, that examination has been replaced by another, which will probably be even more difficult.

From 1977 to 1983, doctors found it very difficult indeed to get into this country unless they came from Canada, where the VQE was not required. Then their next hurdle in applying for residence was to find a medical institution or other suitable place to employ them.

Today, it is again understood that in certain parts of the United States some categories of medical specialties are in short supply. For these specialties, doctors are once again on Schedule A, but not with the benefits that applied before 1977. They still have to pass the VQE and/or the examination that will shortly replace it.

The list of specialties and places in which these specialties are in short supply can be obtained by writing to the Department of Health and Human Resources and asking for its list of health manpower shortage areas. For all practical purposes, this is now the only Schedule A category that doctors will be able to look to when they seek exemption from the normal requirements to apply for labor certification.

Doctors who are internationally famous, and can therefore be considered outstanding members of the sciences, are exempt from the labor certification requirement. These doctors are exempt not only from labor certification, but also from the requirement to take the VQE or its equivalent.

As we've seen in a previous chapter, one rule governing certification is that a job offered to an alien must be generally advertised by the employer. But some hospitals with vacancies of the kind foreign doctors could hope to fill never advertise. They know most of the probable candidates and are in general strongly against the whole idea. Some famous medical institutions are especially insulted by the notion of advertising for jobs.

One of my clients was an English doctor who had been offered a position in the Chicago area as head of an important department in a major hospital. He was highly qualified for the position, but not famous enough to qualify as an outstanding member of the profession. The hospital was horrified when it learned about the rule requiring advertising and flatly refused to help. The local office of the Labor Department was sympathetic but made it clear that it was impossible to bend the rules. In the end, the doctor gave up trying to emigrate to America and went to Australia instead. The hospital eventually hired an American doctor. It was unfortunate for my client, but it was an example of how the law operates in the real world.

Another difficulty confronting doctors under the current regulations is that of the Visa Qualifying Examination (VQE), and now the new examination. It is open to question how many United States– and Canadian-trained doctors could pass this test if they were made to take it. The pass rate among foreign applicants varies according to the quality of medical training in a particular country, but worldwide it is significantly less than 40 percent.

Many doctors who come to the United States have no intention of residing here, and some only form that intention after they have been here for some time on a temporary visa. Temporary visas available to most immigrants are not always available to doctors without complications. For example, doctors may not work in the United States in a clinical capacity on an H visa. They can, however, study in the United States on an F-1. Of course, if doctors visit the United States and have no intention of working here, they can do so on the B-2 visa, which applies to all tourists, and even can do nonclinical work in the United States on a B-1 if the work essentially involves nonremunerative consultancy activity.

Of course, after the physician enters the United States on whatever nonimmigrant visa he chooses, he can change his status either to another nonimmigrant status or to permanent residence if he qualifies after he is here.

There are some special problems that alien doctors should be aware of. For example, many of those who study in America come here under the auspices of the Exchange Visitors Program, which means they use a J visa to get here. One of the great pitfalls of the J visa, however, is that it will usually subject you to living abroad for two years after the program is completed before you can either change to another temporary visa or apply for residence. Consuls know this but are unlikely to warn you of the consequences of entering with a J visa, even though regulations require that the consul must warn each applicant about the pitfalls. Even if warned, many applicants either ignore the warning or assume that when the time comes, they will somehow be able to get around it.

Although a procedure for a waiver of this requirement does exist, it's a complicated process to get it, and it's granted only in certain specified cases—where there is fear of persecution in the home country, extreme hardship, or an offer of employment by a United States government-related agency or organization. If the applicant doesn't fit clearly into one of these categories, the application for such a waiver will not be approved, and he will be forced to return to his home country for a two-year period.

Despite its drawbacks, the J-1 visa has certain advantages that must be considered. One is that it's issued for the duration of the program that sponsors you. The J visa is usually granted on a one-year basis, with extensions permitted for as long as the program is expected to last. That can be for up to a total of five years, but extensions of more than two years at one time are quite difficult to get. With each application for an extension, the Immigration Service will review the facts and determine whether there is indeed a valid reason to extend the visa for an additional year.

The usual length of stay is now two years, unless additional training is required and requested by your home country, and then the extension is given only for a one-year period. If such an extension is necessary, a written request from the sponsoring organization is required.

With approval of your J-1 visa comes a current properly issued Form IAP-66 (see appendix 16), showing the expiration date of your stay in the United States as an exchange visitor. Without this document, neither you nor your spouse and minor children can be admitted to this country. The form must be completed by your sponsor, and it must state the length of stay and the terms of the proposed exchange visit. It must also specify the educational objectives of your projected training program.

You can use the IAP-66 form to apply for J-2 visas for members of your immediate family. If you're going to precede your family into the United States, a copy of this form can be sent to the relatives abroad for use in making their own applications for J-2 entry visas. Copies of the form can be obtained by writing to the Educational Commission for Foreign Medical Graduates, asking for the IAP-66 for the use of dependents. Completed applications must then be returned to the commission. This commission sponsors a contract between a training program and a foreign doctor for only one year, so your IAP-66 has to be renewed every year.

There's an important warning to remember: be careful to stay in status, keep your family in status, and when you apply for extensions, leave enough time for the processing.

The reasoning behind the two-year foreign residence requirement with J-1 visas stems from the visa's purpose. The stated purpose is not to provide an avenue for immigration, but to provide training unavailable in other countries, so that foreign doctors, on their return to their own countries, can use the benefit of this training for their fellow nationals.

It's possible to transfer from one exchange visitor program to another after you're here. In that case, you must apply to the district director of the Immigration Service office nearest the location of the first authorized program. You must apply thirty days before the beginning of the new program. The Service will deny a transfer if it's clearly inconsistent with the doctor's original objective—for example, if a surgeon wants to transfer to a program in psychiatry.

Another extremely important thing to remember: If you engage in activities unrelated to the training program that produces income from American sources, you will lose your status and become deportable.

The H-1 visa does not carry with it the discouraging two-year foreign residence requirement. It's only applicable, however, to physicians coming to the United States to work for a nonprofit public institution or private hospital to do nonclinical work (usually research or teaching). Incidental clinical work for pay is allowed, however, on the H-1 visa, if it occurs as part of the teaching and/or research duties.

In working out an immigration strategy, it's quite possible to use the H-1 visa to enter the United States and, while you're here, to initiate an application for permanent residence. Once this is granted, you will be able to do clinical work of any kind on a permanent basis. For those who want to do such work on a temporary basis, the J visa remains a risky but viable option.

Doctors able to qualify for permanent residence through a procedure not related to their profession (such as marriage to an American citizen) don't have to worry about any special rules for their profession, such as the VQE.

Listed below are the five classes of foreign medical graduates applying for immigration visas who are exempt from the VQE examination and its equivalent:

1. Those who are not coming to the United States primarily to perform medical services as members of the medical profession—that is, medical investigators, drug company employees, and medical school faculty.

2. Those who, as of January 9, 1977, were fully and permanently licensed to practice as doctors of medicine in an American state, held a valid specialty certification from one of the American Boards of Medical Specialties, and were actually practicing medicine in an American state.

3. Alien doctors who are "of national or international renown in the field of medicine." Unfortunately, the word "renown" has neither a legislative nor a practical definition.

4. Those who are graduates of medical schools accredited by a body approved by the United States Commissioner of Education. Such schools need not be in the United States (they might, for instance, be in Canada).

5. Those who seek to enter the United States as close relatives of American citizens or permanent residents. This group does not even need labor certification.

A final word of advice. I'm sure that many doctors reading this chapter are going to feel confused. American immigration laws are an extremely complex maze of rules and exceptions that sometimes baffle even those whose life's work is immigration. Every time the laws are changed, which happens often, the confusion is increased. In the case of foreign medical graduates, they are confronted with additional rules, exceptions, and restrictions that are even more complex and confusing than other immigration regulations.

Consequently, my advice to a foreign doctor contemplating temporary or permanent employment in the United States is to consult an expert to make sure the course chosen is the best one. Doctors do have unusually good access to information from advisers and medical schools, but they should keep checking beyond these sources while the situation for them remains in flux. In particular, they should call the Educational Commission for Foreign Medical Graduates at (215) 386–5900 if they have any questions.

Always remember that in order to get the fullest benefit from the educational and professional opportunities available to alien physicians in America, you must first choose the best pathway to enter the United States. Nearly everything else depends on that choice.

STUDENTS

No one knows exactly how many foreign students come to the United States to study every year, but there may be as many as a hundred thousand. At the last count, there were about two hundred and fifty thousand in residence. In the view of the United States government, they represent both a benefit and a danger.

On the one hand, foreign students are unquestionably a valuable economic asset to private education, which has been in deep trouble for some time, and even to publicly supported institutions, which have been badly hurt by declining enrollments and cuts in federal support. Foreign students introduce a welcome diversity to the lives of their fellow scholars, helping to educate American students away from isolationist, xenophobic viewpoints. Moreover, these visitors from abroad are ambassadors of good will, taking back with them a better appreciation of the American system—or so we hope—which will be useful to us if they become important people in their own countries.

On the other hand, a large number of immigrants who come in

as students don't want to leave when their studies are completed, and that creates labor problems in a tight economy. Many of these students see their visas as a stepping stone that will enable them to stay in this country. Abuse of the visa itself is common. Foreign students often work, which is illegal, and to make things worse, they work "off the books," which means they are paid in cash, on which no taxes are paid. Both students and their spouses are often involved in this particular kind of abuse. Foreign students in elementary schools require special attention that drains the resources of an already overburdened school system.

The student visa issued to foreigners is an F-1 visa for those pursuing an academic course of study, or an M-1 visa for those enrolled in a vocational institution. In each case, a spouse and children are entitled to an F-2 or M-2 visa, respectively. As a precondition to the issuance of the F-1 or M-1 visa, the applicants must indicate that they have been accepted by an accredited institution in the United States. The visa will allow the students to study in this country, and their spouses and children will be allowed to accompany them during the period of time they are here. Generally speaking, no one in the family is permitted to work, although there are certain exceptions that will be discussed later.

I recommend obtaining the student visa abroad through consular processing, rather than in the United States by means of a change-of-status application. I do so because the Immigration Service is very suspicious of an individual who comes here on another visa and soon after requests a change to student status. The INS usually assumes that his original intent was to come here and study, and if this is so it will deny the application.

The first step to the issuance of a student visa is acceptance by an accredited institution. The school will issue the appropriate immigration document, which is Form I-20A (see appendix II). Some institutions will not issue this form until a registration fee is paid. This fee is usually nonrefundable and so will be lost if there is any difficulty in obtaining the student visa.

The I-20A form indicates what it will cost to live for a year at the particular institution, the duration of the program, and other relevant details. You'll need a letter from your bank or some other kind of proof that you can support yourself or get help from your family. An affidavit from someone who can vouch for you financially is a second choice, but consulates and embassies don't like affidavits because they are not always honored.

When you apply at the consulate for a student visa, fill out the regular nonimmigrant visa form, and be very careful to make it clear that you intend to study in America, not to live here. A nonimmigrant visa form for every member of the family who is coming with you will also be necessary, along with photographs. If the consul accepts you, he'll stamp the visa on your passport, then place in a sealed envelope the completed I-20A form and the letter or other proof that you can support yourself. This envelope will be opened by the immigration officer you deal with at the port of entry.

There are some additional points to keep in mind. You'll have to prove that you can support your wife and children if they come with you. Otherwise, the Immigration Service will conclude that a member of the family will have to work here, and this is not permitted. The INS, at the point of entry, may reevaluate the entire application and can refuse to admit you if any doubt exists about your true intent. The examiner will give special consideration to unusual circumstances that may affect a student's application—political chaos in his own country, for example, or whether the applicant seems to be an unsuitable student. If the examiner suspects you are not really coming here to study, or that your I-20A was issued by an "immigration mill," you may not be admitted.

For the kind of consular processing I've been describing, prospective students won't need a lawyer, unless there's some special circumstance. You may need one, however, if you take the change-of-status route.

Many students choose to enter this country as visitors and change to the F-1 visa while they're here. While there's no practical reason why this approach shouldn't work, the government frowns on it, and consequently many such applications are rejected. Yet there are often good reasons to try anyway. Sometimes prospective students don't know where they want to study and wish to inspect several schools. There are sympathetic consuls who recognize such situations and are lenient about giving prospective students a visitor's visa, knowing they will be applying for change of status later. Unfortunately, neither these consuls, inexperienced for the most part, nor those getting the visas appreciate how often applications for change of status are rejected.

To change status means following the procedure I described in chapter 4. You'll need the same documents that you'd require if you were applying from abroad for a student visa. There's only one difference: instead of submitting visa forms, you'll be using the change-of-status form, I-506 (see appendix 9).

The key to a successful change-of-status procedure is filling out Form I-506 intelligently. There's a trap in this form. Among other things, it will ask you why you want to change your status. You must convince the immigration authorities that the idea came to you while you were here, but not so soon after your arrival that officials might conclude that you had it in mind all the time. You'll also have to convince the authorities that you will maintain your student status if it's granted, and that you will not violate it by working.

In filling out Form I-506, pay special attention to questions 13 and 14. They cover the issues I just mentioned. Question 13 says: "I desire to have my nonimmigrant status changed for the following reasons." Question 14 states: "I did not apply to the American consul for a visa in the nonimmigrant status which I am now seeking for the following reasons." It may be better to answer both these questions in a single statement. Many assert that they had no intention of studying here when they came, and that the idea came without any deliberate intent on their part, having been prompted by friends or relatives. You may want to point out that the kind of education you're seeking here isn't available in your own country.

Timing is also important. If you apply for a status change quickly, it will be taken as an intent to do so from the beginning. If you came in on a visitor's visa, that means you may have been admitted for up to six months, and it may be better to wait until several additional months have passed before applying. (But remember that your change-of-status application almost certainly will be denied if you're already *out* of status; you must get an extension of the visa status you do have before it expires.) Even sixty days is often too soon to apply for a change of status. Three to four months is better, but of course that is subject to the immigration officer's judgment. No matter what strategy you follow, the application may be denied anyway. The ideas I've given you here may not work, but they will give you a better chance.

Another important question on Form I-506, number 15, says: "I submit the following documentary evidence to establish that I will maintain the nonimmigrant classification to which I wish to be changed." Here you need to convince Immigration that you can support yourself while you're here, and that you intend to go back home when you've finished studying.

Once you've completed your forms for submission, be very sure that you retain copies of everything, including a receipt for the filing fee, in case the Service loses your documents. While your application is pending, you may *not* legally attend school.

If the application is approved, it means you can stay as long as you are registered in school on a full-time basis. You must be careful, however, if you change schools to get the permission of the Immigration Service and to file Form I-538 (see appendix 12). Your status ends when your studies are completed.

If the application is denied, you should appeal, a procedure for which you'll need a lawyer. The point of the appeal is usually to buy time because it, too, will probably be denied. While your application or appeal is still pending, you are here legally. Time is what's needed, and the bureaucracy inadvertently helps you, because it often takes a ridiculously long time for applications to be processed.

Students who are here legally, with the appropriate F-1 or M-1 visa, usually have no difficulty in traveling out of the United States. Those whose visas have already expired, however, will have to return to a foreign consulate with all the appropriate documents to get new visas before they reenter. If the visas have not yet expired, the students must remember to take with them before they leave the United States a fresh Form I-20A and fresh proof of their ability to support themselves while they are here. They will have to present this proof to an immigration official when they reenter.

Students who entered the United States originally as visitors and who changed status while they were here will encounter a particular problem if they travel abroad. They will have no student visa in their passport, because such visas can only be put there by foreign consuls. Some of these people may be lucky to find an Immigration Service official who will readmit them on presentation of proof of their change of status. More often than not, however, they will be turned away and required to reapply for the student visa abroad before they are allowed back in.

There are some students who shouldn't try to leave the United States at all, because they won't be able to get back in—for example, those who have no residence abroad. If such an alien applies in the United States for change of status and it is denied, he shouldn't leave without exhausting the appeal process in the United States. That might take years, and in the meantime, he might be able to find some other way to stay here legitimately, if that is his wish.

Now let's look at some special considerations. As I've warned previously, it's important to remember that if you work without permission, in violation of your student status, you can be expelled from the country. Those who want to obey the law and not risk expulsion should know that it's possible to work legally by applying to the Immigration Service, showing that your expenses have become greater than your available funds or the ability of your supporter to pay. Sometimes you'll be given permission to do part-time work. This is ironic, because if you had told the authorities this in the first place, when you applied, you might not have been given the visa. You must demonstrate that unforeseen circumstances have arisen leading to an adverse financial situation.

Sometimes, in any case, even though you can explain convincingly that you have a need to work, permission may not be given. A danger lies in accepting unauthorized employment, or permitting any member of your family to do so. You are then in technical violation of your status and are deportable. To apply for work permission, ask for Form I-538 (see appendix 12).

To protect your status, be sure to extend your visa when it expires, and to abide by its terms, especially when it comes to changing schools. It's always wise to guard against loss of your status, but especially so if you happen to come from a country that may have strained relations with the United States—a situation not always foreseeable, of course.

After you've completed your course of study, in most cases you will be allowed a period of practical training. The school you're attending can handle this for you; a lawyer won't be needed. The training period is for six months, with a six-month extension permitted as long as your training is in the same field. After that, you're expected to go home.

Those who have long-term plans to stay in America after their student visas and practical training periods have expired will usually apply for labor certification, which requires proof of at least six months' experience. In this respect the training period is important, for it counts as experience.

If you've decided to stay, it pays to lay out a strategic plan well in advance, before it's time to leave school, because it is often difficult to change from a student visa to another status. An important part of that successful long-term strategy is to remain in status and never work without permission.

Some critics argue that the flow of foreign students to this country ought to be curtailed, or at least supervised more rigorously. But others, of which I'm one, believe that the benefits of educating foreign students in the United States far outweigh the drawbacks. We educate a good many of the world's elite leaders, and many of its professional and technical people. In general, foreign students have maintained a high academic standard in this country, sometimes better than our own students. And finally, their work in America not only aids us indirectly, but also helps to pay our formidable education bills. Clearly, foreign students need us, and we need them.

15

ILLEGAL ALIENS

Illegal aliens are numbered in the millions—so many that the authorities can do no more than estimate their numbers. The lowest figure is six million; the highest, twelve million. Illegal aliens in the United States have created a vast problem, for the country and for themselves, forced as they are to live outside society.

The great importance of this issue has led to recent efforts to revise the immigration law. Legislation will not, however, wholly resolve the conflicting emotions both legislators and the public feel about this matter. There are those who believe strongly that illegals are a drain on America and advocate throwing them all out. It's argued that they undercut American labor, deprive government of legitimate income, and contribute to the crime rate.

On the other hand, there are those who believe we must recognize the fact of illegal aliens' existence in this country and legitimize their presence, since it is plainly impossible as a practical matter to throw them out. Besides, so runs this argument, they are doing a good many jobs Americans don't want to do, and if that undercuts native labor, it's hardly the fault of the illegals. This reasoning goes even further: advocates argue that without such illegals doing certain kinds of work Americans would not do, some segments of our economy would suffer irreparable harm.

While this debate has continued, so has the flow of illegal aliens. A great many sneak in over the borders with Mexico and Canada. Others come in legally, overstay the period allotted at the time of their entry, become illegal, and continue to live here, knowing or believing that it's impossible for them to get a Green Card. People in both these categories live in the hope that they may be eligible for amnesty later.

It does make a difference, however, which category you're in. If you slipped over the border and came in illegally in the first place, under the law you're not officially in this country, and therefore you can't change your status, although it's possible for you to get a preference. You also are entitled to less in the way of due process. But if you came here on some kind of visa and stayed on after it expired, there's hope for an adjustment of status—that is, if you didn't work illegally in the meantime. You are also entitled to due process.

There are other ways to be legitimate. Marriage to an American, of course, will open the way to a Green Card. If you have a close relative in America who has become a legitimate resident, that may also do it. Sometimes just being here long enough—the minimum is eight years—might mean suspension of deportation if you're caught, again depending on whether you were working and on the surrounding circumstances. In such cases, you'll need a lawyer.

While you're here, you can also have your employer file for labor certification. If you didn't sneak in, but were legally admitted, and if you can prove you didn't work illegally while you were here, then you can adjust status to that of a permanent resident. If you did work illegally, labor certification would have to go through consular processing in your home country.

During the past several years, there has been much talk about amnesty and a new immigration bill. It now appears that such a bill may not pass for some time. It is clear, however, that if one does pass, it will involve some limited amnesty for certain categories of illegal aliens. Great public debate has taken place over the issue of amnesty. There are those who believe that it rewards illegality at the expense of those who have obeyed the law, and there are others who believe that it will help to integrate into society many millions of those who are now living underground. Whatever the outcome, even if amnesty is given, it will certainly not solve the problems of many millions who won't qualify under the very technical rules that have been proposed.

If amnesty is given, proof will certainly be required to show that an alien was in this country illegally as of a certain date. Without such proof, the alien will not qualify. As a result of this requirement, the production of phony documents is inevitable.

The hope that a new immigration law will pass lives on. This hope causes many people to make decisions that may seem illogical. Some decide to remain here illegally in the hope that a law will pass and that somehow, miraculously, they will meet its requirements. Meanwhile, they live underground and become part of a growing community of illegal aliens.

Others resort to direct fraud. Some people get involved in phony marriages and divorces in order to create a relationship with an American that will help them get Green Cards. Still others pay high prices for false documents. Unfortunately for the system, many of these tricks work, and the few who get caught do not discourage those who continue to try.

All of us hope the problem of illegal aliens will be resolved, at least to some extent, by legislation. But that may not be forthcoming for some time.

16

BUSINESSMEN
AND INVESTORS

One of the most striking developments in immigration in the past ten years has been the emergence of what has become known as the new immigrant—the businessman or investor. This arrival on our shores tends to be affluent, educated, and sophisticated. A variety of options have been opened to him, giving him great flexibility when he approaches the problem of getting into America.

Certain nonimmigrant visas are especially useful to businessmen and investors who wish to visit or to stay in this country. These visas should be reviewed carefully by anyone who falls within the categories covered by this chapter. What I will do here is to outline briefly the kinds of issues that concern a businessman or an investor and leave it to you to go back to earlier portions of this book and assimilate what is specifically necessary for you to proceed. This chapter should also be read along with chapter 17, on taxation, which is of special importance to businessmen and investors.

For the businessman or investor, an assortment of temporary

visas is available, such as the E, the B-1, the B-2, and the L. Even the H-1 visa may be available to those interested in temporary work here who are professionals.

If permanent residence is the goal, and if the immigrant cannot base his case on a relationship to an American resident or citizen, he has fewer options. Nevertheless, there are some useful loopholes in the legislation.

Foreigners who have businesses outside of the United States, or who have been employed by such businesses for a period of one year before making the decision to enter, can use the L visa, one of the more useful options available under the law. The existence or formation of an American branch, subsidiary, or affiliate is necessary. If no such branch is already in existence, its formation is usually nothing more than a small inconvenience to be attended to.

Earlier in this book, I indicated that the same set of facts that qualify a person for an L visa can also be used for an application to classify an immigrant as a preference. I have already covered this extensively, but it's worth repeating that the primary difference between this category and the L visa is the requirement that the American business must be active for at least a year before the time the application is made.

You already know that if your intention is immigration, applications can be initiated either in the United States or outside. Businessmen and investors must be especially careful to take their tax profile into consideration before reaching a decision about their immigration status.

As I mentioned, chapter 17 deals with taxation. No potential immigrant can afford to ignore the American tax authorities. Businessmen and investors must be especially careful to guard against adverse economic consequences that can occur because of a lack of careful preparation before the the first steps are taken toward immigration to the United States.

There was a period when investors, or retired people of independent means, were able to get into the United States with Green Cards quite easily. That was when the nonpreference portion of the quota was open. Those days have been over for some time, how-

ever, and under present law, a millionaire with substantial investments in the United States is, from a legal point of view, no better
off than his employee. Many people consider this outrageous, because our country has taken the position over and over again that
we want to welcome foreigners who will create jobs for Americans.

To illustrate how to plan a strategy based on current law, here
is how one of my wealthy foreign clients made good his desire to
enter the United States as an immigrant. He was a Frenchman, the
owner of a car franchise in Europe. He had property in California
and for years entered and left the United States on a B-2 visa
without difficulty. Recently, however, he decided that in the long
run it was better to get a Green Card. I raised the subject of
taxation and advised him to calculate the probable tax consequences of becoming a resident. After a careful analysis, we concluded that there were no adverse tax consequences to worry
about.

My client didn't want to go through the labor certification process. Consequently, I formed a corporation for him in the United
States that became a branch of his business in Europe. Since he had
been the head of his company there for more than a year, the L
visa that I aimed for was approved without delay. Once he was
here on an L-1 visa, however, he became impatient with the pros-
pect of waiting a year before he would be able to apply for a
preference. I advised him that the one-year rule could be avoided
if his American corporation were to buy an already functioning
business in this country that was more than a year old. He looked
around for a suitable investment and bought an automobile franchise in the Southwest. As a result of this investment, and because
he qualified as a professional, my client became immediately eligible for a Green Card, which was issued within a matter of three
months.

This avenue is one widely used by foreign businessmen who
want to settle here. It's a classic example of what can be done when
you know how to use the immigration laws to your advantage. The
options available to investors and businessmen are very wide indeed. Not only do these people have access to the complete range
of nonimmigrant visas and the methods of establishing residence

that are available to everyone else, but they also have the capacity to create structures and make investments that can substantially ease the normal problems of immigration and travel that most people come up against.

In this chapter, I have not discussed in detail the E visas that are most often used in these situations because I believe that the recommendations in chapter 4 should be sufficient. I would, however, like to add that the E visa is one of the more flexible tools available to someone who is in a position to do business or invest in the United States. Unfortunately, this category of visa is open only to nationals of certain countries. Other options, such as the L visa and intracompany transfers, are excellent alternatives.

PART V

TAXATION AND NATURALIZATION

TAXATION

Most of those who think about coming to the United States, either on a temporary or permanent basis, don't concern themselves at the beginning with American taxes. Nevertheless, I believe that the consequences of taxation in this country ought to be studied carefully by any alien who intends to live and work here, and that this should take place before he arrives.

In America income taxes are levied by the federal government, by all but a few of the states, and by a great many cities. Worse, these taxes vary from place to place, and even from time to time, as do other kinds of taxes, such as sales and estate taxes.

Consequently, it would be frivolous to try to explain in a few pages all the intricacies of our tax system. What I can do, however, is to discuss a few important possibilities. If they concern you, consider them carefully, with the help of a competent financial adviser, before you plan on coming here.

Our tax system differs from many others in the world. While we have a high rate of taxation, we also have a much greater number of ways to shelter income legally and consequently decrease the tax burden—ways that are unknown in many places outside the United States. But to take advantage of them, you will need sophisticated advice. In the end, it may turn out that you will be better off to be taxable here than in another country.

Foreigners, even if they don't live in the United States, have to pay income taxes on what they earn in this country, depending on the amount of time they have spent here and the nature of the tax treaty, if any, between their country of origin and this one. Furthermore, once the Internal Revenue Service (IRS) considers them residents of the United States, they will be taxed just like Americans on income earned anywhere in the world. If that income happens to be earned in a country where taxes must be paid on it, the alien may have to pay duplicate taxes in the United States, unless there is a tax treaty between both countries.

If such treaties exist, there may not be any problem. As for capital gains, however, there could be significant differences between taxes paid abroad and those paid here. In some countries, such as South Africa, the sale of an asset, regardless of the profit deriving from the sale, does not incur a tax liability. But that isn't so in the United States, so it's important for foreigners to take precautions about potential profit from the sale of capital assets before they get here.

The IRS has several guidelines for the question of residence in the United States as it applies to taxation. They are complex but nevertheless easy to explain in general terms. If all the facts of your case indicate an intention to live permanently in the United States, you may be taxed as an American resident, regardless of how many days you spend here. In general, if you spend more than one hundred and eighty days per year in this country, the IRS considers you a resident for tax purposes, no matter where you may actually live. But even this rule has so many exceptions that it can only be cited as a general guideline. You may need an expert to help you interpret it as it applies to your situation. Ordinarily, however, it's an important rule of thumb and should be taken seriously.

Some tax lawyers will tell you that if you have a Green Card, you're automatically taxable in the United States as a resident regardless of where you live. There are many others, however, who take a different view and will assure you that if you have a Green Card but live outside the United States for nine months of the year, you can avoid American taxation on your worldwide income. If you question closely the lawyers who take the latter view, however, usually you'll find that what they mean is simply that you may be able to win a tax claim filed against you by the IRS. In fact, the probability of winning is not high. And if you do win, you will almost certainly forfeit your right to live in this country and will have to give up your Green Card.

Rich foreigners often use the Green Card as a sort of an insurance policy, never intending to live here. That means risking having to surrender the card if they're discovered, since they don't fill the requirement of "continually manifesting" an intent to reside in the United States. I believe that if more rich aliens were really aware of this risk, and took it as seriously as it deserves to be taken, they might make different decisions.

Very often what would normally be the best kind of immigration advice turns out to produce the worst tax results. In my own practice, I often find myself advising clients to do things that some lawyers would consider wasteful. The advice I render takes into account tax and other considerations, however, which a careful lawyer cannot ignore if he is mindful of all of the needs of his client.

Many foreigners are concerned about estate taxes and gift taxes. Here the IRS rules are somewhat more lenient. You will be told by many lawyers that even if you have a Green Card, these estate and gift taxes will apply to you only if you actually live in the United States most of the year, and if the IRS can prove that your primary residence is in this country.

None of the rules I've been talking about are inflexible and without exceptions. Most of the rules in this area are, in fact, general guidelines that will alter depending on the facts of a particular case.

For example, I have a client who has never had a Green Card but who has for years maintained a home in Connecticut as his primary residence. He also lives in the United States for more than six months a year, but only because he must look after an aging member of his family. His principal residence is actually a yacht that floats from country to country, from season to season, all year. This extremely rich man retains a group of tax lawyers to help him sort out the problems of American taxation on his numerous transactions. In addition, he has consulted at least five of the leading tax lawyers in the United States and several others in Europe. Not one of them has given him exactly the same advice as another.

There's a lesson to be learned here: if your tax situation is complex and your true residence is not clearly established, beware of simple solutions. It's usually safer to take a more conservative approach, even though it may mean paying a higher price in taxation. People whose tax problems are not very unusual may believe that the rules applying to them will be simple, but in reality all tax situations can present complications. There is simply no escape from the realities of taxation. The rich may have much more complicated problems, but those with modest incomes also have their troubles.

I think tax planning should begin before you do anything else. There have been cases in which the IRS has considered aliens taxable from the time they took their first steps toward residence.

When the potential tax burden in the United States is significant, and the Green Card represents more a protective measure—insurance, if you will—than an urgent desire to live here, it may pay a husband and wife to conduct their lives differently from a legal point of view. By this I mean that it may pay a spouse who earns most of the income to remain a resident of a foreign country and let the other spouse who earns less income become a resident of the United States with a Green Card.

People who do this also file separate returns, and so avoid a substantial American tax burden. Of course, the facts of their living situation have to be considered. If, in fact, such a couple live in the United States most of the year, the IRS may consider them taxable in the United States regardless.

During the past few years, the American government has tried to close many of the tax loopholes that have existed for years, not only those applying to foreigners doing business and living here, but also for Americans who do business and live abroad. Since the recent flood of immigration, these issues, once ignored, have come to be much more important. Taxation is something extremely important to almost everyone who intends to work and live in America. There are no shortcuts and few tricks that actually work; those that do are often expensive to employ. Because the stakes can be so high, it's absolutely essential to consult an expert before you arrive here.

18

NATURALIZATION

American law defines U.S. naturalization as the means by which the nationality of the United States is conferred on an individual after birth. Once you've gone through the naturalization process, you become a citizen of the United States with nearly all the rights and privileges of those whose citizenship was automatically conferred upon them at birth. For many readers of this book, naturalization is the ultimate goal of the immigration process.

Superficially, naturalization appears to be the least complicated part of immigration law. You've moved to the United States as a permanent resident, obtained a job, lived here for a certain amount of time, and have finally decided to become a citizen. Newspapers often show the end result of this process—a roomful of people holding up their right hands as they're sworn in as full citizens of the country.

It would be nice to think that most people who become citizens through the naturalization process do so because they believe in our system of government and endorse the American way of life.

People decide to become citizens of this country for many other reasons, however. For example, they may want to confer the benefits of American residence on a close family relation. Others may become citizens to help them with international travel, or because of a fear of harassment by the Immigration Service. Still others may decide to be citizens because it makes them eligible for certain rights—state and federal aid and employment, political office, even Social Security. These are rights granted only to American citizens, not to permanent residents of the United States.

Let's discuss, then, the basic requirements for naturalization:

1. First, you must be a permanent resident of the United States.

2. From the date permanent residence was issued to you, you must prove continuous residence in this country for at least five years immediately before filing your application for naturalization. If your residence was based on marriage to an American citizen, the time requirement is cut to three years.

3. In most cases, you must prove physical presence within the United States for at least one-half of a five- or three-year period, depending on the basis of your residence claim.

4. You must demonstrate residence within the state from which you're filing your application for at least six months before the time of the filing.

5. You must show that your residence in this country (meaning your actual home, not your physical presence) has been continuous from the date of your application until the moment citizenship is conferred on you.

6. You must indicate your intention to live in the United States permanently.

7. You must be able to read, write, and speak English fluently, at least in an elementary manner, and you must also have a knowledge of the fundamentals of our history and government.

8. You must be of good moral character, and indicate your allegiance to the principles of the Constitution.

These rules aren't complicated, obviously. If you've satisfied the requirements for naturalization, in normal circumstances you will be able to proceed without an attorney. The next step is to prepare and file the following documents:

1. Form N-400 (see appendix 32).
2. Form G-325A (see appendix 18).
3. Three passport-size photographs.
4. Completed fingerprint charts (see appendix 24).

The only unfamiliar item on this list is Form N-400, which is straightforward and uncomplicated. Clearly, you won't need an attorney to fill this form out and to apply for naturalization. All you have to do is to file the applications and documents listed above with the INS office having jurisdiction over your place of residence.

You can file anywhere, but remember that you must first live for at least six months in the state in which you are filing. Depending on the state in which you file, the waiting period until the next step is reached can be anywhere from two months to a year and a half. For example, as I write, California is very slow in processing applications; the delay varies from state to state, sometimes from county to county. Before you go ahead, you should check with your local immigration office to see how long it will take to go through the process.

After you file, you'll be called in for a preliminary interview. At that time, your application will be reviewed with you to establish your eligibility.

During the initial interview, you'll be questioned to determine whether you were physically present in the United States for the required period of time. The examiner will look at every absence from the country, beginning from the time nearest to the interview and working backward. He'll also review the other requirements for naturalization.

Assuming that the examiner finds you eligible, he will file your petition for naturalization with the court. Once the petition is filed, there is a statutory waiting period of thirty days before the final hearing and swearing in take place in federal court. During this thirty-day period, a final investigation may take place. The examiner who questioned you will make a recommendation for or against the application. If the court is then satisfied, you will be considered qualified for naturalization, and be given a specific date to appear before the court for swearing in as a citizen.

Let me emphasize that the single most important requirement is to be a lawful permanent resident before you apply. That means you must not only have your Green Card, but must also swear under oath that you are a lawful permanent resident when you apply for naturalization. Simply possessing a Green Card for the statutory period is not enough, especially if a naturalization officer can demonstrate that you are no longer entitled to permanent residence.

If you get divorced, for instance, two years or less after your marriage, and that marriage was the basis for your residence in the United States, your application for naturalization will be carefully scrutinized. That doesn't mean the INS will revoke your residence automatically, or fail to grant you naturalization. It does mean that the authorities may look into the circumstances surrounding your marriage very carefully, to see if they were what you claimed them to be.

When you file for naturalization, your entire permanent residence application, and the time you've spent in this country (and out of it), may be reexamined by the INS. Any discrepancies in your various applications will come back to haunt you, if you can't explain them. This is why I've emphasized over and over in this book how essential it is to fill out every form truthfully, accurately, and consistently.

During such a reexamination, other kinds of visa fraud might come to light that would prevent your naturalization. If, for instance, you entered the United States for permanent residence as a worker but then failed to work for the employer who filed your labor certification, you may not be naturalized unless you can show that some local law or other unavoidable event prevented you from working. Maybe you began but didn't continue the kind of employment for which you were certified. Or maybe you were a nonpreference "investor" but didn't maintain your business status after you were given permanent residence. In these and other cases, the burden of proof is on you to show that you came into the country in a lawful manner, at the time and place prescribed by law, and that you carried out the intent described in your application.

Now let's examine, in a little more detail, some of the other potential stumbling blocks to naturalization. For example, there are rules about the length of permanent residence. You'll have to show that after your entry for that purpose, or during the five years before your citizenship application (three years if you were married to an American citizen), you lived in the United States for more than 50 percent of this period. The residency period doesn't begin until after permanent residence is granted, so that if you came in earlier under a nonimmigrant status—as a visitor or student, for instance—it won't count toward the required period. It's easy to establish your entrance date; it appears on your Green Card.

Another thing about the residence requirement: you must not be physically absent from the country for periods totaling more than thirty months during the three- or five-year waiting period. The INS can easily check your absences by looking at your passport. Further, if, within the three- or five-year waiting period, you're out of the country for more than a year, that absence breaks the continuity required for residence.

It's clear from the above that, in the period before you apply for naturalization, it will be an excellent idea to keep track of all your trips outside the country, noting carefully your date of departure, your date of return, and the airlines and flight numbers. These facts may be requested at the time of filing your application for naturalization. If you're one of those who travel frequently, and can't possibly remember details of all the trips you've taken, you may have a problem if you do not keep careful records or cannot reconstruct them to the satisfaction of the immigration examiner who questions you when you are called for your naturalization interview.

It's possible to take certain steps that have the effect of preserving your permanent residence in the United States, despite prolonged absence from the country. Before your anticipated lengthy departure (that is, for more than a year), you should apply for a reentry permit (Form I-131; see appendix 26). This permit is valid for one year, and it can be extended to cover an additional year. By obtaining it, you can remain out of the United States for more than a year without forfeiting your permanent residence, and it won't interrupt the residency requirement for citizenship.

There are certain other cases where you would be protected. If, for instance, you've been physically present within the United States for at least a year after your lawful admission for permanent residence, and you've since been employed abroad by an American firm engaged in the development of foreign trade and commerce, such employment won't break the continuity of your residence. The form covering this circumstance is Form N-470, Application to Preserve Residence for Naturalization Purposes (see appendix 33). It can be filed either before or after your employment begins, but it must be done before the expiration of a full year of absence from the country.

One requirement for naturalization may seem odd—the declaration that you intend to live in the United States permanently. It often happens, however, that people move to another country to live within five years after they've been naturalized. It may then be presumed that they falsely stated their intention to live in the United States. Their naturalization may be revoked if no rebutting proof is submitted.

The evidence you would need to disprove any accusation of false intent would be, for instance, proof that a sudden transfer of employment occurred that you couldn't have been aware of at the time you applied for naturalization. Or that you fell ill after becoming a citizen and had to return to your own country for certain specialized care unavailable here. In short, proof should consist of showing that the decision to live abroad occurred *after* the naturalization petition was filed.

One phrase in the naturalization law looks so vague that it requires an explanation. What does it mean when it says you must be of "good moral character"? There isn't anything vague about the way the INS authorities interpret that phrase. Your moral character is regarded as impaired, if not wholly absent, if you're a habitual drunkard, if you've committed adultery, or if you belong to several other classes of persons somewhat similar to classifications that would exclude you from the United States in the first place. Your application can be denied if your income is derived primarily from illegal gambling, or if you've been convicted of two or more gambling offenses during the required three- or five-year period of your residence here. Likewise if you've given false testimony to obtain any benefits under the Naturalization Act. You'll be denied if you've been convicted and confined to a penal institution for an aggregate period of 188 days or more, whether or not this offense, or offenses, was committed within the statutory period. You'll be denied if at any time you've been convicted of murder.

There are still further grounds that would bar you from being naturalized. For example, your being a possible deportee, a "subversive," a draft evader, or inexcusably absent from duty in the armed forces. Advocating certain political ideas (for example, communism), or membership in various political groups (Communist, or those considered Communist fronts, for instance), are also grounds for disqualification. Another area closely scrutinized will be your past tax-paying history. You must declare emphatically, and in certain cases you must document it, that during the time you claim permanent residence in the United States you paid all the taxes that were due, based on that status and your employment.

It's not difficult to see, then, that the United States regards your behavior during the three or five years before you file your petition as critical, and in practice, the naturalization court may consider conduct that occurred even earlier. Consequently, if you admit to adulterous sexual activity and cohabitation, to criminal conviction, to nonsupport of dependents, or to making willful misstatements when you applied for naturalization benefits—any of these, at any time—you may be prevented from even trying to demonstrate your good moral character.

Times change, however, and sometimes the "good moral character" clause begins to change with them. Homosexuality is a case in point. When it was raised in the past (and that was only when someone was noted for homosexual behavior), there was virtually no chance such a person could become a citizen. Today the question is raised more often than it used to be, and whether or not it will bar you from naturalization depends on where you live. Most states have laws against homosexual behavior, but some do not. If you admit to having had homosexual relations in a state where such acts are considered criminal, you may be cited as lacking good moral character. But in more tolerant states, such an admission won't count against you, at least not by itself.

People often worry about the language, literacy, and civics requirements. If through some disability you're physically unable to demonstrate literacy, you're exempt from having to prove English reading, writing, or spelling ability. This is also true if you're fifty or more years old at the time of filing, and have been a lawful permanent resident of the United States for twenty years. Even then, however, the examination in history and government is still required, although it can be taken in your preferred language.

In administering both literacy and government tests, the INS is required to use excerpts from *Federal Textbooks on Citizenship* for the examinations. These books are written at the elementary level, and you can buy them from the Superintendent of Documents, Government Printing Office, Washington, DC 20402, or at any government bookstore. The test on government must be limited to the subject matter in these books, and in grading, the examiner must also give consideration to education, background, age, length of residency, and, as the language of the law says, "Opportunities available and efforts made to acquire the requisite knowledge, and any other elements or factors relevant" to the government test. So, in the end, the examiner does have considerable latitude. And if you don't pass the test the first time, you'll get at least two more opportunities after your petition is filed.

The touchiest requirement for naturalization is the one that concerns "loyalty." No one would argue that an applicant for naturalization should show an attachment to constitutional principles and profess loyalty to the United States. The idea, at least, is to exclude "subversives." But what does "loyalty" mean? A sentimental attachment to one's native country does not preclude loyalty to the U.S. government. A belief that the United States Constitution isn't perfect—a belief shared by many native Americans—does not, fortunately, constitute disloyalty. Nor is it considered disloyal if you've taken the Fifth Amendment in response to questions from congressional committees.

That's as far as the law's liberality goes, however. You can be denied naturalization if you have held active membership in an organization ruled "subversive" by the Attorney General. Your membership must have been voluntary, and it must have been entered into when you were more than sixteen. You can also be denied if you're among those "unwilling to bear arms" for the United States, if you've been a deserter in wartime, or if you claim to be exempt from service solely on the basis of being an alien. Nevertheless, there's a provision for naturalizing people who conscientiously object to bearing arms, and it's also worth noting that those who "evaded military service" between August 4, 1961, and March 28, 1973, have been granted an unconditional pardon by the President.

You should know, however, that when Selective Service registration was reinstated by presidential proclamation in 1980, it was meant to apply not only to citizens but to all male immigrant aliens as well. If you were born in 1963 or anytime after that date, you are required to register within thirty days of your eighteenth birthday. If you fail to register, you expose yourself to legal penalties. Therefore every male alien over the age of eighteen should check with the local Selective Service office when he becomes a resident to make certain that no violation of the law will occur.

Among the special classes of applicants for naturalization, probably the most important are the spouses and children of citizens. As I pointed out earlier, if you're married to an American citizen, you can be naturalized in three years instead of five if you satisfy the permanent residence and "good moral character" qualifications. But other qualifications are stipulated by the law, and all of them must be fulfilled in the three years immediately before you file your petition. You must have been a permanent resident, your spouse must have been an American citizen, and you must have been living together in a marital relationship during that time.

This means, for instance, that if your spouse has been a citizen for only two years during your three years of residency, you won't qualify. Nor will you if you've been married to a citizen for three years but weren't a permanent resident until the second year of the marriage. Nor if you've been physically separated from a citizen spouse for a substantial part of the three-year period.

Most of the other rules also apply. You must have been physically present in the United States for a minimum total of eighteen months and have lived in the state where the petition is filed for six months before you file your petition. And, of course, you have to demonstrate good moral character and attachment to constitutional ideals, just as the five-year applicants do.

An exception is made for spouses of American citizens who have qualifying employment with corporations in the United States, religious groups, research institutions, or the federal government. The requirements for physical presence, residence, and moral character are less stringent for them, as they are for surviving spouses of citizens who died while on active military duty.

Children can get citizenship status if they're born abroad to a citizen parent or parents; this is called "acquisition." They can also derive citizenship if a parent or parents have been naturalized after the child's admission for permanent residence; this is known as "derivation." An American citizen parent may also file petition for naturalization on their behalf.

Citizenship status can be acquired by children, too, if the U.S. citizen parent or parents lived in the United States before the birth of a child abroad. The definition and duration of American residence required by the parent and/or the child vary according to the law that was in effect when the child was born. One of the few cases where a child born to a U.S. citizen parent (or parents) is not automatically a U.S. citizen at birth occurs when a child is born outside the United States whose parent (or parents) did not have the required residence in the United States at the time of the child's birth. In such a case, a specific citizenship petition for the child must be filed by the parent (or parents) in order for the child to become a U.S. citizen.

There are other specific rules relating to children depending on their specific birth dates, but they are so technical that I suggest an expert be consulted if any further elaboration is required.

Any child born abroad derives citizenship automatically without court action if one or both parents were naturalized before the child attained the required statutory age of adulthood and length of permanent residence. An easy way to distinguish "derivation" from "acquisition" is to remember that, for acquisition, on the date of the child's birth abroad the parent or parents must already be citizens. The rules for both vary, however, depending on the date the parent or parents were naturalized. Consult your local INS office for the law as it applies to your child.

Children who don't qualify for either acquisition or derivation can be naturalized anyway by petition from the parent or parents. In this case, the parent must be an American citizen either by birth or naturalization, and the child must be under eighteen and a lawful permanent resident, although no period of residence or physical presence is required. A recent law permits a petition on behalf of a child adopted while under fourteen, if the child has lawful permanent resident status, and if he is in the custody of the adoptive parent or parents when the petition is filed.

In general, because of the long processing time in some back-logged counties, it's advisable for you to file your application several months before the date of your eligibility, so that by the time you're called for your interview you'll be eligible. This may save you several months of waiting.

If there's some reason for you to be naturalized quickly, a lawyer can be helpful in speeding up things. The problem is to show need. Circumstances of employment, for instance, often constitute a convincing reason for expediting matters.

Finally, naturalization is like every other aspect of immigration law: it varies widely from place to place.

APPENDIXES

APPENDIXES

APPENDIX 1

District Offices of the Immigration and Naturalization Service

ALASKA
Room 401
632 West Sixth Avenue
Anchorage, AK 99501

ARIZONA
Federal Building
230 North First Avenue
Phoenix, AZ 85025

CALIFORNIA
300 North Los Angeles
   Street
Los Angeles, CA 90012

880 Front Street
San Diego, CA 92188

Appraisers Building
630 Sansome Street
San Francisco, CA 94111

COLORADO
17027 Federal Office
   Building
Denver CO 80202

CONNECTICUT
900 Asylum Avenue
Hartford, CT 96105

DISTRICT OF COLUMBIA
1025 Vermont Avenue,
   N.W.
Washington, DC 20538

FLORIDA
Room 1324
Federal Building
51 S.W. First Avenue
Miami, FL 33130

GEORGIA
Room 406
1430 West Peachtree Street,
   N.W.
Atlanta, GA 30309

HAWAII
P.O. Box 461
595 Ala Moana Boulevard
Honolulu, HI 96809

ILLINOIS
Dirksen Federal Office
   Building
219 South Dearborn Street
Chicago, IL 60604

LOUISIANA
New Federal Building
701 Loyola Avenue
New Orleans, LA 70113

MAINE
76 Pearl Street
Portland, ME 04112

MARYLAND
Room 124
Federal Building
31 Hopkins Plaza
Baltimore, MD 21201

MASSACHUSETTS
John Fitzgerald Kennedy
Federal Building
Government Center
Boston, MA 02203

MICHIGAN
Federal Building
333 Mt. Elliott Street
Detroit, MI 48207

MINNESOTA
Room 932
New Post Office Building
180 East Kellogg Boulevard
St. Paul, MN 55101

MISSOURI
Room 819
U.S. Courthouse
811 Grand Avenue
Kansas City, MO 64106

MONTANA
Federal Building
Helena, MT 59601

NEBRASKA
Room 8411
215 North 17th Street
Omaha, NE 68102

NEW JERSEY
Federal Building
970 Broad Street
Newark, NJ 07102

NEW YORK
68 Court Street
Buffalo, NY 14202

26 Federal Plaza
New York, NY 10007

OHIO
Room 1917
Federal Office Building
1240 East 9th Street
Cleveland, OH 44199

OREGON
Room 333
U.S. Courthouse
S.W. Broadway and Main
Street
Portland, OR 97205

PENNSYLVANIA
Room 1321
U.S. Courthouse
Independence Mall West
601 Market Street
Philadelphia, PA 19106

PUERTO RICO
GPO Box 5068
San Juan, PR 00936

TEXAS
Room 1C13
Federal Building
1100 Commerce Street
Dallas, TX 75202

Room 343
U.S. Courthouse
P.O. Box 9398
El Paso, TX 79984

Federal Building
U.S. Courthouse
P.O. Box 61630
515 Rusk Avenue
Houston, TX 77208

U.S. Federal Building
Suite A301
727 Durango
San Antonio, TX 78206

VERMONT
Federal Building
P.O. Box 591
St. Albans, VT 05478

WASHINGTON
815 Airport Way South
Seattle, WA 98134

APPENDIX 2

Regional Offices
of the
Immigration and Naturalization Service

EASTERN REGION
Federal Building
Burlington, Vermont 05401

NORTHERN REGION
Federal Building
Fort Snelling
Twin Cities, Minnesota 55111

SOUTHERN REGION
First International Building
1201 Elm Street, Room 2300
Dallas, Texas 75270

WESTERN REGION
Terminal Island
San Pedro, California 90731

APPENDIX 3

Preference Quota Classifications

On the chart below, the listing of the date under any class indicates that the class is oversubscribed; "C" means current—i.e., that numbers are available for all qualified applicants; "U" means unavailable—i.e., that no numbers are available.

	PREFERENCE						
Chargeability	First	Second	Third	Fourth	Fifth	Sixth	Nonpreference
All chargeability areas except those listed below	C	01-15-83	C	C	08-01-80	07-01-81	U
China-mainland born	C	01-15-83	C	C	01-01-79	U	U
India	C	01-15-83	01-01-83	C	07-15-80	10-08-80	U
Korea	C	01-15-83	C	C	07-01-79	07-01-81	U
Mexico	C	09-01-74	U	U	U	U	U
Philippines	C	09-15-79	09-01-70	05-22-77	11-01-71	09-22-79	U
Hong Kong	C	07-08-77	10-01-74	11-24-78	11-01-72	01-22-79	U

St. Christopher-Nevis has been removed from the list of oversubscribed areas.

The Department of State has available a recorded message with visa-availability information which can be heard at: (area code 202) 632-2919. This recording is updated in the middle of each month with information on cutoff dates for the following month.

APPENDIX 4

Nonimmigrant Visas

A-1	Ambassador, public minister, career diplomatic or consular officer, and members of immediate family
A-2	Other foreign government official or employee, and members of immediate family
A-3	Attendant, servant, or personal employee of A-1 and A-2 classes, and members of immediate family
B-1	Temporary visitor for business
B-2	Temporary visitor for pleasure
B-1 and B-2	Temporary visitor for business and pleasure
C-1	Alien in transit
C-2	Alien in transit to United Nations Headquarters District
C-3	Foreign government official, members of immediate family, attendant, servant, or personal employee, in transit
D	Crewman (seaman or airman)
E-1	Treaty trader, spouse and children
E-2	Treaty investor, spouse and children
F-1	Student
F-2	Spouse or child of student
G-1	Principal resident representative of recognized foreign member government to international organization, his staff, and members of immediate family
G-2	Other representative of recognized foreign member government to international organization, and members of immediate family
G-3	Representative of nonrecognized or nonmember foreign government to international organization, and members of immediate family
G-4	International organization officer or employee, and members of immediate family
G-5	Attendant, servant, or personal employee of G-1,

	G-2, G-3, and G-4 classes, and members of immediate family
H-1	Temporary worker of distinguished merit and ability
H-2	Temporary worker performing services unavailable in the United States
H-3	Industrial trainee
I	Representative of foreign information media, spouse, and children
J-1	Exchange visitor
J-2	Spouse or child of exchange visitor
K-1	Alien fiancé or fiancée of U.S. citizen
K-2	Children of alien fiancé or fiancée of U.S. citizen
L-1	Intracompany transferee
L-2	Spouse and children of intracompany transferee
M-1	Student at vocational school
M-2	Spouse or child of student at vocational school
NATO 1-5	There are several different kinds of NATO visas, which are not discussed in this book

APPENDIX 5

Form I-94

| I-94 | IMMIGRATION AND NATURALIZATION SERVICE ARRIVAL/DEPARTURE RECORD | Form Approved OMB No. 1115-077 Expires 8-31-85 |

WELCOME TO THE UNITED STATES

INSTRUCTIONS

- ALL PERSONS EXCEPT U.S. CITIZENS MUST COMPLETE THIS FORM. A SEPARATE FORM MUST BE COMPLETED FOR EACH PERSON IN YOUR GROUP.

- TYPE OR PRINT LEGIBLY WITH PEN IN ALL CAPITAL LETTERS. USE ENGLISH. DO NOT WRITE ON THE BACK OF THIS FORM.

- This form is in two parts, an ARRIVAL RECORD (Items 1 through 7), and a DEPARTURE RECORD (Items 8 through 10). *You must complete both parts.* Enter exactly the same information in spaces 8, 9, and 10 as you enter in spaces 1, 2, and 3.

  Item 7. If you entered the United States by land, enter "LAND" in this space.

- WHEN YOU HAVE COMPLETED ALL REQUIRED ITEMS, PRESENT THIS FORM TO THE U.S. IMMIGRATION AND NATURALIZATION INSPECTOR.

ADMISSION NUMBER
995-01059446   I-94 ARRIVAL RECORD (Rev. 1-1-83)N

1. FAMILY NAME (SURNAME) *(leave one space between names)*

FIRST (GIVEN) NAME *(do not enter middle name)*

2. DATE OF BIRTH   DAY MO. YR.

3. COUNTRY OF CITIZENSHIP

4. COUNTRY OF RESIDENCE *(country where you live)*

5. ADDRESS WHILE IN THE UNITED STATES *(Number and Street)*

City   State

6. CITY WHERE VISA WAS ISSUED

7. AIRLINE & FLIGHT NO. OR SHIP NAME*

THIS FORM IS REQUIRED BY THE IMMIGRATION AND NATURALIZATION SERVICE, UNITED STATES DEPARTMENT OF JUSTICE.

WARNING
- A nonimmigrant who accepts unauthorized employment is subject to deportation.

IMPORTANT
- Retain this permit in your possession; you must surrender it when you leave the U.S. Failure to do so may delay your entry into the U.S. in the future.

ADMISSION NUMBER
995-01059446

8. FAMILY NAME (SURNAME) *(same as Family Name in Item 1 above)*

FIRST (GIVEN) NAME *(same as First Name in Item 1 above)*

9. DATE OF BIRTH *(same as Item 2)*   DAY MO. YR.

10. COUNTRY OF CITIZENSHIP *(same as Item 3 above)*

SEE REVERSE SIDE FOR OTHER IMPORTANT INFORMATION

U.S. IMMIGRATION AND NATURALIZATION SERVICE   I-94 DEPARTURE RECORD (Rev. 1-1-83)N   STAPLE HERE

THIS SIDE FOR GOVERNMENT USE ONLY
(DO NOT WRITE BELOW THIS LINE)

PRIMARY INSPECTION

NAME _____

II NUMBER _____ DATE/TIME REFERRED _____

REASON REFERRED _____

SECONDARY INSPECTION

II NUMBER _____ END TIME SECONDARY _____

DISPOSITION _____

11. OCCUPATION

12. SCHOOL

13. ITINERARY

14. PETITION NUMBER

15. INS FILE NO.
A:

16. WAIVERS

IMPORTANT NOTICE

- You are authorized to stay in the U.S. only until the date written on this form. To remain past this date, without permission from immigration authorities, is a violation of law.

SURRENDER THIS PERMIT WHEN YOU LEAVE THE UNITED STATES

- *By sea or air,* to transportation line.
- *Over Canadian border,* to Canadian Official.
- *Over Mexican border,* at the designated location.

RECORD OF CHANGES

DEPARTURE RECORD

Port:
Date:
Carrier:

APPENDIX 6

Form 156

1. SURNAMES OR FAMILY NAMES *(Exactly as in Passport)*	DO NOT WRITE IN THIS SPACE
2. FIRST NAME AND MIDDLE NAME *(Exactly as in Passport)*	
3. OTHER NAMES *(Maiden. Religious. Professional. Aliases)*	

4. DATE OF BIRTH			7. PASSPORT NUMBER
DAY	MONTH (letters)	YEAR	DATE PASSPORT ISSUED
5. PLACE OF BIRTH *(City, State, Country)*			DATE PASSPORT EXPIRES
6. NATIONALITY			PASSPORT ISSUED AT *(City)*

8. RESIDENTIAL ADDRESS *(Include apartment no. and post zone)*

9. NAME AND ADDRESS OF EMPLOYER OR SCHOOL

10. HOME TELEPHONE NUMBER	11. BUSINESS TELEPHONE NUMBER

12. SEX ☐ Female ☐ Male	13. COLOR OF HAIR	14. COLOR OF EYES
15. COMPLEXION	16. HEIGHT	17. MARITAL STATUS ☐ Married ☐ Single ☐ Widowed ☐ Divorced ☐ Separated
18. MARKS OF IDENTIFICATION		

19. NAMES AND RELATIONSHIPS OF PERSONS TRAVELING WITH YOU *(Spouse. children. parents. etc.)*

26. PRESENT PROFESSION OR OCCUPATION *(If retired. State Past Profession)*

27. HOW LONG HAVE YOU LIVED IN THIS COUNTRY

____Years____Months

20. HAVE YOU EVER APPLIED FOR A UNITED STATES VISA OF ANY KIND? ☐ Yes   ☐ No
(If YES, state where, when and type of visa)

28. WHAT IS THE PURPOSE OF YOUR TRIP?

21. INDICATE WHETHER: ☐ Visa was granted ☐ Visa was refused	22. HAS YOUR U.S. VISA EVER BEEN CANCELED? ☐ Yes ☐ No

23. NAME, RELATIONSHIP AND ADDRESS OF SPONSOR. FIRM. OR SCHOOL IN U.S.A.

29. WHEN DO YOU INTEND TO ARRIVE IN THE U.S.A.?

30. HOW LONG DO YOU PLAN TO STAY IN U.S.A.?

24. WHO WILL PAY FOR YOUR TICKETS TO LEAVE THE U.S.A. at the end of your temporary visit? If not yourself, please explain

31. HOW MUCH MONEY WILL YOU TAKE?

32. HAVE YOU EVER BEEN IN THE U.S.A.?

☐ Yes   ☐ No If YES, when, and for how long?

25. WHO WILL FURNISH FINANCIAL SUPPORT?

NONIMMIGRANT VISA APPLICATION

OPTIONAL FORM 156X (Rev.9/81) PAGE 1

COMPLETE ALL QUESTIONS ON REVERSE OF FORM

APPENDIX 6, *cont.*

33. AT WHAT ADDRESS WILL YOU STAY IN THE U.S.A.?	34. DO YOU INTEND TO WORK OR STUDY IN THE U.S.A.? □ Yes □ No If YES, explain

35. HAS ANYONE EVER FILED AN IMMIGRANT VISA PETITION ON YOUR BEHALF: HAS A LABOR CERTIFICATION FOR EMPLOYMENT IN THE UNITED STATES EVER BEEN REQUESTED BY YOU OR ON YOUR BEHALF: HAVE YOU OR ANYONE ACTING FOR YOU EVER INDICATED TO A U.S. CONSULAR OR IMMIGRATION OFFICER OR EMPLOYEE A DESIRE TO IMMIGRATE TO THE U.S.?
□ Yes   □ No

36. ARE ANY OF THE FOLLOWING IN THE U.S.A.? *(If YES, check appropriate box(es) and indicate in blank space what their status is, i.e. student, working, etc.)*
□ HUSBAND/WIFE_____   □ FIANCE/FIANCEE_____   □ BROTHER/SISTER_____

□ FATHER/MOTHER_____   □ SON/DAUGHTER_____

37. PLEASE LIST THE COUNTRIES WHERE YOU HAVE LIVED FOR MORE THAN SIX MONTHS DURING THE PAST FIVE YEARS

COUNTRIES	CITIES	APPROXIMATE DATES

38. TO WHAT ADDRESS DO YOU WISH YOUR VISA AND PASSPORT SENT?

39. IMPORTANT: ALL APPLICANTS MUST READ AND ANSWER THE FOLLOWING:

(1) U.S. law prohibits the issuance of a visitor visa to persons who plan to remain in the United States indefinitely or who will accept unauthorized employment. A VISITOR MAY NOT WORK except as explained in the attached visitors visa information.

(2) A visa may not be issued to persons who are within specific categories defined by law as inadmissible to the United States (except when a waiver is obtained in advance). Complete information regarding these categories and whether any may be applicable to you can be obtained from this office. Generally, they include persons afflicted with contagious diseases (such as tuberculosis) or who have suffered serious mental illness; persons who have been arrested, convicted for any offense or crime even though they may have been the subject of a pardon, amnesty or other such legal action; narcotic addicts or traffickers; persons who have been deported from the U.S.A.; persons who have sought to obtain a visa by means of misrepresentation or fraud; persons who are or have been members of certain organizations including communist organizations and those affiliated therewith; and persons who participated in the persecution of any person because of race, religion, national origin, or political opinion under the direction of the Nazi Government of Germany.

DO ANY OF THE FOREGOING RESTRICTIONS APPEAR TO APPLY TO YOU?

YES □   NO □

If YES, or if you have any question in this regard, personal appearance at this office is recommended. If it is not possible at this time, attach a statement of facts in your case to this application.

40. I certify that I have read and understood all the questions set forth in this application, and the answers I have furnished on this form are true and correct to the best of my knowledge and belief. I understand that possession of a visa does not entitle the bearer to enter the United States of America upon arrival at a port of entry if he or she is found inadmissible.

DATE OF APPLICATION _____

APPLICANT'S SIGNATURE_____

If this application has been prepared by a travel agency or another person on your behalf, the agent should indicate name and address of agency or person with appropriate signature of individual preparing form.

SIGNATURE OF PERSON PREPARING FORM _____

DO NOT WRITE IN THIS SPACE

37mm x 37mm
1½ inches x 1½ inches

——— PHOTO ———

Sign name on reverse
side of photo

OPTIONAL FORM 156X (Rev.9/81) PAGE 2   *(This form is free of charge)*

APPENDIX 7

Form I-539

UNITED STATES DEPARTMENT OF JUSTICE
IMMIGRATION AND NATURALIZATION SERVICE

READ INSTRUCTIONS CAREFULLY
FEE WILL NOT BE REFUNDED

Form Approved
OMB 43-R0068

FEE STAMP

APPLICATION TO EXTEND TIME OF TEMPORARY STAY

I HEREBY APPLY TO EXTEND MY TEMPORARY STAY IN THE UNITED STATES

PRESS FIRMLY—LEGIBLE COPY REQUIRED. PRINT OR TYPE YOUR NAME EXACTLY AS IT APPEARS ON YOUR ARRIVAL—DEPARTURE RECORD FORM I-94. IF YOUR MAILING ADDRESS IN THE U.S. IS WITH SOMEONE WHOSE FAMILY NAME IS DIFFERENT FROM YOURS, INSERT THAT PERSON'S NAME IN THE C/O BLOCK.

6. DATE TO WHICH EXTENSION IS REQUESTED

1. YOUR NAME — FAMILY NAME (CAPITAL LETTERS) FIRST MIDDLE

IN CARE OF — C/O

7. REASON FOR REQUESTING EXTENSION

2. MAILING ADDRESS IN U.S. — NUMBER AND STREET (APT. NO.) / FILE NUMBER
CITY STATE ZIP CODE

3. DATE OF BIRTH (MO./DAY/YR.) COUNTRY OF BIRTH COUNTRY OF CITIZENSHIP

4. PRESENT NONIMMIGRANT CLASSIFICATION DATE ON WHICH AUTHORIZED STAY EXPIRES

5. DATE AND PORT OF LAST ARRIVAL IN U.S. NAME OF VESSEL, AIRLINE, OR OTHER MEANS OF LAST ARRIVAL IN U.S.

8. REASON FOR COMING TO THE U.S.

FOR GOVERNMENT USE ONLY

☐ EXTENSION GRANTED TO (DATE) — DATE OF ACTION

☐ EXTENSION DENIED V.D. TO (DATE) — DD OR OIC OFFICE

9. HAS AN IMMIGRANT VISA PETITION EVER BEEN FILED IN YOUR BEHALF?
☐ YES ☐ NO IF "YES", WHERE WAS IT FILED?

10. HAVE YOU EVER APPLIED FOR AN IMMIGRANT VISA OR PERMANENT RESIDENCE IN THE U.S.? ☐ YES ☐ NO IF "YES", WHERE DID YOU APPLY?

11. I INTEND TO DEPART FROM THE U.S. ON (DATE)
I AM IN POSSESSION OF A TRANSPORTATION TICKET FOR MY DEPARTURE ☐ YES ☐ NO

12. PASSPORT NO.* EXPIRES ON (DATE) ISSUED BY (COUNTRY) 13. NUMBER, STREET, CITY, PROVINCE (STATE) AND COUNTRY OF PERMANENT RESIDENCE

14. MY USUAL OCCUPATION IS: 15. SOCIAL SECURITY NO. (IF NONE, STATE "NONE")

16. I ☐ AM ☐ AM NOT MARRIED. IF YOU WISH TO APPLY FOR EXTENSION FOR YOUR SPOUSE & CHILDREN, GIVE THE FOLLOWING: (SEE INSTRUCTIONS #1)

NAME OF SPOUSE AND CHILDREN	DATE OF BIRTH	COUNTRY OF BIRTH	PASSPORT ISSUED BY (COUNTRY) AND EXPIRES ON (DATE)

NOTE IF SPOUSE AND CHILDREN FOR WHOM YOU ARE SEEKING EXTENSION DO NOT RESIDE WITH YOU, GIVE THEIR COMPLETE ADDRESS ON A SEPARATE ATTACHMENT

17. I INSERT "HAVE" OR "HAVE NOT") _____ BEEN EMPLOYED OR ENGAGED IN BUSINESS IN THE UNITED STATES (IF YOU HAVE BEEN EMPLOYED OR ENGAGED IN BUSINESS IN THE UNITED STATES, COMPLETE THE REST OF THE BLOCK.)

NAME AND ADDRESS OF EMPLOYER OR BUSINESS	INCOME PER WEEK	DATES EMPLOYMENT OR BUSINESS BEGAN & ENDED

I certify that the above is true and correct
SIGNATURE OF APPLICANT DATE

SIGNATURE OF PERSON PREPARING FORM, IF OTHER THAN APPLICANT

I declare that this document was prepared by me at the request of the applicant and is based on all information on which I have any knowledge.
SIGNATURE ADDRESS DATE

ATTACH YOUR FORM I-94 OR I-144 –*DO NOT SEND YOUR PASSPORT	RECEIVED	TRANS IN	RET D.-TRANS OUT	COMPLETED

Form I-539 (Rev. 10-15-80)N

APPENDIX 8

Form I-134

UNITED STATES DEPARTMENT OF JUSTICE
Immigration and Naturalization Service

Form approved
OMB No. 43–R423

AFFIDAVIT OF SUPPORT

(ANSWER ALL ITEMS; FILL IN WITH TYPEWRITER OR PRINT IN BLOCK LETTERS IN INK.)

I, _____, residing at _____
(Name)   (Street and Number)

_____
(City)   (State)   (ZIP Code if in U.S.)   (Country)

BEING DULY SWORN DEPOSE AND SAY:

1. I was born on _____ at _____
(Date)   (City)   (Country)

If you are not a native born United States citizen, answer the following as appropriate:

  a. If a United States citizen through naturalization, give certificate of naturalization number _____

  b. If a United States citizen through parent(s) or marriage, give citizenship certificate number _____

  c. If United States citizenship was derived by some other method, attach a statement of explanation.

  d. If a lawfully admitted permanent resident of the United States, give 'A' number _____

2. That I am _____ years of age and have resided in the United States since (date)_____

3. That this affidavit is executed in behalf of the following person:

_____
(Name)   (Sex)   (Age)

_____
(Citizen of — Country)   (Marital Status)   (Relationship to Deponent)

_____
(Presently resides at — Street and Number)   (City)   (State)   (Country)

4. That this affidavit is made by me for the purpose of assuring the United States Government that the person named in item 3 will not become a public charge in the United States.

5. That I am willing and able to receive, maintain and support the person named in item 3. That I am ready and willing to deposit a bond, if necessary, to guarantee that such person will not become a public charge during his or her stay in the United States, or to guarantee that the above named will maintain his or her nonimmigrant status if admitted temporarily and will depart prior to the expiration of his or her authorized stay in the United States.

6. That I understand this affidavit will be binding upon me for a period of three (3) years after entry of the person named in item 3 and that the information and documenation provided by me may be made available to the Secretary of Health and Human Services.

7. That I am employed as, or engaged in the business of _____ with _____
(Type of business)   (Name of concern)

at _____
(Street and Number)   (City)   (State)   (ZIP Code)

I derive an annual income of (if self-employed, I have attached a copy of my last income tax return or report of commercial rating concern which I certify to be true and correct to the best of my knowledge and belief. See instruction for nature of evidence of net worth to be submitted.) $_____

I have on deposit in savings banks in the United States $_____

I have other personal property, the reasonable value of which is $_____

I have stocks and bonds with the following market value, as indicated on the attached list which I certify to be true and correct to the best of my knowledge and belief. $_____

I have life insurance in the sum of $_____
With a cash surrender value of $_____

I own real estate valued at $_____
With mortgages or other encumbrances thereon amounting to $_____

Which is located at _____
(Street and number)   (City)   (State)   (ZIP Code)

Form I-134
(Rev. 9–30–80) N

APPENDIX 8, *cont.*

8. That the following persons are dependent upon me for support: (Place a check √ in the appropriate column to indicate whether the person named is wholly or partially dependent upon you for support.)

NAME OF PERSON	WHOLLY DEPENDENT	PARTIALLY DEPENDENT	AGE	RELATIONSHIP TO ME

9. That I have previously submitted affidavit(s) of support for the following person(s). If none, state none.

Name   *Date submitted*

_____   _____

_____   _____

_____   _____

10. That I have submitted visa petition(s) to the Immigration and Naturalization Service on behalf of the following person(s). If none, state none.

Name   *Relationship*   *Date submitted*

_____   _____   _____

_____   _____   _____

11. (Complete this block only if the person named in item 3 will be in the United States temporarily.) That I ☐ do intend ☐ do not intend, to make specific contributions to the support of the person named in item 3. (If you check "do intend", indicate the exact nature and duration of the contributions. For example, if you intend to furnish room and board, state for how long and, if money, state the amount in United States dollars and state whether it is to be given in a lump sum, weekly, or monthly, and for how long.)

_____

_____

OATH OR AFFIRMATION OF DEPONENT

I swear (affirm) that I know the contents of this affidavit signed by me and the statements are true and correct.

Signature of deponent _____

Subscribed and sworn to (affirmed) before me this _____ *day of* _____, 19 _____

at _____. *My commission expires on* _____

Signature of Officer Administering Oath _____ *Title* _____

If affidavit prepared by other than deponent, please complete the following:
I declare that this document was prepared by me at the request of the deponent and is based on all information of which I have any knowledge.

_____
(Signature)   *(Address)*   *(Date)*

APPENDIX 8, *cont.*

(Please tear off this sheet before submitting Affidavit)

UNITED STATES DEPARTMENT OF JUSTICE
Immigration and Naturalization Service

AFFIDAVIT OF SUPPORT

INSTRUCTIONS

I. EXECUTION OF AFFIDAVIT.

A separate affidavit must be submitted for each person. You must sign the affidavit in your full, true, and correct name and affirm or make it under oath. If you are *in the United States* the affidavit may be sworn or affirmed before an immigration officer without the payment of fee, or before a notary public or other officer authorized to administer oaths for general purposes, in which case the official seal or certificate of authority to administer oaths must be affixed. If you are *outside the United States* the affidavit must be sworn to or affirmed before a United States consular or immigration officer.

II. SUPPORTING EVIDENCE.

The deponent should submit in duplicate evidence of income and resources, as appropriate:

A. Statement from an officer of the bank or other financial institution in which you have deposits giving the following details regarding your account:
   1. Date account opened.
   2. Total amount deposited for past year.
   3. Present balance.

B. Statement of your employer, preferably on business stationery, showing:
   1. Date and nature of employment.
   2. Salary paid.
   3. Whether position is temporary or permanent.

C. If self-employed:
   1. Copy of last income tax return filed or,
   2. Report of commercial rating concern.

D. List containing serial numbers and denominations of bonds and name of record owner(s).

III. SPONSOR AND ALIEN LIABILITY.

Effective September 30, 1980 amendments to section 1614(f) of the Social Security Act and Part A of Title XVI of the Social Security Act establish certain requirements for determining the eligibility of aliens for Supplemental Security Income (SSI) benefits. These amendments require that the income and resources of any person who, as the sponsor of an alien's entry into the United States, executed an affidavit of support or similar agreement on behalf of the alien, and the income and resources of the sponsor's spouse, shall be deemed to be the income and resources of the alien under formulas for determining eligibility for SSI benefits during the three years following the alien's entry into the United States.

An alien applying for SSI must make available to the Social Security Administration any documentation concerning his or her income or resources or those of the sponsor which were provided in support of the application for an immigrant visa or adjustment of status. The Secretary of Health and Human Services is authorized to obtain copies of any such documentation from other agencies.

The Social Security Act also provides that an alien and his or her sponsor shall be jointly and severally liable to repay any SSI benefits which are incorrectly paid because of misinformation provided by a sponsor or because of sponsor's failure to provide information, and any incorrect payments which are not repaid will be withheld from any subsequent payments for which the alien or sponsor are otherwise eligible under the Social Security Act.

These provisions do not apply to an alien who becomes blind or disabled after admission into the United States for permanent residency. They also will not apply to aliens admitted as refugees or granted political asylum by the Attorney General.

IV. AUTHORITY/USE/PENALTIES.

Authority for the collection of the information requested on this form is contained in 8 U.S.C. 1182(a)(15), 1184(a), and 1258. The information will be used principally by the Service, or by any consular officer to whom it may be furnished, to support an alien's application for benefits under the Immigration and Nationality Act and specifically the assertion that he or she has adequate means of financial support and will not become a public charge. Submission of the information is voluntary. It may also, as a matter of routine use, be disclosed to other federal, state, local and foreign law enforcement and regulatory agencies, including the Department of Health and Human Services, the Department of State, the Department of Defense and any component thereof (if the deponent has served or is serving in the armed forces of the United States), the Central Intelligence Agency, and individuals and organizations during the course of any investigation to elicit further information required to carry out Service functions. Failure to provide the information may result in the denial of the alien's application for a visa, or his exclusion from the United States.

U.S. GOVERNMENT PRINTING OFFICE : 1981 O - 358-599

Form I-134
(Rev. 9-30-80) N

For sale by the Superintendent of Documents, U.S. Government Printing Office
Washington, D.C. 20402

APPENDIX 9

Form I-506

UNITED STATES DEPARTMENT OF JUSTICE
IMMIGRATION AND NATURALIZATION SERVICE

Form Approved
OMB No. 43-R0342

Fee Stamp

APPLICATION FOR CHANGE
OF NONIMMIGRANT STATUS
(Under Section 248 of the Immigration and Nationality Act)

➡ **Please read the instructions on the first page**

I hereby apply to have my status in the United States changed to that of a nonimmigrant_____
(Student, visitor, etc.)

I wish to remain in the United States in that new status until_____
(Month, Day, Year)

This application is submitted together with the required documents which are made a part hereof and, if applicable, the fee of $10.

PRESS FIRMLY—LEGIBLE COPY REQUIRED. PRINT OR TYPE YOUR NAME EXACTLY AS IT APPEARS ON YOUR ARRIVAL-DEPARTURE RECORD FORM I-94. IF YOUR MAILING ADDRESS IN THE U.S. IS WITH SOMEONE WHOSE FAMILY NAME IS DIFFERENT FROM YOURS, INSERT THAT PERSON'S NAME IN THE C/O BLOCK.

1. YOUR NAME	FAMILY NAME *(Capital Letters)*	GIVEN	MIDDLE
IN CARE OF	C/O		FILE NUMBER *(If Known)*

2. MAILING ADDRESS IN U.S.	NUMBER AND STREET *(Apt. No.)*		
	CITY	STATE	ZIP CODE

3. DATE OF BIRTH *(Month, Day, Year)*	COUNTRY OF BIRTH	COUNTRY OF CITIZENSHIP

4. PRESENT NONIMMIGRANT CLASSIFICATION	DATE ON WHICH AUTHORIZED STAY EXPIRES

5. DATE AND PORT OF LAST ARRIVAL IN UNITED STATES	NAME OF VESSEL, AIRLINE, OR OTHER MEANS OF LAST ARRIVAL IN U.S.

6. I AM IN POSSESSION OF PASSPORT

NUMBER:*
ISSUED BY (Country)

WHICH EXPIRES ON: (Month, Day, Year)

7. MY I-94 IS ATTACHED ☐ YES ☐ NO
If "No", it was ☐ Lost ☐ Stolen ☐ Destroyed
☐ Other (Specify)_____

8. I ENTERED WITH NONIMMIGRANT VISA NO.

9. MY NONIMMIGRANT STATUS IN THE UNITED STATES ☐ HAS ☐ HAS NOT BEEN CHANGED
SINCE MY ENTRY (if changed, give details)

Reclassification to — FOR GOVERNMENT USE ONLY

☐ STAY GRANTED TO (Date) — DATE OF ACTION

☐ Application DENIED. V.D. TO (Date) — DD OR OIC OFFICE

10. MY PERMANENT ADDRESS OUTSIDE THE UNITED STATES IS: (Street) (City or Town) (County, District, Province or State) (Country)

11. I RESIDED AT THE ADDRESS IN ITEM 10 FROM: (Month, Day, Year) TO: (Month, Day, Year)

12. SINCE MY ENTRY INTO THE UNITED STATES, I HAVE RESIDED AT THE FOLLOWING PLACES:

(Street and No.) (City or Town) (State)	FROM: (Month, Day, Year)	TO: (Month, Day, Year)
		Present Time

13. I DESIRE TO HAVE MY NONIMMIGRANT STATUS CHANGED FOR THE FOLLOWING REASONS:

14. I DID NOT APPLY TO THE AMERICAN CONSUL FOR A VISA IN THE NONIMMIGRANT STATUS WHICH I AM NOW SEEKING FOR THE FOLLOWING REASONS:

15. I SUBMIT THE FOLLOWING DOCUMENTARY EVIDENCE TO ESTABLISH THAT I WILL MAINTAIN THE NONIMMIGRANT CLASSIFICATION TO WHICH I WISH TO BE CHANGED:

ATTACH YOUR FORM I-94 .*DO NOT SEND YOUR PASSPORT

RECEIVED	TRANS. IN	RET'D. TRANS. OUT	COMPLETED

FORM I-506 (REV. 10-22-79)

APPENDIX 9, *cont.*

16. (COMPLETE THIS BLOCK ONLY IF YOU ARE APPLYING FOR CHANGE TO STUDENT STATUS.)
THE COUNTRY IN WHICH I INTEND TO LIVE AND WORK AFTER I COMPLETE MY SCHOOLING IN THE UNITED STATES IS _____

(IF YOU ARE SEEKING TO ATTEND A VOCATIONAL OR BUSINESS SCHOOL, COMPLETE THE FOLLOWING ADDITIONAL STATEMENTS BY CHECKING THE APPROPRIATE BOXES.)

THE SCHOOLING I AM SEEKING ☐ IS ☐ IS NOT AVAILABLE IN MY COUNTRY.

I ☐ INTEND ☐ DO NOT INTEND TO ENGAGE IN THE OCCUPATION FOR WHICH THAT SCHOOLING WILL PREPARE ME.

17. MY OCCUPATION IS:	18. SOCIAL SECURITY NO. (If none, state "none")

19. I ☐ HAVE ☐ HAVE NOT BEEN EMPLOYED OR ENGAGED IN BUSINESS SINCE ENTERING THE UNITED STATES. IF ANSWER IS IN THE AFFIRMATIVE, COMPLETE THE FOLLOWING:
NATURE OF OCCUPATION OR BUSINESS IN WHICH I ☐ AM ☐ WAS EMPLOYED:

NAME OF EMPLOYER OR BUSINESS FIRM	ADDRESS

MY EMPLOYMENT OR ENGAGEMENT IN BUSINESS BEGAN ON: (Month, Day, Year)	AND ENDED ON: (Month, Day, Year)

MY MONTHLY INCOME FROM EMPLOYMENT OR BUSINESS ☐ IS ☐ WAS: $ _____

20. IF NOT EMPLOYED OR ENGAGED IN BUSINESS IN THE UNITED STATES, DESCRIBE FULLY THE SOURCE AND AMOUNT OF YOUR INCOME ABROAD AND HOW SUPPORTED WHILE IN THE UNITED STATES: (If applying for change to student status, see Instruction # 4.)

21. I ☐ AM ☐ AM NOT MARRIED

Name of Spouse	Present address of Spouse	Citizenship (Country) of Spouse

22. I HAVE _____ (Number) CHILDREN: (List children below)

Name	Age	Place of Birth	Present Address

23. I HAVE _____ (Number) RELATIVES IN THE UNITED STATES OTHER THAN MY SPOUSE AND/OR CHILDREN: (List relatives below)

Name	Relationship	Immigration Status	Present Address

24. I ☐ HAVE ☐ HAVE NOT SUBMITTED THE ADDRESS REPORTS REQUIRED BY THE ALIEN REGISTRATION ACT OF 1940, AS AMENDED, AND BY SECTION 265 OF THE IMMIGRATION AND NATIONALITY ACT.

25. I ☐ HAVE ☐ HAVE NOT BEEN ARRESTED OR CONVICTED OF ANY CRIMINAL OFFENSE IN THE UNITED STATES OR IN ANY FOREIGN COUNTRY. IF ANSWER IS IN THE AFFIRMATIVE. GIVE DETAILS:

26. I certify that the above is true and correct to the best of my knowledge and belief. (If form prepared by other than applicant, that person must execute item 27.)

(Signature of Applicant)	(Date)

SIGNATURE OF PERSON PREPARING FORM, IF OTHER THAN APPLICANT

27. I declare that this document was prepared by me at the request of the applicant and is based on all information of which I have any knowledge.

(Signature)	(Address)	(Date)

APPENDIX 10

Form I-126

United States Department of Justice
Immigration and Naturalization Service

Form approved
OMB No. 43-RO297

REPORT OF STATUS
BY TREATY TRADER OR INVESTOR

Alien Registration Number

Read instructions on other side before filling out this report

| 1. Name | (Last, in capital letters) | (First) | (Middle) | 2. Date of Birth |

| 3. Place of Birth | (City or Town) | (State or Province) | (Country) | 4. Present Nationality |

| 5. United States Mailing Address | (Apt. No.) | (No. and Street) | (City or Town) | (State) | (Zip Code) |

| 6. Foreign Residence | (Street) | (City or Town) | (State or Province) | (Country) |

| 7. Resided at above foreign address | From (Month, day, year) | To (Month, day, year) | 8. Date of Entry (Month, day, year) |

| 9. Port of Entry | (City) | (State) | 10. Name of vessel or other conveyance |

| 11. Visa | Issued on (Mo., day, year) | Visa Issued at (City) | (Country) |

| 12. Passport Number | Issued on (Mo., day, year) | Issued at (City) | (Country) | Expiration Date |

13. Information Concerning Business Engaged in Pursuant to Treaty of Commerce and Navigation with the United States:

A. Name of Country Signatory to Treaty with United States

B. Name and address of business or enterprise in which engaged or employed

C. Nature of business or enterprise

D. List all countries engaged in trade with the company named in item B and the amount derived from each country

E. Percentage of Business or Enterprise Owned by Nationals of Country of Which You Are a National

F. Title of My Position or Occupation

G. Brief Description of My Duties

H. (Check box and fill in blank as appropriate)

☐ I am an employee of the business or enterprise named in item 13B.

☐ I am an independent developer or director of operations of the business or enterprise named in item 13B, in which I have personally invested or am in the process of investing cash or other capital in the amount of $ _____ .

14. Documents attached in support of this report (See Instructions)

☐ Arrival-Departure Record (Form I-94)   ☐ Letter from Employer

☐ Application for Extension of Stay (Form I-539)   ☐ Application for Change of Nonimmigrant Status (Form I-506)

Form I-126 (Rev. 3-26-76)N   OVER

APPENDIX 10, *cont.*

15. Marital Status	☐ Married	☐ Divorced	☐ Widowed	☐ Never Married

Name of Spouse

Nationality of Spouse	Passport Issued By (Country)	Expires on (Date)

Present Address of Spouse

16.	Name of Children	Date of Birth	Country of Birth	Passport Issued by (Country) and Expires on (Date)

Note: If the children for whom you are seeking extension or change of nonimmigrant status do not reside with you, give their complete address on a separate attachment to this application.

17. I certify that all information furnished in this report is true and correct.

Date _____   _____
Signature of Treaty Trader or Investor or applicant seeking such status

18. Signature of person preparing form, if other than Treaty Trader or Investor or applicant seeking such status

I declare that this document was prepared by me at the request of the Treaty Trader or Investor or applicant seeking such status and is based upon all information of which I have any knowledge.

_____
Signature

Date _____   Address _____

INSTRUCTIONS

If you were admitted to this country as a Treaty Trader prior to December 24, 1952, this report must be submitted annually, 30 days prior to each anniversary of your entry, to the immigration office having jurisdiction over your place of residence; and, in that case, no application for extension of temporary stay need be submitted.

If you are seeking to acquire status as a Treaty Trader or Investor, this report must be attached to your Application for Change of Nonimmigrant Classification, Form I-506.

If you acquired status as a Treaty Trader or Investor on or after December 24, 1952, this report must be attached to your Application for Extension of Temporary Stay (Form I-539).

Submit with this report your temporary entry permit (Form I-94, Arrival-Departure Record). If your temporary entry permit is attached to your passport, the permit should be removed for this purpose. DO NOT SEND IN YOUR PASSPORT. However, you must be in possession of a passport valid for at least six (6) months beyond the date to which your stay may be extended.

If you are employed, submit with this report a letter from your employer stating your present and intended position and duties. Name and title or position of person signing the letter should be clearly indicated. If your employer is a person and not an organization, the letter from your employer should indicate whether or not he is an E-1 or E-2 nonimmigrant.

A Treaty Trader or Investor may include in this report any alien dependent spouse and unmarried, minor children who are in the United States. If this application includes your wife and children, their Forms I-94 must be submitted with the application. They too must be in possession of passports valid for at least six months beyond the expiration date of the extensions requested. In all other cases separate reports must be made.

DO NOT WRITE IN THIS SPACE
(For use of Immigration and Naturalization Service Officer)

☐ Status maintained   ☐ Status not maintained   ☐ See Form I-506 for action taken.

Date _____   _____
District Director

GPO 901-767

APPENDIX II

Form I-20A

U.S. Department of Justice
Immigration and Naturalization Service
Please read instructions on PAGE 4

**Certificate of Eligibility
for Nonimmigrant
(F-1) Student Status**

Form Approved
OMB. No. RO397

E   126889   B

This page must be completed and signed in the U.S. by an authorized school official.

Name of Student—Family Name (Capital Letters) Given Name Middle Name	Visa Issuing Post
Date of Birth (Mo., day, year) Country of Birth Country of Nationality	For Immigration Official
Name of School	
School Official to be notified of student's arrival in U.S. (Name and Title)	
Address of School (Include Zip Code)	

1. This certificate is issued to the student named above for (check and fill out as appropriate):
- ☐ Initial attendance at this school.
- ☐ Continued attendance at this school after a temporary absence from the United States, or
- ☐ Use by spouse and/or children in acquiring nonimmigrant F-2 classification.
  The student's authorized stay, as it appears on his/her Form I-94, expires on (date): _____
- ☐ Other (specify): _____

2. The student named above has been accepted for a full course of study at this institution (complete each of the following):
Majoring in the field of _____
The student is expected to report to the school not later than (date)_____and complete studies not later
than (date)_____.

3. Proficiency in the English language ☐ is ☐ is not required (check and fill out as appropriate):
- ☐ The school has determined that the student has the required proficiency.
- ☐ If the student is not yet proficient, he or she will be given instruction consisting of _____.
- ☐ English IS NOT a requirement (explain): _____

4. This school estimates the student's average MONTHLY costs to be the following:

Tuition and fees	$_____	
Living expenses	$_____	
Expenses of dependent(s):	$_____	
Other (specify):	$_____	TOTAL $_____

5. This school has information showing the following as the student's means of support, estimated on a MONTHLY basis:

Personal funds of the student:	$_____	
Family funds from abroad:	$_____	
Funds from this school (Specify type): _____	$_____	
Funds from another source (Specify type/source): _____	$_____	
On-campus employment, if applicable:	$_____	TOTAL $_____

6. Remarks (complete as appropriate): _____

7. This school is approved by the Immigration and Naturalization Service for attendance by nonimmigrant students (fill out all blanks):
Under the name of (School/School District)_____
Approval was granted on (date)_____and the school was given the file number of _____.

I CERTIFY under penalty of law that:
All information provided above was completed before I signed this form, and is true and correct to the best of my knowledge;
The school has determined that the above-named student's qualifications meet all standards for admission to the school;
The student will be required to pursue a full course of study as defined by 8 CFR 214.2(f)(1a); and
I am a designated official of the above named school and I am authorized to issue this form.

Signature of School Official	Title	Date Issued	Place Issued (city and state)

I-20A (REV. 2/14/81)Y

APPENDIX II, *cont.*

I-20A Student

Please read instructions on PAGE 4

CERTIFICATE BY NONIMMIGRANT STUDENT
Under Section 101 (a) (15) (F) (i) of the Immigration and Nationality Act

PAGE

1. My full name is: (Family name)   (Given name)   (Middle name) | **2.** My anticipated stay is (months or years):

3. My educational objective is: (Degree or certificate sought; Major field of study) | **4.** My passport was issued by (country): and the number on it is:

5. I am financially able to support myself for the entire period of my stay in the United States while pursuing a full course of study, by: (State source and amount of support—Documentary evidence of means of actual support must be attached to this form):

6. I last attended (Name of school)   (City)   (State)   (Country)

7. My major field of studies was: | **8.** I completed those studies on: (Date)

9. The person most closely related to me who lives OUTSIDE the United States is (Name)   (Relationship)   (Address):

10. The person most closely related to me who lives IN the United States is: (If you have no relative in the U.S., give the name of a friend.) (Family name):   (Given name):   (Middle name):   (Relationship):   (Address):

11. PLEASE READ CAREFULLY, and be sure that you understand the following, before signing below:

SCHOOL
A. If I am applying for entry to the United States for the first time after being issued an F-1 visa, I will not be admitted unless I plan to attend the school specified in that visa. If, before I depart for the United States, I decide to attend another school, I will present an I-20 from that school to the issuing Consular office to have that school specified in my visa.

EMPLOYMENT
B. I am not permitted to work off-campus or to engage in business unless I have received permission to do so from the Immigration and Naturalization Service. If I require employment, I will apply for permission to work (on Form I-538). My application must be based on financial need arising after receiving student status, or the need to obtain practical training. My alien spouse or child (F-2 Classification) may not work in the United States.

PERIOD OF STAY
C. I am permitted to remain in the United States only while maintaining nonimmigrant student status. I must also maintain a passport which is valid for a period of no less than 6 months, unless exempt from passport requirements. I may not stay longer than authorized on my Form I-94, unless I apply to the Immigration and Naturalization Service (On Form I-538) for an extension. To get an extension, I must apply between 15 and 60 days before the date that my authorized stay expires. I may stay while the application is being processed and if it is approved, until the expiration of the extension.

NOTICE OF ADDRESS
D. Each year I am in the United States on the first day of January, I must submit, by the 31st day of January, a notice of my address to the Immigration and Naturalization Service. I must also send a notice within 10 days after any change of address. Regardless of whether I move, I must file a notice of my address every 3 months. (The forms to be used to make each of these reports are available at any United States Immigration Office or Post Office.)

ARRIVAL/ DEPARTURE
E. When I depart from the United States, I must give my "Arrival-Departure Record" (Form I-94) to a representative of the steamship or airline if I leave via a seaport or airport, to a Canadian Immigration Officer if I leave across the Canadian border or to a United States Immigration Officer if I leave across the Mexican border. However, I may keep my I-94 for reentering the United States from Mexico or Canada, or from adjacent islands other than Cuba, if I return to the U.S. within 30 days.

SCHOOL TRANSFER
F. I may remain in the United States only to pursue a full course of study at a specified school. If, after being admitted, I want to transfer to another school, I must first apply (on Form I-538) and be granted permission to do so. The application must be submitted to the Immigration and Naturalization Service Office having jurisdiction over the school from which I wish to transfer. A Form I-20, completed by the school to which I wish to transfer, must be with my application. My application will be denied if I have not taken a full course of study at the school I was last authorized to attend, unless I establish that failure to do so was beyond my control or was otherwise justified.

RE-ENTRY
G. If I want to reenter the United States as a nonimmigrant student, after a temporary absence, I must be in possession of the following: (1) A valid student visa, unless I am exempt from visa requirements; (2) a passport valid for at least 6 months beyond the period of readmission, unless I am exempt from passport requirements, and (3) a current copy of Form I-20A or I-20B. (Only the "A" copy of Form I-20 is required if I am returning from a temporary absence from the United States, to continue studies at the school which the Immigration and Naturalization Service last authorized me to attend.)

PENALTY
H. If I do not register at the school named in my "Arrival-Departure Record" (Form I-94), or if I stop attending school, or take less than a full course of study, or accept unauthorized employment, I fail to maintain my status and may be deported from the United States.

I AUTHORIZE the named school, and any school to which I transfer, to release any information from my records which is needed to determine if I am maintaining the lawful status in which I was admitted to the United States. I further authorize the school to report to the Immigration and Naturalization Service if I fail to register within 60 days of the time expected, to carry a full course of study, or to attend classes to the extent required, or if I become employed and/or terminate attendance at the school. The school is authorized to provide the Service with my name, country of birth, current address, and any other directory information on a regular basis or upon request.

I CERTIFY that all information provided on this form refers specifically to me and is true and correct to the best of my knowledge. I certify that I seek to enter or remain in the United States temporarily, and solely for the purpose of pursuing a full course of study at the school named on Page 1 of this form.

I AGREE to comply with the above terms and with any other conditions of my admission, and those of any extension of stay.

Signature of Student | Address (City) | (State or Province) | (Country) | (Date)

Signature of Parent or Guardian if Student is under 18 years of age   (Relationship)   Address (City)   (State or Province)   (Country)   (Date)

APPENDIX 12

Form I-538

UNITED STATES DEPARTMENT OF JUSTICE
IMMIGRATION AND NATURALIZATION SERVICE

APPLICATION BY NONIMMIGRANT STUDENT (F-1)
FOR EXTENSION OF STAY, SCHOOL TRANSFER
OR PERMISSION TO ACCEPT OR CONTINUE EMPLOYMENT

PART I — TO BE FILLED IN BY ALL APPLICANTS

I AM APPLYING FOR (CHECK AND COMPLETE AS APPROPRIATE)

☐ EXTENSION OF TEMPORARY STAY UNTIL (SPECIFY DATE) _____

☐ PERMISSION TO TRANSFER TO ANOTHER SCHOOL

☐ PERMISSION TO ACCEPT EMPLOYMENT OR TO CONTINUE PREVIOUSLY AUTHORIZED EMPLOYMENT

PRESS FIRMLY—LEGIBLE COPY REQUIRED. PRINT OR TYPE YOUR NAME EXACTLY AS IT APPEARS ON YOUR ARRIVAL-DEPARTURE RECORD FORM I-94 IF YOUR MAILING ADDRESS IN THE U S IS WITH SOMEONE WHOSE FAMILY NAME IS DIFFERENT FROM YOURS, INSERT THAT PERSON S NAME IN THE C/O BLOCK

1. YOUR NAME	FAMILY NAME (Capital Letters)	FIRST	MIDDLE	7. DATE OF INTENDED DEPARTURE FROM U.S.
IN CARE OF	C/O		FILE, NUMBER (If Known)	
2. MAILING ADDRESS IN U.S.	NUMBER AND STREET (Apt. No.)			8. I ☐ AM ☐ AM NOT IN POSSESSION OF A TRANSPORTATION TICKET FOR MY DEPARTURE
	CITY STATE	ZIP CODE		9. PASSPORT NUMBER *
3. DATE OF BIRTH (Month, Day, Year)	COUNTRY OF BIRTH		COUNTRY OF CITIZENSHIP	
4. PRESENT NONIMMIGRANT CLASSIFICATION		DATE ON WHICH AUTHORIZED STAY EXPIRES		10. PASSPORT ISSUED BY (Country)
5. DATE AND PORT OF LAST ARRIVAL IN UNITED STATES		NAME OF VESSEL, AIRLINE, OR OTHER MEANS OF LAST ARRIVAL IN U.S.		11. PASSPORT EXPIRES ON (Date)

6. THE PERMIT NUMBER ON MY FORM I-94 IS:

☐ EXTENSION GRANTED TO (Date)

☐ EXTENSION DENIED V.D. TO (Date)

IF TRANSFER GRANTED SHOW NEW SCHOOL, CITY, STATE.

THIS SECTION FOR GOVERNMENT USE ONLY

DATE OF ACTION		
DD OR OIC OFFICE	EMPLOYMENT ☐ GRANTED ☐ DENIED	
	TRANSFER ☐ GRANTED ☐ DENIED	

12. Number, Street, City, Province (State) and Country of Permanent Residence

13. Has an immigrant visa petition ever been filed in your behalf? ☐ Yes ☐ No. If "Yes", where was it filed?

14. Have you ever applied for an immigrant visa or permanent residence in the U.S.? ☐ Yes ☐ No. If "Yes", where did you apply?

15. I ☐ AM ☐ AM NOT married. If married and you wish to apply for extension for your F-2 spouse and children, give the following: (See Instruction #1)

NAMES OF SPOUSE AND CHILDREN	DATE OF BIRTH	COUNTRY OF BIRTH	PASSPORT ISSUED BY (Country) AND EXPIRES ON (Date)

NOTE: If spouse and children for whom you are seeking extension do not reside with you, give their complete address on a separate attachment to this application.

16. OCCUPATION	17. SOCIAL SECURITY NUMBER (If none, state "none")

18. (Insert "Have" or "Have Not") _____

BEEN EMPLOYED OR ENGAGED IN BUSINESS IN THE UNITED STATES. IF YOU HAVE BEEN EMPLOYED OR ENGAGED IN BUSINESS IN THE UNITED STATES, COMPLETE THE REST OF THE BLOCK. NAME AND ADDRESS OF EMPLOYER OR BUSINESS

KIND OF EMPLOYMENT OR BUSINESS	INCOME PER WEEK	DATES SUCH EMPLOYMENT OR BUSINESS BEGAN AND ENDED

19. MEANS AND SOURCE OF SUPPORT WHILE IN THE UNITED STATES

20. (COMPLETE THIS ITEM ONLY IF YOU ARE APPLYING FOR A SCHOOL TRANSFER)
I ☐ Have ☐ Have not been a full-time student at the school which I was last authorized by the Immigration and Naturalization Service to attend (If you checked "Have not" state the reasons fully)

I am requesting this transfer because:

ATTACH YOUR FORM I-94 * DO NOT SEND YOUR PASSPORT	RECEIVED	TRANS. IN	RET'D-TRANS. OUT	COMPLETED

FORM I-538 (REV. 9-12-77)Y

APPENDIX 12, *cont.*

PART I — (CONTINUED) — TO BE FILLED IN BY ALL APPLICANTS

21. CHECK ITEM (A) OR (B) AND COMPLETE THE ITEM CHECKED *(See Instruction No. 1; also, if you are applying for a transfer see Instruction No. 4.)*

	NAME AND LOCATION OF SCHOOL I AM ATTENDING IS	I ☐ WAS ☐ WAS NOT AUTHORIZED BY THE IMMIGRATION AND NATURALIZATION SERVICE TO ATTEND THAT SCHOOL. IF ANSWER IS "WAS NOT", ATTACH A STATEMENT GIVING NAME AND LOCATION OF THE SCHOOL YOU WERE LAST AUTHORIZED TO ATTEND AND WHY YOU ARE NOT ATTENDING THAT SCHOOL.		
☐ (A) I AM ATTENDING SCHOOL	NUMBER OF CLASSROOM HOURS I ATTEND SCHOOL WEEKLY	DAY OR EVENING CLASSES (SPECIFY)	MAJOR FIELD OF STUDY	DATE EXPECTED TO COMPLETE
☐ (B) I AM NOT ATTENDING SCHOOL	MY REASON FOR NOT ATTENDING IS:			
	NAME AND LOCATION OF SCHOOL I WAS LAST AUTHORIZED BY IMMIGRATION AND NATURALIZATION SERVICE TO ATTEND	DATE OF GRADUATION OR LAST ATTENDANCE (SPECIFY)	MAJOR FIELD OF STUDY	

PART II — TO BE FILLED IN BY APPLICANT FOR PERMISSION TO ACCEPT OR CONTINUE EMPLOYMENT

22. I DESIRE PERMISSION TO ACCEPT EMPLOYMENT FOR THE FOLLOWING REASON: *(CHECK ONE)*

(A) ☐ TO OBTAIN OR CONTINUE PRACTICAL TRAINING IN A FIELD RELATED TO MY COURSE OF STUDY AND RECOMMENDED BY THE SCHOOL.

(B) ☐ TO OBTAIN OR CONTINUE PART-TIME EMPLOYMENT NEEDED BECAUSE OF ECONOMIC NECESSITY WHICH AROSE AS A RESULT OF UNFORESEEN CHANGE IN FINANCIAL CIRCUMSTANCES. *(If you checked this item, explain in block 23.)*

23. (FILL IN IF YOU CHECKED (B) IN ITEM 22.)

	My yearly expenses at time of initial F-1 entry were:	My yearly expenses currently are:		My yearly income at time of initial F-1 entry was:	My yearly income currently is:
Tuition	$	$	Parents	$	$
Room			Other (specify)		
Board				— Totals —	
Other (Specify)					
	— Totals —		Occupation of Father		

EXPLAIN the unforeseen change in your financial circumstances which arose after your entry into the United States and why parent, relative, organization or other sponsor is unable to furnish you the additional funds needed to cover expenses.

Annual Income $ _____

Occupation of Mother _____

Annual Income $ _____

24. DESCRIPTION OF PROPOSED EMPLOYMENT

25. (IF YOU CHECKED (A) IN ITEM 22 ABOVE, CHECK AND FILL IN THE APPLICABLE STATEMENT BELOW.)
☐ I HAVE PREVIOUSLY BEEN GRANTED PERMISSION TO ENGAGE IN EMPLOYMENT FOR PRACTICAL TRAINING FROM _____ (date) TO _____ (date)
☐ I HAVE PREVIOUSLY PARTICIPATED IN AN OFF-CAMPUS WORK-STUDY PROGRAM.
☐ I HAVE NEVER PREVIOUSLY BEEN GRANTED PERMISSION TO ENGAGE IN EMPLOYMENT FOR PRACTICAL TRAINING.

26. IF YOU HAVE PREVIOUSLY SUBMITTED AN APPLICATION TO ACCEPT OR CONTINUE EMPLOYMENT, FURNISH THE FOLLOWING INFORMATION.

OFFICE OF THE IMMIGRATION & NATURALIZATION SERVICE TO WHICH LAST SUBMITTED: *(CITY AND STATE)*	SUCH APPLICATION WAS ☐ GRANTED ☐ DENIED	DATE GRANTED OR DENIED

PART III — TO BE FILLED IN BY ALL APPLICANTS

27. Signature of Applicant I CERTIFY that the information above is true and correct	30. Signature of Person Preparing the Form If Other Than Applicant I DECLARE that this application was prepared by me at the request of the applicant and is based on all information of which I have any knowledge.
(Signature)	(Signature)
(Date Signed)	(Address) (Date Signed)

PLEASE NOTE: Enclose your Temporary Entry Permit (Form I-94, ARRIVAL DEPARTURE RECORD) (See Instruction # 2)

PART IV—(Must be completed by an authorized official of the school student was last authorized by the Immigration and Naturalization Service to attend)

28. I hereby certify as follows:
To the best of my information and belief the facts in the application are true and correct.
The applicant: (Check one; if item (D) is checked, complete that item.)

(A) ☐ is taking a full course of studies at this school.

(B) ☐ is taking less than a full course of studies at this school.

(C) ☐ completed or will complete his course of study at this school on _____ While

(D) ☐ did not complete his course of studies but terminated his attendance on _____ while attending, he ☐ was ☐ was not taking a full course of studies.

If application is for permission to accept or continue employment: (Check one)

(A) ☐ the proposed employment is recommended for practical training of the student in his field of study. To the best of my belief such training will not be available to him in the country of his foreign residence.

(B) ☐ the proposed employment is recommended because of economic necessity due to an unforeseen change in the student's financial circumstances. The employment will not interfere with the student's ability to carry successfully a full course of study.

This school (or if approval was not in its own name, the _____ school district under which it operates or the _____ school of which it is a part) was approved for attendance by non-immigrant students by the Immigration and Naturalization Service, and such approval has not been withdrawn.

DATE	NAME OF SCHOOL	SIGNATURE OF SCHOOL OFFICIAL	TITLE

Form I-129B

UNITED STATES DEPARTMENT OF JUSTICE Immigration and Naturalization Service	Date Filed		Form approved OMB No. 43–R0348
PETITION TO CLASSIFY NONIMMIGRANT AS TEMPORARY WORKER OR TRAINEE		Fee Stamp	
		File No.	

(To be submitted in duplicate, with supplementary documents described in instructions, to the District Director having administrative jurisdiction over the place in the United States in which it is intended the alien(s) be employed or trained)

(THIS BLOCK NOT TO BE FILLED OUT BY PETITIONER)

The Secretary of State is hereby notified that the alien(s) for whom this petition was filed is (are) entitled to the nonimmigrant status checked below:

☐ H-1 ☐ H-3 ☐ H-2 ☐ L-1 **REMARKS:**	The validity of this petition will expire on_____. The admission of the alien(s) may be authorized to the above date.	DATE OF ACTION DD DISTRICT

(PETITIONER NOT TO WRITE ABOVE THIS LINE)
(PLEASE FILL IN WITH TYPEWRITER OR PRINT IN BLOCK LETTERS IN INK)

I hereby petition, pursuant to the provisions of section 214(c) of the Immigration and Nationality Act, for the following: (Check one.)

H-1 ☐   Alien(s) of distinguished merit and ability to perform services of an exceptional nature requiring such merit and ability.

H-2 ☐   Alien(s) to perform temporary service or labor for which a bona fide need exists. (One who is to perform duties which are themselves temporary in nature.)

H-3 ☐   Alien trainee(s). (One who seeks to enter at the invitation of an individual, organization, firm, or other trainer for the purpose of receiving training in any field of endeavor. Incidental production necessary to the training is permitted provided a United States worker is not thereby displaced.)

L-1 ☐   Intra-company transferee. (One who has been employed continuously for one year and who seeks to enter in order to continue to render services to the same employer or a subsidiary or affiliate thereof in a managerial or executive capacity or in a capacity which involves specialized knowledge.)

1. NAME OF PETITIONER	2. DATE BUSINESS ESTABLISHED

3. ADDRESS (NUMBER, STREET, CITY, STATE, ZIP CODE)

4. DESCRIPTION OF PETITIONER'S BUSINESS, INCLUDING ITS NATURE, NUMBER OF EMPLOYEES, AND GROSS ANNUAL INCOME

5. LOCATION OF AMERICAN CONSULATE AT WHICH ALIEN(S) WILL APPLY FOR VISA(S):	(City in Foreign Country)	(Foreign Country)

(If petition is to be made for more than one H alien and application for visas will be made at more than one American Consulate, a separate petition must be submitted for each consulate at which H visa applications will be made. Separate petition must be filed for each L-1 alien.)

6. THE ALIEN(S) WILL PERFORM SERVICES OR LABOR FOR OR RECEIVE TRAINING FROM THE FOLLOWING ESTABLISHMENT IN THE U.S.: (Name of Establishment)

(Street and Number)	(City or Town)	(State)	(Zip Code)

7. PERIOD REQUIRED TO COMPLETE SERVICES OR TRAINING			8. WAGES PER WEEK	8A. HOURS PER WEEK	9. OVERTIME RATE
From (date)	To (date)	No. of days or months			

10. OTHER COMPENSATION (Explain)	10A. VALUED AT $ WEEKLY	11. BY WHOM PAID?	

Form I-129B
(Rev. 6–20–80)N

	RECEIVED	TRANS. IN	RET'D-TRANS. OUT	COMPLETED

APPENDIX 13, *cont.*

(Page

ALL PETITIONERS COMPLETE ITEMS 12A THROUGH 22. If petition is for more than one H alien, give required information for each additional alien in space provided on page 3. If the identity of the H aliens is not known at present, you must furnish information concerning them as soon as that information becomes known to you.

12A. ALIEN'S NAME (Family name in capital letters)   (First name)   (Middle name)

12B. OTHER NAMES (Show all other past and present names. including maiden name if married woman.) | **12C. NUMBER OF ALIENS INCLUDED IN THIS PETITION**

13. ADDRESS TO WHICH ALIEN WILL RETURN   (Street and Number)   (City)   (Province)   (Country)

14. PRESENT ADDRESS   **15. PROPOSED PORT OF ENTRY**

16. DATE OF BIRTH | **17. PLACE OF BIRTH** | **18. PRESENT NATIONALITY OR CITIZENSHIP** | **19. PRESENT OCCUPATION**

20. HAS AN IMMIGRANT VISA PETITION EVER BEEN FILED ON THE ALIEN'S BEHALF? ☐ YES ☐ NO
If "Yes", where was it filed?

21. HAS THE ALIEN EVER APPLIED FOR AN IMMIGRANT VISA OR PERMANENT RESIDENCE IN THE U.S.? ☐ YES ☐ NO
If "Yes", where did he apply?

22. TO YOUR KNOWLEDGE, HAS ANY VISA PETITION FILED BY YOU OR ANY OTHER PERSON OR ORGANIZATION FOR THE NAMED ALIEN(S) BEEN DENIED? ☐ YES ☐ NO
If you answered "yes", complete the following: Date of filing of each denied petition_____
Place of filing of each denied petition (city)_____
TO YOUR KNOWLEDGE, HAVE ANY OF THE NAMED ALIEN(S) EVER BEEN IN THE U.S.? ☐ YES ☐ NO (If "yes" identify each on Page 3)

23. NONTECHNICAL DESCRIPTION OF SERVICES TO BE PERFORMED BY OR TRAINING TO BE RECEIVED BY ALIEN(S) (THIS BLOCK NEED NOT BE COMPLETED IF PETITION IS FOR H-2 WORKERS)

24. (If you are petitioning for an H–1 physician or nurse, complete this block.)
DOES THE LAW GOVERNING THE PLACE WHERE THE ALIEN'S SERVICES WILL BE PERFORMED RESTRICT HIM/HER FROM PERFORMING ANY OF THE DESIRED SERVICES? ☐ YES ☐ NO If the answer is "yes", attach statement listing the restricted services and setting forth the reason for the restriction. (See instructions for Physicians and Nurses.)

25. (If you are petitioning for a trainee, complete this block.)
A. IS SIMILAR TRAINING AVAILABLE IN ALIEN'S COUNTRY? ☐ YES ☐ NO
B. WOULD ALIEN'S TRAINING RESULT IN DISPLACEMENT OF UNITED STATES WORKER? ☐ YES ☐ NO

26. (If you are petitioning for an L-1 alien, complete this block.) (Check appropriate boxes.)

a. The alien has been employed in an ☐ executive; ☐ managerial capacity; ☐ in a capacity which involves specialized knowledge

by _____   since _____
              (name and address of employer)   (date)

b. The petitioner is ☐ the same employer ☐ subsidiary ☐ an affiliate of the employer abroad.

FILL IN ITEMS 27 THROUGH 31 INCLUSIVE ONLY IF PETITION IS FOR H-2 ALIEN(S)

27. DESCRIPTIVE JOB TITLE OF WORK TO BE PERFORMED BY ALIEN(S) (Use title which corresponds to that used in job order placed with state Employment Service or Agency by petitioner for same type of labor. Where work in more than one job classification is to be performed by aliens, state number to be employed in each job classification.)

28. IS (ARE) ALIEN(S) SKILLED IN WORK TO BE PERFORMED? ☐ YES ☐ NO ☐ UNKNOWN

29. IS ANY LABOR ORGANIZATION ACTIVE IN THE LABOR FIELD(S) SPECIFIED IN ITEM 27? ☐ YES ☐ NO
(If "yes", specify organization(s) and labor field(s).)

30. IS THE PETITIONER INVOLVED IN, OR ARE THERE THREATENED, ANY LABOR RELATIONS DIFFICULTIES, INCLUDING STRIKES OR LOCK-OUTS? (Specify)

31. I HAVE NOT BEEN ABLE TO FIND IN THE UNITED STATES ANY UNEMPLOYED PERSON(S) CAPABLE OF PERFORMING THE DUTIES OF THE POSITION(S) TO BE FILLED. THE FOLLOWING EFFORTS HAVE BEEN MADE TO FIND SUCH PERSON(S): (Complete only if labor certification not attached.)

ALL PETITIONERS FILL IN ITEMS 32 THROUGH 34B.

32. LIST DOCUMENTS SUBMITTED IN SUPPORT OF THIS PETITION.

APPENDIX 13, *cont.*

33. THE DOCUMENTS SUBMITTED HEREWITH ARE HEREBY MADE A PART OF THIS PETITION.

I am willing (unwilling) to post bond required as a condition to the approval of this petition.
I agree that as soon as known I shall furnish the District Director to whom this petition is being submitted with the names of those alien(s) not named herein.
If the petition is for temporary worker(s), I certify that I have a bona fide need of such worker(s).
If the petition is for trainee(s), I certify he/she is coming to the United States to participate in a bona fide training program.
I certify that the statements and representations made in this petition are true and correct to the best of my knowledge and belief.

34A. SIGNATURE OF PETITIONER	DATE	34B. TITLE (Must be petitioner or authorized agent of petitioner)

SIGNATURE OF PERSON PREPARING FORM, IF OTHER THAN PETITIONER

35. I declare that this document was prepared by me at the request of the petitioner and is based on all information of which I have any knowledge.

(Signature)	(Address)	(Date)

If this petition is for more than one alien of distinguished merit and ability (H-1) or trainee (H-3), use spaces below to give required information. If additional space is needed, attach separate sheet executed in same general manner.

NAME	DATE OF BIRTH	PLACE OF BIRTH	NATIONALITY	OCCUPATION

PRESENT ADDRESS

ADDRESS TO WHICH ALIEN WILL RETURN

NONTECHNICAL DESCRIPTION OF SERVICES TO BE PERFORMED BY OR TRAINING TO BE RECEIVED BY ALIEN

NAME	DATE OF BIRTH	PLACE OF BIRTH	NATIONALITY	OCCUPATION

PRESENT ADDRESS

ADDRESS TO WHICH ALIEN WILL RETURN

NONTECHNICAL DESCRIPTION OF SERVICES TO BE PERFORMED BY OR TRAINING TO BE RECEIVED BY ALIEN

NAME	DATE OF BIRTH	PLACE OF BIRTH	NATIONALITY	OCCUPATION

PRESENT ADDRESS

ADDRESS TO WHICH ALIEN WILL RETURN

NONTECHNICAL DESCRIPTION OF SERVICES TO BE PERFORMED BY OR TRAINING TO BE RECEIVED BY ALIEN

If this petition is for more than one (H-2) alien to perform temporary service or labor, use spaces below to give required information. If additional space is needed, attach separate sheet executed in same general manner. Identify each alien who has been in the U.S., by placing an "X" in the last column.

NAME	NATIONALITY	DATE AND PLACE OF BIRTH	PRESENT ADDRESS	X

APPENDIX 14

Form I-171C

UNITED STATES DEPARTMENT OF JUSTICE
Immigration and Naturalization Service

**NOTICE OF APPROVAL OF NONIMMIGRANT VISA PETITION OR
OF EXTENSION OF STAY OF NONIMMIGRANT H OR L ALIEN**

NAME OF BENEFICIARY OR BENEFICIARIES

NAME AND ADDRESS OF EMPLOYER OR TRAINER

CLASSIFICATION

FILE NO.

DATE OF APPROVAL

PLEASE BE ADVISED THAT APPROVAL OF THE PETITION CONSTITUTES A DETERMINATION THAT THE BENEFICIARY IS CLASSIFIABLE UNDER A SPECIFIED NONIMMIGRANT CLASSIFICATION. THE APPROVAL CONSTITUTES NO ASSURANCE THAT THE BENEFICIARY WILL BE FOUND ELIGIBLE FOR VISA ISSUANCE, ADMISSION TO THE UNITED STATES OR CHANGE OF NONIMMIGRANT STATUS. ELIGIBILITY FOR VISA ISSUANCE IS DETERMINED ONLY WHEN APPLICATION THEREFOR IS MADE TO A CONSULAR OFFICER; ELIGIBILITY FOR ADMISSION OR CHANGE OF STATUS IS DETERMINED ONLY WHEN APPLICATION THEREFOR IS MADE TO AN IMMIGRATION OFFICER. ALSO, PLEASE NOTE THE ITEMS BELOW WHICH ARE INDICATED BY "X" MARKS CONCERNING THIS PETITION:

THE PETITION HAS BEEN APPROVED AND FORWARDED TO THE UNITED STATES CONSULATE AT WHICH THE BENEFICIARY OR BENEFICIARIES WILL APPLY FOR VISA ISSUANCE. ANY INQUIRY CONCERNING VISA ISSUANCE SHOULD BE DIRECTED TO THE CONSULATE AT _____

THIS SERVICE WILL BE UNABLE TO ANSWER ANY INQUIRY CONCERNING VISA ISSUANCE.

☐ THE PETITION HAS BEEN APPROVED. IT IS INDICATED THAT THE BENEFICIARY(IES) WILL NOT REQUIRE VISA(S) TO ENTER THE UNITED STATES. NOTICE OF APPROVAL OF THE PETITION HAS BEEN FORWARDED TO THE INTENDED UNITED STATES PORT OF ENTRY. PLEASE NOTIFY THIS OFFICE IMMEDIATELY OF ANY CHANGE IN THE INTENDED PORT OF ENTRY.

☐ THE PETITION HAS BEEN APPROVED. IT IS INDICATED THAT THE BENEFICIARY IS IN THE UNITED STATES. THE BENEFICIARY MAY APPLY TO CHANGE HIS STATUS TO THE NONIMMIGRANT CLASSIFICATION SHOWN ABOVE BY SUBMITTING THE ENCLOSED FORM I-506 TO THIS OFFICE. NO ASSURANCE IS MADE THAT SUCH APPLICATION WILL BE GRANTED.

☐ THE APPROVED PETITION IS VALID UNTIL _____ .

☐ THE PETITION HAS BEEN APPROVED. THE BENEFICIARY WILL BE NOTIFIED OF THE DECISION ON HIS APPLICATION FOR CHANGE OF NONIMMIGRANT STATUS.

☐ THE TEMPORARY STAY OF THE BENEFICIARY(IES) IS AUTHORIZED TO _____

☐ REMARKS _____
_____ .

☐ DOCUMENTS WHICH YOU SUBMITTED IN SUPPORT OF YOUR PETITION HAVE SERVED OUR PURPOSE AND ARE RETURNED.

IMPORTANT

1. THE BENEFICIARY(IES) OF YOUR NONIMMIGRANT VISA PETITION MAY NOT REMAIN IN THE U.S. BEYOND THE PERIOD FOR WHICH THE PETITION IS VALID OR ANY EXTENSION OF STAY AUTHORIZED BY THIS SERVICE.

2. YOU ARE REQUIRED TO NOTIFY THIS OFFICE PROMPTLY IF THE EMPLOYMENT OR TRAINING SPECIFIED IN THIS PETITION IS TERMINATED BEFORE THE EXPIRATION OF THE AUTHORIZED STAY IN THE UNITED STATES OF THE BENEFICIARY(IES).

3. PLEASE ADVISE THE BENEFICIARY(IES) THAT THE ACCEPTANCE OF EMPLOYMENT OR TRAINING NOT SPECIFIED IN THIS PETITION WILL BE A VIOLATION OF NONIMMIGRANT STATUS.

INFORMATION REGARDING BENEFICIARY'S DEPARTURE AND RETURN

DO NOT MAKE COPIES OF THIS NOTICE. YOU MAY FURNISH IT TO ONLY ONE OF THE BENEFICIARIES WHO IS NOT IN POSSESSION OF A VALID "H" OR "L" VISA AND WHO DESIRES TO DEPART FROM AND RETURN TO THE UNITED STATES TO RESUME THE SAME EMPLOYMENT OR TRAINING DURING THE PERIOD FOR WHICH THE PETITION IS VALID OR FOR WHICH HIS STAY IN THIS COUNTRY HAS BEEN AUTHORIZED. A SIMILAR FORM NEEDED FOR ANY OTHER BENEFICIARY WHO WILL BE DOING SO MAY BE ISSUED BY THIS OFFICE UPON WRITTEN REQUEST BY THE EMPLOYER OR TRAINER FURNISHING THE NAME OF THE BENEFICIARY, FILE NUMBER, AND DATE OF APPROVAL AS SHOWN ON THIS FORM. IF A BENEFICIARY HAS AN "H" OR "L" VISA WHICH HAS EXPIRED, HE MAY APPLY TO THE DIRECTOR, VISA OFFICE, DEPARTMENT OF STATE, WASHINGTON, D.C., FOR REVALIDATION OF THAT VISA PRIOR TO DEPARTURE AND MAY SUBMIT THIS NOTICE WITH THAT APPLICATION. ALTERNATIVELY, IF A NEW VISA IS REQUIRED, HE SHOULD PRESENT THIS NOTICE TO AN AMERICAN CONSUL ABROAD. IF HE IS EXEMPT FROM THE VISA REQUIREMENT, HE SHOULD PRESENT THIS NOTICE AT A UNITED STATES PORT OF ENTRY. IF THE BENEFICIARY DESIRES TO RETURN TO THE SAME EMPLOYMENT OR TRAINING SHOWN IN THIS FORM. AFTER THE EXPIRATION OF THE VALIDITY OF THE PETITION OR AUTHORIZED TEMPORARY STAY SHOWN IN THIS FORM, A NEW PETITION WILL BE REQUIRED. THE BENEFICIARY MAY BE READMITTED TO THIS COUNTRY ONLY IF FOUND ADMISSIBLE UNDER THE IMMIGRATION LAWS WHEN HE RETURNS.

Form 1-171C
Rev. 9-1-77)Y

DISTRICT DIRECTOR

APPENDIX 15

ETA-750

OMB Approval No. 44-R1301

U.S. DEPARTMENT OF LABOR
Employment and Training Administration

APPLICATION

FOR

ALIEN EMPLOYMENT CERTIFICATION

IMPORTANT: READ CAREFULLY BEFORE COMPLETING THIS FORM

PRINT legibly in ink or use a typewriter. If you need more space to answer questions on this form, use a separate sheet. Identify each answer with the number of the corresponding question. SIGN AND DATE each sheet in original signature.

To knowingly furnish any false information in the preparation of this form and any supplement thereto or to aid, abet, or counsel another to do so is a felony punishable by $10,000 fine or 5 years in the penitentiary, or both (18 U.S.C. 1001).

PART A. OFFER OF EMPLOYMENT

1. Name of Alien *(Family name in capital letter, First, Middle, Maiden)*

2. Present Address of Alien *(Number, Street, City and Town, State ZIP Code or Province, Country)*

3. Type of Visa *(If in U.S.)*

The following information is submitted as evidence of an offer of employment.

4. Name of Employer *(Full name of organization)*

5. Telephone *(Area Code and Number)*

6. Address *(Number, Street, City or Town, Country, State, ZIP Code)*

7. Address Where Alien Will Work *(if different from item 6)*

8. Nature of Employer's Business Activity	9. Name of Job Title	10. Total Hours Per Week		11. Work Schedule *(Hourly)*	12. Rate of Pay	
		a. Basic	b. Overtime	a.m. / p.m.	a. Basic $ per	b. Overtime $ per hour

13. Describe Fully the Job to be Performed *(Duties)*

14. State in detail the MINIMUM education, training, and experience for a worker to perform satisfactorily the job duties described in Item 13 above.

15. Other Special Requirements

EDUCATION *(Enter number of years)*	Grade School	High School	College	College Degree Required *(specify)*
				Major Field of Study

TRAINING	No. Yrs.	No. Mos.	Type of Training

EXPERIENCE	Job Offered		Related Occupation		Related Occupation *(specify)*
	Yrs.	Mos.	Yrs.	Mos.	

Number

16. Occupational Title of Person Who Will Be Alien's Immediate Supervisor ► ►

17. Number of Employees Alien will Supervise ►

◄ ENDORSEMENTS *(Make no entry in section - for government use only)*

Date Forms Received	
L.O.	S.O.
R.O.	N.O.
Ind. Code	Occ. Code
Occ. Title	

Replaces MA 7-50A, B and C (Apr. 1970 edition) which is obsolete.

ETA 750 (Oct. 1979)

APPENDIX 15, *cont.*

18. COMPLETE ITEMS ONLY IF JOB IS TEMPORARY			19. IF JOB IS UNIONIZED *(Complete)*	
a. No. of Openings To Be Filled By Aliens Under Job Offer	b. Exact Dates You Expect To Employ Alien		a. Number of Local	b. Name of Local
	From	To		
				c. City and State

20. STATEMENT FOR LIVE-AT-WORK JOB OFFERS *(Complete for Private Household Job ONLY)*						
a. Description of Residence		b. No. Persons Residing at Place of Employment				c. Will free board and private room not shared with anyone be provided? *("X" one)*
("X" one)	Number of Rooms	Adults	Children	Ages		
☐ House			BOYS			☐ YES ☐ NO
☐ Apartment			GIRLS			

21: DESCRIBE EFFORTS TO RECRUIT U.S. WORKERS AND THE RESULTS. *(Specify Sources of Recruitment by Name)*

22. Applications require various types of documentation. Please read PART II of the instructions to assure that appropriate supporting documentation is included with your application.

23. EMPLOYER CERTIFICATIONS

By virtue of my signature below, I HEREBY CERTIFY the following conditions of employment.

a. I have enough funds available to pay the wage or salary offered the alien.

b. The wage offered equals or exceeds the prevailing wage and I guarantee that, if a labor certification is granted, the wage paid to the alien when the alien begins work will equal or exceed the prevailing wage which is applicable at the time the alien begins work.

c. The wage offered is not based on commissions, bonuses, or other incentives, unless I guarantee a wage paid on a weekly, bi-weekly or monthly basis.

d. I will be able to place the alien on the payroll on or before the date of the alien's proposed entrance into the United States.

e. The job opportunity does not involve unlawful discrimination by race, creed, color, national origin, age, sex, religion, handicap, or citizenship.

f. The job opportunity is not:

(1) Vacant because the former occupant is on strike or is being locked out in the course of a labor dispute involving a work stoppage.

(2) At issue in a labor dispute involving a work stoppage.

g. The job opportunity's terms, conditions and occupational environment are not contrary to Federal, State or local law.

h. The job opportunity has been and is clearly open to any qualified U.S. worker.

24. DECLARATIONS

DECLARATION OF EMPLOYER ▶ Pursuant to 28 U.S.C. 1746, I declare under penalty of perjury the foregoing is true and correct.

SIGNATURE	DATE
NAME *(Type or Print)*	TITLE

AUTHORIZATION OF AGENT OF EMPLOYER ▶ I HEREBY DESIGNATE the agent below to represent me for the purposes of labor certification and I TAKE FULL RESPONSIBILITY for accuracy of any representations made by my agent.

SIGNATURE OF EMPLOYER	DATE
NAME OF AGENT *(Type or Print)*	ADDRESS OF AGENT *(Number, Street, City, State, ZIP Code)*

APPENDIX 15, *cont.*

PART B. STATEMENT OF QUALIFICATIONS OF ALIEN

FOR ADVICE CONCERNING REQUIREMENTS FOR ALIEN EMPLOYMENT CERTIFICATION: *If alien is in the U.S., contact nearest office of Immigration and Naturalization Service. If alien is outside U.S., contact nearest U.S. Consulate.*

IMPORTANT: READ ATTACHED INSTRUCTIONS BEFORE COMPLETING THIS FORM.

Print legibly in ink or use a typewriter. If you need more space to fully answer any questions on this form, use a separate sheet. Identify each answer with the number of the corresponding question. Sign and date each sheet.

1. Name of Alien *(Family name in capital letters)*	First name	Middle name	Maiden name

2. Present Address *(No., Street, City or Town, State or Province and ZIP Code*	Country	3. Type of Visa *(If in U.S.)*

4. Alien's Birthdate *(Month, Day, Year)*	5. Birthplace *(City or Town, State or Province)*	Country	6. Present Nationality or Citizenship *(Country)*

7. Address in United States Where Alien Will Reside

8. Name and Address of Prospective Employer if Alien has job offer in U.S.	9. Occupation in which Alien is Seeking Work

10. "X" the appropriate box below and furnish the information required for the box marked

a. ☐ Alien will apply for a visa abroad at the American Consulate in ⟶	City in Foreign Country	Foreign Country

b. ☐ Alien is in the United States and will apply for adjustment of status to that of a lawful permanent resident in the office of the Immigration and Naturalization Service at ⟶	City	State

11. Names and Addresses of Schools, Colleges and Universities Attended *(include trade or vocational training facilities)*	Field of Study	FROM Month	Year	TO Month	Year	Degrees or Certificates Received

SPECIAL QUALIFICATIONS AND SKILLS

12. Additional Qualifications and Skills Alien Possesses and Proficiency in the use of Tools, Machines or Equipment Which Would Help Establish if Alien Meets Requirements for Occupation in Item 9.

13. List Licenses *(Professional, journeyman, etc.)*

14. List Documents Attached Which are Submitted as Evidence that Alien Possesses the Education, Training, Experience, and Abilities Represented

Endorsements	DATE REC. DOL
(Make no entry in this section — FOR Government Agency USE ONLY)	O.T. & C.

(Items continued on next page)

APPENDIX 15, *cont.*

15. WORK EXPERIENCE. *List all jobs held during past three (3) years. Also, list any other jobs related to the occupation for which the alien is seeking certification as indicated in item 9.*			
a. NAME AND ADDRESS OF EMPLOYER			
NAME OF JOB	DATE STARTED Month Year	DATE LEFT Month Year	KIND OF BUSINESS
DESCRIBE IN DETAILS THE DUTIES PERFORMED, INCLUDING THE USE OF TOOLS, MACHINES, OR EQUIPMENT			NO. OF HOURS PER WEEK
b. NAME AND ADDRESS OF EMPLOYER			
NAME OF JOB	DATE STARTED Month Year	DATE LEFT Month Year	KIND OF BUSINESS
DESCRIBE IN DETAIL THE DUTIES PERFORMED, INCLUDING THE USE OF TOOLS, MACHINES, OR EQUIPMENT			NO. OF HOURS PER WEEK
c. NAME AND ADDRESS OF EMPLOYER			
NAME OF JOB	DATE STARTED Month Year	DATE LEFT Month Year	KIND OF BUSINESS
DESCRIBE IN DETAIL THE DUTIES PERFORMED, INCLUDING THE USE OF TOOLS, MACHINES, OR EQUIPMENT			NO. OF HOURS PER WEEK

16. DECLARATIONS

DECLARATION OF ALIEN ➤➤	*Pursuant to 28 U.S.C. 1746, I declare under penalty of perjury the foregoing is true and correct.*	
SIGNATURE OF ALIEN		DATE
AUTHORIZATION OF AGENT OF ALIEN ➤➤	*I hereby designate the agent below to represent me for the purposes of labor certification and I take full responsibility for accuracy of any representations made by my agent.*	
SIGNATURE OF ALIEN		DATE
NAME OF AGENT *(Type or print)*	ADDRESS OF AGENT *(No., Street, City, State, ZIP Code)*	

APPENDIX 16

Form IAP-66

PLEASE DO NOT STAPLE THIS FORM

APPROVED OMB
1116-0008

United States Information Agency
EXCHANGE VISITOR FACILITATIVE STAFF GC/V
CERTIFICATE OF ELIGIBILITY FOR EXCHANGE VISITOR (J-1) SATUS

A555539

PART I — IT IS HEREBY CERTIFIED THAT:

( ) Male
( ) Female

(FAMILY NAME OR EXCHANGE VISITOR)   (FIRST NAME)   (MIDDLE NAME)

Born ⌊_⌋ ⌊_⌋ ⌊_⌋ in _____ , _____
      (Mo.) (Day) (Yr.)   (City)   (Country)

legal permanent resident of _____ , ⌊____⌋ whose position in
                              (Country)   (Code)

that country is _____ ⌊____⌋
                          (Pos Code)

U.S. address

will be sponsored by _____

_____ to participate in Exchange Visitor Program No ⌊___⌋·⌊___⌋·⌊___⌋, which is still valid and is officially described as follows:

THE PURPOSE OF THIS FORM IS TO:

1 ( ) Begin a new program
2 ( ) Extend an on going program
3 ( ) Transfer to a different program
4 ( ) Replace a lost form
5 ( ) Permit visitor's immediate family to enter U.S. separately.

This form covers the period from ⌊_⌋ ⌊_⌋ ⌊_⌋ to ⌊_⌋ ⌊_⌋ ⌊_⌋ (one year maximum.)
                                  (Mo.) (Day) (Yr.)   (Mo.) (Day) (Yr.)
If this form is for family travel or replaces a lost form, the expiration date on the exchange visitor's I-94 is _____

The category of this visitor is 1 ( ) Student, 2 ( ) Trainee, 3 ( ) Teacher, 4 ( ) Professor, 5 ( ) Research Scholar or Specialist, 6 ( ) International Visitor, 7 ( ) Medical Trainee, 8 ( ) Alien employee of the Bureau of Broadcasting. The specific field of study, research, training or professional activity is _____ verbally
                              (Subj/Field Code)
described as follows:

During the period covered by this form, it is estimated that the following financial support (in U.S. $) will be provided to this exchange visitor by:

a. ( ) The Program Sponsor in item 2 above $ _____

Financial support from organizations other than the sponsor will be provided by one or more of the following:

b1. ( ) U.S. Government Agency(ies): _____ (Agency Code), $ _____ , b2 _____ (Agency Code), $ _____
c1. ( ) International Organization(s): _____ (Int. Org. Code), $ _____ , c2 _____ (Int. Org. Code), $ _____
d. ( ) The Exchange Visitor's Government $ _____   (If necessary, use above spaces
e. ( ) The binational Commission of the visitor's Country $ _____   for funding by multiple U.S.
f. ( ) All other organizations providing support $ _____   Agencies or Intl. Organizations)
g. ( ) Personal funds $ _____

I.N.S. USE

7. _____
   (Name of Official Preparing Form)   (Title)

   _____
   (Address)

   _____
   (Signature of Responsible Officer or Alternate R.O.)   (Date)

PART II—ENDORSEMENT OF CONSULAR OR IMMIGRATION OFFICER REGARDING SECTION 212(e) OF THE I.N.S.

(Name)
(Title)

have determined that this alien in the above program

( ) is not subject to the two year residence requirement;
( ) is subject, based on: A. ( ) government financing and/or
                          B. ( ) the Exchange visitor skills list and/or
                          C. ( ) PL 94 484 as amended.

(Signature of Officer)   (Date)

PART III—STATEMENT OF RESPONSIBLE OFFICER FOR RELEASING SPONSOR (FOR TRANSFER OF PROGRAM)

Date _____ . Transfer of this exchange visitor from
program No _____ sponsored by

to the program specified in item (2) is necessary or highly desirable and is in conformity with the objectives of the Mutual Educational and Cultural Exchange Act of 1961.

(Signature of Officer)   (Date)

IAP-66 (9-83)   **Copy 1 - For Immigration and Naturalization Service**   PAGE 1

APPENDIX 16, *cont.*

INSTRUCTIONS FOR AND CERTIFICATION BY the alien beneficiary named on page 1 of this Form:

Read and complete this page prior to presentation to a United States consular or immigration official.

1.   I understand that the following conditions are applicable to exchange visitors:

    (a) *Extension of Stay and Program Transfers:* The initial period of stay in the United States authorized for an exchange visitor may not exceed one year, notwithstanding the fact that a sponsorship beyond that period may be contemplated. The completed Form IAP-66, which is required in order to apply for an extension or transfer, may be obtained from or with the assistance of the sponsor. It must be submitted to the appropriate office of the Immigration and Naturalization Service within fifteen to sixty days before the expiration of the authorized period of stay.

    (b) *Limitation on Stay:* STUDENTS -as long as they pursue a substantial scholastic program leading to recognized degrees or certificate. Students for whom the sponsor recommends practical training may be permitted to remain for such purpose for an additional period of up to 18 months after receiving their degree or certificate. BUSINESS AND INDUSTRIAL TRAINEES - 18 months. TEACHERS, PROFESSORS, RESEARCH SCHOLARS, and SPECIALISTS - 3 years. INTERNATIONAL VISITORS - 1 year. MEDICAL TRAINEES: Graduate Nurses - 2 years. Medical Technologists, Medical Record Librarians, Medical Record Technicians, Radiologic Technicians, and other participants in similar categories - the length of the approved training program plus a maximum of 18 months for practical experience, not exceeding a total of 3 years. Medical Interns and Residents - the time typically required to complete the medical specialty involved but limited to 7 years with the possibility of extension if such extension is approved by the Director of the United States Information Agency.

    (c) *Documentation Required for Admission or Readmission as an Exchange Visitor:* To be eligible for admission or readmission to the United States, an exchange visitor must present the following at the port of entry: (1) A valid nonimmigrant visa bearing classification J-1, unless exempt from nonimmigrant visa requirements; (2) A passport valid for six months beyond the anticipated period of admission, unless exempt from passport requirements; (3) A properly executed Form IAP-66. Copies one and two of Form IAP-66 must be surrendered to a United States immigration officer upon arrival in the United States. Copy three may be retained for re-entries within a period of previously authorized stay.

    (d) *Change of Status:* Exchange visitors are expected to leave the United States upon completing their objective. An exchange visitor who is subject to the two-year home-country physical presence requirement is not eligible to change his/her status while in the United States to any other nonimmigrant category except, if applicable, that of official or employee of a foreign government (A) or of an international organization (G) or member of the family or attendant of either of these types of officials or employees.

    (e) *Two-Year Home Country Physical Presence Requirement:* Any exchange visitor whose program is financed in whole or in part, directly or indirectly by either his/her own government or by the United States Government is required to reside in his/her own country for two years following completion of his/her program in the United States before he/she can become eligible for permanent residence (immigration) or for status as a temporary worker ("H") or as an intracompany transferee ("L"). Likewise, if an exchange visitor is acquiring a skill which is in short supply in his/her own country (these skills appear on the *Exchange Visitor Skills List*) he/she will be subject to this same two-year home-country residence requirement as well as alien physicians entering the U.S. to receive graduate medical education or training (Section 212(e) of the Immigration and Nationality Act and PL 94 484, as amended)

2.   I seek to enter into, or remain temporarily in, the United States as an exchange visitor under Section 101(a)(15)(J) of the Immigration and Nationality Act, as amended, for a total maximum stay of _____ *(months or years)* for the purpose of (state type of degree, certificate, or other objective toward which your program participation will be directed. Doctors of medicine should indicate their medical specialty): _____

    and I understand that I shall be permitted to perform only those activities described in Item 2 and 4 on page 1 of this Form.

3.   My passport numbered _____ issued by _____ *(Country)* expires on _____
    _____ *(Mo./Day/Yr.)*

4.   I ☐ have ☐ have not *(check one)* been in the United States previously as an exchange visitor. (If you have been in the United States previously as an exchange visitor, show total length of time: _____ , and dates: _____):

5.   (To be completed only if application is being made for extension of stay or Program transfer. Use a continuation sheet if necessary.) I first entered the United States as an exchange visitor, or acquired exchange visitor status, on _____ *(Mo. Day/Yr.)* and have engaged in the following activities under the sponsorship of respective institutions listed for each activity (include program numbers,

    _____

6.   I understand that a Consular or Immigration Officer will determine whether I am subject to the two year home country physical presence requirement described in Item 1(e) above. If such officer determines that I am subject, I will accept that determination and comply with the requirement. I understand that the determination will be endorsed in Part II, Page 1 of this form.

7.   I certify that I have read and I understand the foregoing.

_____   _____   _____
    (Signature of Applicant)   *(Place)*   *(Date: Mo., Day, Yr.)*

IAP-66

APPENDIX 17

Grounds of Excludability

The complete list, as furnished by the Immigration and Naturalization Service, is too technical to be reproduced here exactly and in entirety. The following are several of the more important general categories covered:

Mental and physical classes:
  Mentally retarded persons
  Insane persons
  Persons having had one or more attacks of insanity
  Persons afflicted with psychopathic personality, sexual deviation, or a mental defect
  Narcotic drug addicts or chronic alcoholics
  Persons afflicted with any dangerous contagious disease (such as tuberculosis or leprosy)
  Persons having limiting disabilities
Paupers, beggars, and vagrants
Certain criminal classes
Polygamists
Persons engaged in immoral acts
Persons likely to become public charges
Persons previously arrested and deported, excluded and deported
Stowaways
Various kinds of visa-fraud cases
Persons who departed the United States to avoid military service
Persons who have been convicted for possession and/or trafficking of narcotics
Persons who are illiterate
Persons who are members of subversive groups and organizations (Communists, for instance)

APPENDIX 18

Form G-325A

FORM G-325A (REV. 6-18-80) Y

Form Approved
OMB No. 43-R436

UNITED STATES DEPARTMENT OF JUSTICE
Immigration and Naturalization Service

BIOGRAPHIC INFORMATION

(Family name)	(First name)	(Middle name)	☐ MALE ☐ FEMALE	BIRTHDATE (Mo. Day Yr.)	NATIONALITY	FILE NUMBER A

ALL OTHER NAMES USED (Including names by previous marriages)	CITY AND COUNTRY OF BIRTH	SOCIAL SECURITY NO. (If any)

	FAMILY NAME	FIRST NAME	DATE, CITY AND COUNTRY OF BIRTH (If known)	CITY AND COUNTRY OF RESIDENCE
FATHER				
MOTHER (Maiden name)				

HUSBAND (If none, so state) OR WIFE	FAMILY NAME (For wife, give maiden name)	FIRST NAME	BIRTHDATE	CITY & COUNTRY OF BIRTH	DATE OF MARRIAGE	PLACE OF MARRIAGE

FORMER HUSBANDS OR WIVES (If none, so state) FAMILY NAME (For wife, give maiden name)	FIRST NAME	BIRTHDATE	DATE & PLACE OF MARRIAGE	DATE AND PLACE OF TERMINATION OF MARRIAGE

APPLICANT'S RESIDENCE LAST FIVE YEARS. LIST PRESENT ADDRESS FIRST

STREET AND NUMBER	CITY	PROVINCE OR STATE	COUNTRY	FROM MONTH	FROM YEAR	TO MONTH	TO YEAR
						PRESENT TIME	

APPLICANT'S LAST ADDRESS OUTSIDE THE UNITED STATES OF MORE THAN ONE YEAR

STREET AND NUMBER	CITY	PROVINCE OR STATE	COUNTRY	FROM MONTH	FROM YEAR	TO MONTH	TO YEAR

APPLICANT'S EMPLOYMENT LAST FIVE YEARS. (IF NONE, SO STATE.) LIST PRESENT EMPLOYMENT FIRST

FULL NAME AND ADDRESS OF EMPLOYER	OCCUPATION SPECIFY	FROM MONTH	FROM YEAR	TO MONTH	TO YEAR
				PRESENT TIME	

Show below last occupation abroad if not shown above. (Include all information requested above.)

THIS FORM IS SUBMITTED IN CONNECTION WITH APPLICATION FOR: ☐ NATURALIZATION ☐ STATUS AS PERMANENT RESIDENT ☐ OTHER (SPECIFY):	SIGNATURE OF APPLICANT	DATE

IF YOUR NATIVE ALPHABET IS IN OTHER THAN ROMAN LETTERS, WRITE YOUR NAME IN YOUR NATIVE ALPHABET IN THIS SPACE.

Are all copies legible? ☐ Yes

PENALTIES: SEVERE PENALTIES ARE PROVIDED BY LAW FOR KNOWINGLY AND WILLFULLY FALSIFYING OR CONCEALING A MATERIAL FACT.

APPLICANT: BE SURE TO PUT YOUR NAME AND ALIEN REGISTRATION NUMBER IN THE BOX OUTLINED BY HEAVY BORDER BELOW.

COMPLETE THIS BOX (Family name)	(Given name)	(Middle name)	(Alien registration number)

(OTHER AGENCY USE)	INS USE (Office of Origin) OFFICE CODE: TYPE OF CASE: DATE:

FORM G-325A

(1) IDENT.

APPENDIX 19

Form OF-169
Preliminary Questionnaire for Residence
(Sometimes Known as Packet Three)

I A. FIRST Complete and return immediately to this office the enclosed Optional Form 179 (formerly DSP-70), Biographic Data for Visa Purposes.

   B. SECOND Obtain the documents listed in Part II. As you obtain each document check the box before each item listed in Part II.

   C. THIRD Notify this office when you have assembled the documents which are applicable to your case listed in Part II by completing Part III on page 4 and submitting the entire form to this office.

PLEASE DO NOT SEND OR BRING ANY DOCUMENTS TO THIS OFFICE UNTIL YOU ARE SPECIFICALLY REQUESTED TO DO SO. A FINAL DETERMINATION CONCERNING THEIR ADEQUACY CAN ONLY BE MADE BY A CONSULAR OFFICER AT THE TIME OF YOUR FORMAL INTERVIEW.

OF.169
May 83

APPENDIX 19, *cont.*

-2-

II

/ / 1. PASSPORTS: A passport must be valid for at least six months and be endorsed by the issuing authority for travel to the United States. British regular passports meet this consideration. Each child 16 years of age or older, who is included in the parent's passport but whose photograph does not appear in such passport must obtain his own separate passport.

/ / 2. BIRTH CERTIFICATES: Two birth certificates are required for each person, including children, applying for a visa. The certificates must state your date and place of birth and names of both your parents and be certified copies of an original issued by the Registrar or other official keeper of the records. Alternatively, two photographic copies of an original or certified copy may be presented provided the original or certified copy is also produced for comparison purposes at the formal visa application.

In addition, you should assemble one long form birth certificate for any of your children under 21 who will not be accompanying you to the United States. UNOBTAINABLE BIRTH CERTIFICATE: In rare cases, it may be impossible to obtain a birth certificate because records have been destroyed, or the government will not issue one. In such a case, a baptismal certificate, in duplicate, may be submitted for consideration provided it contains the date and place of the applicant's birth and information concerning parentage and provided the baptism took place shortly after birth. Should a baptismal certificate be unobtainable, a close relative, preferably the applicant's mother, should prepare a notarized statement, in duplicate, stating the place and date of the applicant's birth, the names of both parents and maiden name of the mother. The statement must be executed before an official authorized to administer oaths or affirmations.

/ / 3. ADOPTION CERTIFICATE: Obtain original and two copies in cases of applicants who have been adopted.

/ / 4. DEED POLL: For applicants who have ever changed their names (except by marriage) original and two copies of the Deed Poll, or other legal evidence of the change in name should be furnished.

/ / 5. POLICE CERTIFICATES: (Certificates of Good Conduct).
Please state below the name of the country or countries from which you or accompanying members of your family have obtained Police Certificates.

_____

_____

Each visa applicant aged 16 years or over is required to submit a police certificate, in duplicate, to cover any period of residence of six months or more since reaching the age of sixteen. The term "police certificate" as used in this paragraph means a certification by the appropriate police authorities stating either there is no record or what their records show concerning the

APPENDIX 19, *cont.*

-3-

applicant including any and all arrests, the reasons therefor and the disposition of each case of which there is a record.

Police certificates are not issued by the police in the United Kingdom. You need not concern yourself with this requirement (but see item 6, Court and Prison Records).

(SEE PAGE 2 OF SUPPLEMENT 1 TO THIS FORM 169 FOR ADDITIONAL INFORMATION CONCERNING APPLICATION FOR POLICE CERTIFICATES)

/__/ 6. COURT AND PRISON RECORDS: Persons who have been convicted of a crime must obtain two certified copies of the court record relating to each offense for which they have been convicted. This is necessary regardless of the fact that they may have subsequently benefited from an amnesty, pardon or other act of clemency or a Rehabilitation of Offenders Act.

/__/ 7. MILITARY RECORDS: Two certified copies of any military record should be obtained covering periods spent in military service including wartime or national service.

/__/ 8. PHOTOGRAPHS: Three color photographs for each visa applicant, including infants, regardless of age. The photographs must be color photographs with a white background. They must be glossy, unretouched and not mounted; the dimension of facial image should be about 1 inch from chin to top of hair; the subject should be shown in 3/4 frontal view showing right side of face with the right ear visible.

If you have difficulty in obtaining photographs to these specifications you may defer obtaining them until the time of your medical examination and formal interview as such photographs can be obtained in London.

/__/ 9. EVIDENCE OF SUPPORT: Any evidence which will show that you and the members of your family also immigrating are not likely to become a public charge while in the United States. This is required of all visa applicants including the spouse of a United States citizen. The enclosed information sheet, Optional Form 167 - formerly DSL-845, lists evidence which may be presented to meet this requirement of the law. Such evidence must be less than 1 year old.

/__/ 10. MARRIAGE CERTIFICATE: Present original and two copies of the marriage certificate for each marriage. (three copies if husband and wife are planning to travel separately.)

/__/ 11. DIVORCE OR DEATH CERTIFICATES: Proof of the termination of any of your marriages must also be furnished in the form of a divorce, death or annulment certificate in duplicate. A decree nisi is not acceptable, it must be a final divorce decree.

/__/ 12. TRANSLATIONS: All documents not in the more common languages must be accompanied by certified translations into English in duplicate.

APPENDIX 19, *cont.*

-4-

III

    C. THIRD: As soon as you have obtained all of the documents listed in items 1 to 12 which are applicable to your case, read carefully the statement below then complete this form by giving the information requested below and return the entire form to this office.

Enclosures:
1. Optional Form 179 (DSP-70)
2. Optional Form 167 (DSL-845)

I have in my possession and am prepared to present all of the documents listed in items 1 through 12 which apply to my case, as indicated by the check marks I have placed in the appropriate boxes. I fully realize that no advance assurance can be given that a visa will actually be issued to me and I also understand that I should NOT give up my job, dispose of property, nor make any final travel arrangements until a visa is actually issued to me. At such time as it is possible for me to receive an appointment to make formal visa application, I intend to apply:
(check appropriate box)

/__/   1. Alone   /__/ 2. With my spouse

/__/   3. With my spouse & following minor children:
             (print full names of each child)

_____

_____

DATE OF INTENDED TRAVEL_____

_____
                 SIGNATURE

_____
           NAME IN BLOCK LETTERS

_____
                ADDRESS

_____

_____
             CASE NUMBER

PLEASE QUOTE YOUR CASE NUMBER AND FULL NAME WHEN CORRESPONDING WITH THIS OFFICE.

APPENDIX 19, *cont.*

SUPPLEMENT 1 TO OPTIONAL FORM 169

BIRTH CERTIFICATES

A person born in India or Pakistan must present the registration certificate if his birth was registered. If it was not registered, either in the locality or, if a Christian, in a church, sworn affidavits may be submitted. Such an affidavit must be executed before an official authorized to take oaths (i.e., a magistrate, commissioner of oaths, justice of the peace or the like) by the mother. If she is deceased the father may swear to the affidavit. The affidavit should indicate:

(1) that the applicant's birth was not registered;

(2) the full maiden name of the mother of the applicant;

(3) the full name of the father of the applicant;

(4) the date of the applicant's birth;

(5) the place of the applicant's birth.

If neither parent is alive, the next closest relative, who was old enough and of such relationship as to have personal knowledge of the birth at the time and place it occurred, may execute the affidavit.

A statement from the High Commission concerning your birth is not acceptable.

A person who has used a different name from the one shown on the birth certificate, must produce a document explaining the use of such name.

The following documents are commonly available as evidence:

(1) Baptismal certificate

(2) Deed Poll

(3) School records showing early use of adopted name.

If none of the foregoing documents are available any other document, or combination of documents, which appear to resolve the difference in names will be considered. Your personal sworn statement is not acceptable unless there is other evidence to substantiate it.

OF.169 SUPPLEMENT 1
NOV.79

SEE OVER:

APPENDIX 19, *cont.*

- Page 2 -

POLICE CERTIFICATES

If you or accompanying member(s) of your family now applying for a visa have resided in another country or countries, certificates covering residences of six months or more must be obtained. Generally, application for such certificates should be made directly to police authorities in the district in which you resided. If you have any questions about where or how to apply for police certificates in other countries you may communicate directly with this office.

Do not attempt to obtain police certificates covering residence in any of the following countries or areas, as they either are not available or may be obtained only by this office:

AFGHANISTAN	MONGOLIA
ALBANIA	MOZAMBIQUE
BERMUDA	NEPAL
BOTSWANA	NETHERLANDS
BRAZIL	NEW ZEALAND
BRUNEI	NICARAGUA
BULGARIA	NORTHERN IRELAND
BURMA	ROMANIA
CHAD	SAUDI ARABIA
CHILE	SCOTLAND
COLOMBIA	SIERRA LEONE
CUBA	SOMALIA
ENGLAND	SOUTH AFRICA
EQUATORIAL GUINEA	SOVIET UNION
ESTONIA	SRI LANKA
ETHIOPIA	SURINAM
FIJI	TOGO
GHANA	TURKEY
INDONESIA	UNITED ARAB EMIRATES
IRAQ	UNITED KINGDOM
KOREA	UNITED STATES OF AMERICA
KUWAIT	VANUATU
LAOS	VENEZUELA
LATVIA	VIETNAM
MALAWI	WALES
MALAYSIA	ZIMBABWE

APPENDIX 19, *cont.*

SUPPLEMENT 2 TO OPTIONAL FORM 169

Every applicant for an immigrant visa who has a child or children is by regulation required to submit to the interviewing consular officer the birth and/or baptismal certificate for each child. If your wife or husband has a child or children by a previous marriage who had not attained the age of eighteen years at the time of your marriage, or a child born out of wedlock, the birth and/or baptismal certificate for each such child must also be obtained for examination by the consular officer. This requirement applies even though one or more of the children of either spouse has no current intention to apply for an immigrant visa to the United States.

A CHILD AS DEFINED IN THE IMMIGRATION AND NATIONALITY ACT IS AN UNMARRIED PERSON NOT YET 21 YEARS OF AGE.

I (we) have the following children who will NOT accompany me (us) to the United States:

FAMILY NAME   FIRST NAME   MIDDLE NAMES   DATE & COUNTRY OF BIRTH

_____

_____

_____

_____

_____

_____

I (we) have obtained birth and/or baptismal certificates for each child, and these will be retained in my (our) possession for presentation to the consular officer on the date of my (our) formal application for an immigrant visa.

_____   _____

(Signature of Principal Applicant)   (Signature of spouse)

PLEASE RETURN THIS FORM TO THE CONSULAR OFFICER WHEN YOU RETURN OPTIONAL FORM 169

DO NOT SEND ANY DOCUMENTS TO THIS OFFICE UNLESS SPECIFICALLY REQUESTED TO DO SO.

OF. 169 SUPPLEMENT 2

APPENDIX 19, *cont.*

EMBASSY OF THE
UNITED STATES OF AMERICA

Visa Branch
5 Upper Grosvenor Street
London W1A 2JB

EVIDENCE WHICH MAY BE PRESENTED TO MEET THE
PUBLIC CHARGE PROVISIONS OF THE LAW

GENERAL

The Immigration and Nationality Act requires an applicant for a visa to establish to the satisfaction of the consular officer at the time of his application for a visa, and also to the satisfaction of the United States immigration officials at the time of his application for admission into the United States, that he is not likely at any time to become a public charge.

An applicant for an immigrant visa may generally satisfy this requirement of the law by the presentation of documentary evidence, in duplicate, establishing that:

1.　he has, or will have, in the United States funds of his own sufficient to provide for the support of himself and members of his family; or

2.　he has employment awaiting him in the United States which will provide an adequate income for himself and members of his family; or

3.　he is skilled in a profession or occupation which has been determined to be in short supply in the United States and can show that he has funds adequate for transportation to the United States and for the support of himself and members of his family until he is able to locate employment in his profession or occupation; or

4.　relatives or friends in the United States will assure his support.

APPLICANTS OWN FUNDS

An applicant who expects to be able to meet the public charge provisions of the law under 1 or to present evidence of funds required under 3 above may submit to the consular officer one or more of the following items:

(a)　statement from an officer of a bank showing present balance of applicant's account, date account was opened, and average balance during the year. If there have been recent unusually large deposits, an explanation therefor should be given;

(b)　proof of ownership of property or real estate, in the form of a letter from a lawyer, banker or responsible real estate agent showing its present valuation. Any mortgages or loans against the property must be stated;

Optional Form 167
Formerly DSL-845
Feb. 80

APPENDIX 19, *cont.*

-2-

(c) letter or letters verifying ownership of stocks and bonds, with present market value indicated;

(d) statement from insurance company showing policies held and present cash surrender value;

(e) proof of income from business investments or other sources.

EMPLOYMENT

Applicants having prearranged employment should submit evidence thereof, in duplicate, from the prospective employer on his business letterhead or if he has no letterhead in the form of a contract or affidavit. An applicant whose employment has been certified by the Department of Labor need not furnish a statement or contract of employment, unless specifically requested to do so by the consular officer.

The letter, contract or affidavit should:

(a) contain a definite offer of employment;

(b) state whether the employment will be immediately available upon the applicant's arrival in the United States;

(c) specify the location, type, and duration (whether seasonal, temporary, or indefinite) of the employment offered;

(d) specify the rate or range of compensation to be paid;

(e) be of recent date; and

(f) if the prospective employer is an individual rather that a firm, some evidence proving that the individual is in a financial position to carry out the offer of employment.

AFFIDAVIT OF SUPPORT

There are no prescribed forms to be used by persons in the United States who desire to furnish sponsorship in the form of an affidavit of support for presentation to the consul.

Each sponsor should furnish a statement, in duplicate, in affidavit form setting forth his willingness and financial ability to contribute to the applicant's support and his reasons in detail for sponsoring the applicant.

The sponsor's statement should include:

(a) information regarding his income;

(b) where material, information regarding his resources;

(c) his obligations for the support of members of his own family and other persons, if any;

(d) his other obligations and expenses;

APPENDIX 19, *cont.*

-3-

(e) plans and arrangements made for the applicant's reception and support; and

(f) an expression of willingness to deposit a bond, if necessary, with the Immigration and Naturalization Service to guarantee that the applicant will not become a public charge in the United States.

The sponsor should include in his affidavit a statement concerning his status in the United States. If the sponsor is an American citizen he should state how he acquired United States citizenship. If naturalized, he should indicate in the affidavit the date of naturalization, the name and location of the court, and the number of his certificate of naturalization since reproduction thereof is prohibited by law and severe legal penalties are prescribed for such reproduction. If the sponsor is an alien who has been lawfully admitted into the United States for permanent residence, he should state in the affidavit the date and place of his admission for permanent residence and the alien registration number which appears on his Alien Registration Receipt Card (Form I-151). In no case should a copy be made of Form I-151 since the reproduction of this document, like a certificate of naturalization, is also prohibited by law and severe legal penalties are prescribed for such reproduction.

To substantiate the information regarding his income and resources the sponsor should attach one or more of the following items to his affidavit:

(a) notarized copies of his latest income tax return;

(b) a statement, in duplicate, from his employer showing his salary and the length and permanancy of employment;

(c) a statement, in duplicate, from an officer of a bank regarding his account, showing the date the account was opened and the present balance;

(d) any other evidence adequate to establish his financial ability to carry out his undertaking toward the applicant for what might be an indefinite period of time.

If the sponsor is a well established businessman, he may submit a rating from a recognized concern in lieu of the foregoing.

If the sponsor is married, the affidavit should be jointly signed by both husband and wife.

Affidavits of support should be of recent date when presented to the consular officer. They are unacceptable if more than a year has elapsed from the date of execution.

A sponsor may prefer to forward his affidavit of support direct to the consular officer where the visa application will be made, in which event the contents will not be divulged to the applicant.

IMPORTANT: An applicant who expects to meet the public charge provisions of the law through the presentation of an affidavit of support is encouraged to forward this information sheet to his sponsor so as to assist him in preparing his affidavit.

APPENDIX 19, *cont.*

IMPORTANT - This document must be read and signed by persons wishing to submit an affidavit of support on behalf of an alien applying for an immigrant visa. A signed copy of this document must be attached to each copy of any affidavit of support submitted on behalf of an applicant.

The Social Security Act, as amended, establishes certain requirements for determining the eligibility of aliens for Supplemental Security Income (SSI) and Aid to Families with Dependent Children (AFDC) benefits. The Food Stamp Act, as amended, contains similar provisions. These amendments require that the income and resources of any person (and that person's spouse) who executes an affidavit of support or similar agreement on behalf of an immigrant alien, be deemed to be the income and resources of the alien under formulas for determining eligibility for SSI, AFDC, and Food Stamp benefits during the three years following the alien's entry into the United States.

The eligibility of aliens for SSI, AFDC, and Food Stamp benefits will be contingent upon their obtaining the cooperation of their sponsors in providing the necessary information and evidence to enable the Social Security Administration and/or State Welfare Agencies to carry out these provisions. An alien applying for SSI, AFDC, or Food Stamp benefits must make available to the Social Security Administration and/or State Welfare Agencies documentation concerning his income or resources or those of his sponsors, including information which he provided in support of his application for an immigrant visa or adjustment of status. The Secretary of Health and Human Services and/or State Welfare Agencies are authorized to obtain copies of any such documentation from other agencies.

The Social Security Act and the Food Stamp Act also provide that an alien and his or her sponsor shall be jointly and severally liable to repay any SSI, AFDC, and Food Stamp benefits which are incorrectly paid because of misinformation provided by sponsor or because of sponsor's failure to provide information. Also, any incorrect payments of SSI and AFDC benefits which are not repaid will be withheld from any subsequent payments for which the alien or sponsors are otherwise eligible under the Social Security Act.

These provisions do not apply to aliens admitted as refugees or granted political asylum by the Attorney General. They also will not apply to the SSI eligibility of aliens who become blind or disabled after entry into the United States. The AFDC provisions do not apply to aliens who are dependent children of the sponsor or sponsor's spouse.

I, _____ , residing at _____
       (name)   (number and street)

_____ ,
(City)   (State)

acknowledge that I have read the above and am aware of my responsibilities as an immigrant sponsor under the Social Security Act, as amended, and the Food Stamp Act, as amended. This statement is submitted on behalf of the following persons:

Name	Sex	Age	Country of Birth	Married or Single	Relationship to Sponsor

OF-167A
Mar 83   Signature of Sponsor(s)

APPENDIX 20

Form OF-179

Post Symbol: L N D	Department of State BIOGRAPHIC DATA FOR VISA PURPOSES	

INSTRUCTIONS

Complete this form for your entire family (yourself, spouse and unmarried children under 21 years of age).

1. NAME (Family name)	(First name)	(Middle names)

OTHER NAMES, ALIASES (If married woman, maiden name and surname of any previous spouses)

2. PLACE OF BIRTH (City)	(State or Province)	(Country)

DATE OF BIRTH (Month) (Day) (Year)	SEX / / Male / / Female

PRESENT NATIONALITY	PAST NATIONALITY

3. NAME OF FATHER	4. MAIDEN NAME OF MOTHER

5. FATHER'S BIRTHPLACE (City)	(State or Province)	(Country)

6. MOTHER'S BIRTHPLACE (City)	(State or province)	(Country)

7. NAME OF SPOUSE (Maiden/family name)	(First name)	(Middle name)

8. SPOUSE'S BIRTHPLACE (City)	(State or province)	(Country)

9. SPOUSE'S BIRTHDATE (Month)(Day)(Year)	10. WILL SPOUSE IMMIGRATE WITH YOU?	/ / Yes / / No

11. NAME OF SPOUSE'S FATHER	12. NAME OF SPOUSE'S MOTHER

13. BIRTHPLACE OF (City) SPOUSE'S FATHER	(State or province)	(Country)

14. BIRTHPLACE OF (City) SPOUSE'S MOTHER	(State or province)	(Country)

15. LIST UNMARRIED CHILDREN UNDER 21 YEARS, NOT U.S. CITIZENS WHO WILL ACCOMPANY YOU.

NAME OF CHILD	PLACE OF BIRTH (City)	(State or province) (Country)	BIRTHDATE

16. IF YOU OR YOUR SPOUSE ARE NOW, OR HAVE BEEN, IN THE UNITED STATES, STATE:

/ / APPLICANT	WHERE WAS VISA OBTAINED	WHEN WAS VISA GRANTED
/ / SPOUSE		

CHECK TYPE OF VISA USED FOR SUCH ENTRY:
/ / Immigrant
/ / Visitor
/ / Exchange Visitor
/ / Other Nonimmigrant (Specify)

17. IF YOU OR YOUR SPOUSE WERE PREVIOUSLY IN THE UNITED STATES, STATE: ⎿⎽⏌ Applicant ⎿⏌ Spouse

DATE ADMITTED	DATE DEPARTED	REASON FOR DEPARTURE

OF-179   /over

APPENDIX 20, *cont.*

FORM OF-179 Nov.82   Page 2

18. Latest or Last Address in the United Kingdom.

19. List Below in Date Order All Places Where You, Your Spouse and Unmarried Children Named on the Other Side Have Lived Since Reaching the Age of Sixteen. You need not list those places where you have lived less than six months.

First name of Family Member	Town, City, Province, Country	Occupation	From Month Year	To Month Year

20. On separate sheet, give following information on each family member who resided in:

ARGENTINA – Cedula number; date, place of issue and complete address in Argentina.
BAHAMAS – Number, date and place of issue of passport.
BERMUDA – Date of arrival in Bermuda, occupation and places of employment in Bermuda.
CAMEROON – Place of employment there.
HONDURAS – Passport number and date of issuance.
ISRAEL – Israeli Identity Card number or passport number if non-Israeli; name used in Israel, name used on arrival, date of arrival and exact address in Israel.
JAPAN – Registered domicile in Japan and, if Japanese, Chinese or Korean, give name in Chinese (Kanji characters).
JERUSALEM – (see Israel above)
MALAYSIA – National Registration Identity Card number and, if Chinese, full name and parents' names and parents' names in Chinese characters.
NETHERLANDS Full street addresses in the Netherlands.
SINGAPORE – Singapore Identity card number for Singapore citizens and permanent residents. If Chinese, full name and names of spouse and parents in Chinese characters.

21. Membership or affiliation in organizations in each country named in item 19:
Cultural, Social, Labor or Political

ORGANIZATION	FROM	TO

I certify that all information given is complete and correct.

DATE   SIGNATURE AND PRESENT ADDRESS   'PHONE NO.

NOTE: If space above is insufficient to answer any questions properly, the additional information may be printed on a separate sheet of paper and attached to this form.

APPENDIX 21

Form 230

OPTIONAL FORM 230
(FORMERLY FS-610 ENGLISH)
MARCH 1975
DEPT. OF STATE

Form Approved.
Budget Bureau No. 47-R

APPLICATION FOR IMMIGRANT VISA AND ALIEN REGISTRATION

INSTRUCTIONS: This form must be filled out in DUPLICATE by typewriter, or if by hand in legible block letters. ALL questions r be answered, if applicable. Questions which are not applicable should be so marked. If there is insufficient room on the form, ans on separate sheets, in duplicate using the same numbers as appear on the form. Attach the sheets to the forms. DO NOT S this form until instructed to do so by the consular officer. The fee for filing this application for an immigrant visa is $5.00. The should be paid in United States dollars or local currency equivalent or by bank draft, when you appear before the consular officer

WARNING: Any false statement or concealment of a material fact may result in your permanent exclusion from the United States. Even th you should be admitted to the United States, a fraudulent entry could be grounds for your prosecution and/or deportation.

1. Family name	First name	Middle name

2. Other names used or by which known (*If married woman, give maiden name*)

3. Full name in native alphabet (*If Roman letters not used*)

4. Date of birth (Day) (Month) (Year)	5. Age	6. Place of birth (City or town) (Province) (Country)

7. Nationality	8. Sex ☐ Male ☐ Female	9. Marital status ☐ Single (*never married*) ☐ Married ☐ Widowed ☐ Divorced ☐ Separa Including my present marriage, I have been married .... times.

10. Occupation	11. Present address

12. Purpose in going to the United States	13. Name and address of wife/husband (*Give maiden name of wife*)

14. Names and addresses of children under 21 years of age	15. Person(s) named in 13 and 14 (will) (will not) accomp or follow me to the United States. (*Cross out words that d apply*)

16. Length of intended stay (*If permanently, so state*)	17. Intended port of entry

18. Final address in the United States	19. Do you have a ticket to final destination?

20. Person you intend to join (*Give name, address and relationship, if any*)	21. Name and address of sponsoring person or organize (*If different from 20*)

22. Personal description	23. Marks of identification
(a) Color of hair — (c) Height .... feet .... inches	
(b) Color of eyes — (d) Complexion	

24. The following documents are submitted in support of this application

☐ Birth certificate ☐ Death certificate ☐ Evidence of own assets ☐ Medical record(s)
☐ Police certificate(s) ☐ Divorce decree ☐ Affidavit of support ☐ Photographs
☐ Marriage certificate ☐ Military record ☐ Offer of employment ☐ Other (describe)

THIS FORM MAY BE OBTAINED **GRATIS** AT CONSULAR OFFICES OF THE UNITED STATES OF AMERICA   5023

This shows only the first page of the four-page document.

APPENDIX 22

Form I-485

Immigration and Naturalization Service

APPLICATION FOR STATUS AS PERMANENT RESIDENT

Form Approved - O.M.B. No. 43—R0400

FEE STAMP

File No.

APPLICATION FOR THE BENEFITS OF SECTION:

- [ ] Sec. 203(a)(7) and Sec. 245, I&N Act
- [ ] Sec. 245, I&N Act
- [ ] Sec. 214(d), I&N Act
- [ ] Sec. 249 I&N Act
- [ ] Sec. 13, Act of 9/11/57

(DO NOT WRITE ABOVE THIS LINE.) (SEE INSTRUCTIONS BEFORE FILLING IN APPLICATION. IF YOU NEED MORE SPACE TO ANSWER FULLY ANY QUESTION ON THIS FORM, USE A SEPARATE SHEET AND IDENTIFY EACH ANSWER WITH THE NUMBER OF THE CORRESPONDING QUESTION. FILL IN WITH TYPEWRITER OR PRINT IN BLOCK LETTERS IN INK.)

1. I hereby apply for the status of a lawful permanent resident alien on the following basis: (Check box A, B, C, D, E, or F)

A. [ ] As a refugee to whom an immigrant visa is immediately available (Section 203(a)(7) and Section 245, I&N Act).

B. [ ] As a person who entered the U.S. with a visa issued to me as the fiancee or fiance of a U.S. citizen whom I married within 90 days after my entry, or as a child of such fiancee or fiance (Sec. 214(d), I&N Act).

C. [ ] As a former government official, or as a member of the immediate family of such official (Section 13, Act of September 11, 1957).

D. [ ] As a person to whom an immigrant visa is immediately available, other than one described above (Section 245, I&N Act).

E. [ ] As a person who has resided in the United States continuously since prior to July 1, 1924 (Section 249, I&N Act).

F. [ ] As a person who has resided in the United States continuously since a date on or after July 1, 1924, but before June 30, 1948 (Section 249, I&N Act).

2. My name is (Last in capital letters)   (First Name)   (Middle Name)

3. Sex [ ] Male [ ] Female   Phone number

4. I reside in the United States at: (c/o) (No. and Street) (Apt. No.) (City) (State) (ZIP Code)

5. Have you ever applied before for permanent resident status in the U.S.? [ ] Yes [ ] No (If "Yes", give the date and place of filing and final disposition.)

My alien registration number is   7. I am a citizen of (Country)   8. Date of Birth (Month) (Day) (Year)

Place of Birth (City or Town)   (County, Province, or State)   (Country)

Name as appears on nonimmigrant document (Form I-94)

I last arrived in the United States at the port of (City and State)   on (Month) (Day) (Year)   by (Name of vessel or other means of travel)

as a (visitor, student, crewman, parolee, etc.)

I [ ] was [ ] was not inspected.

My nonimmigrant visa, number _____ was issued by the United States Consul at (City) (Country)   on (Month) (Day) (Year)

12. I am [ ] single [ ] married [ ] divorced [ ] widowed

I have been married _____ times, including my present marriage, if now married. (If you are now married give the following:)

a. Number of times my husband or wife has been married   b. Name of husband or wife (Wife give maiden name)

My husband or wife resides [ ] with me [ ] apart from me at Address (Apt. No.) (No. & Street) (Town or City) (Province or State) (Country)

a. I have _____ sons or daughters as follows: (Complete all columns as to each son or daughter; if living with you state "with me" in last column; otherwise give city and state or country of son's or daughter's residence.)

Name	Sex	Place of Birth	Date of Birth	Now living at

The following members of my family are also applying for permanent resident status:

I list below all organizations, societies, clubs, and associations, past or present, in which I have held membership in the United States or a foreign country, and the periods and places of such membership. (If you have never been a member of any organization, state "None".)

UNITED STATES DEPARTMENT OF JUSTICE
Immigration and Naturalization Service
Form I-485 (Rev. 11-26-79) N

RECEIVED	TRANS. IN	RET'D TRANS. OUT	COMPLETED

(Page 1.

APPENDIX 22, *cont.*

16. I ☐ have ☐ have not been treated for a mental disorder, drug addiction or alcoholism. (If you have been, explain.)

17. I ☐ have ☐ have not been arrested, convicted or confined in a prison. (If you have been, explain.)

18. I ☐ have ☐ have not been the beneficiary of a pardon, amnesty, rehabilitation decree, other act of clemency or similar action. (If you have been explain.)

19. APPLICANTS FOR STATUS AS PERMANENT RESIDENTS MUST ESTABLISH THAT THEY ARE ADMISSIBLE TO THE UNITED STATES. EXCEPT AS OTHERWISE PROVIDED BY LAW, ALIENS WITHIN ANY OF THE FOLLOWING CLASSES ARE NOT ADMISSIBLE TO THE UNITED STATES AND ARE THEREFORE INELIGIBLE FOR STATUS AS PERMANENT RESIDENTS:

Aliens who have committed or who have been convicted of a crime involving moral turpitude (does not include minor traffic violations); aliens who have been engaged in or who intend to engage in any commercialized sexual activity; aliens who are or at any time have been, anarchists, or members of or affiliated with any Communist or other totalitarian party, including any subdivision or affiliate thereof; aliens who have advocated or taught, either by personal utterance, or by means of any written or printed matter, or through affiliation with an organization, (i) opposition to organized government, (ii) the overthrow of government by force or violence, (iii) the assaulting or killing of government officials because of their official character, (iv) the unlawful destruction of property, (v) sabotage, or (vi) the doctrines of world communism, or the establishment of a totalitarian dictatorship in the United States; aliens who intend to engage in prejudicial activities or unlawful activities of a subversive nature; aliens who have been convicted of violation of any law or regulation relating to narcotic drugs or marihuana, or who have been illicit traffickers in narcotic drugs or marihuana; aliens who have been involved in assisting any other aliens to enter the United States in violation of law; aliens who have applied for exemption or discharge from training or service in the Armed Forces of the United States on the ground of alienage and who have been relieved or discharged from such training or service; medical graduates (other than those for whom Relative petitions have been approved) coming principally to perform services as members of the medical profession, unless they have passed Parts I and II of the National Board of Medical Examiners Examination (or an equivalent examination as determined by the Secretary of Health, Education, and Welfare) and who are competent in oral and written English.

Do any of the foregoing classes apply to you? ☐ Yes ☐ No *(If answer is Yes, explain)*

20. *(COMPLETE THIS BLOCK ONLY IF YOU CHECKED BOX "A", "B", "C", or "D" OF BLOCK 1)*

APPLICANTS WHO CHECKED BOX "A" "B" "C" OR "D" OF BLOCK 1 (INCLUDING REFUGEES) IN ADDITION TO ESTABLISHING THAT THE ARE NOT MEMBERS OF ANY OF THE INADMISSIBLE CLASSES DESCRIBED IN BLOCK 10 ABOVE MUST, EXCEPT AS OTHERWISE PROVIDED BY LAW, ALSO ESTABLISH THAT THEY ARE NOT WITHIN ANY OF THE FOLLOWING INADMISSIBLE CLASSES:

Aliens who are mentally retarded, insane, or have suffered one or more attacks of insanity; aliens afflicted with psychopathic personality, sexual diviatic mental defect, narcotic drug addiction, chronic alcoholism or any dangerous contagious disease; aliens who have a physical defect, disease or disabili affecting their ability to earn a living; aliens who are paupers, professional beggars or vagrants; aliens who are polygamists or advocate polygamy; alie who intend to perform skilled or unskilled labor and who have not been certified by the Secretary of Labor (see Instruction 10); aliens likely to become public charge; aliens who have been excluded from the United States within the past year, or who at any time have been deported from the United State or who at any time have been removed from the United States at Government expense; aliens who have procured or have attempted to procure a visa fraud or misrepresentation; aliens who have departed from or remained outside the United States to avoid military service in time of war or nation emergency; aliens who are former exchange visitors who are subject to but have not complied with the two year foreign residence requirement.

Do any of the foregoing classes apply to you? ☐ Yes ☐ No *(If answer is Yes, explain)*

21. I ☐ do ☐ do not intend to seek gainful employment in the United States. If you intend to seek gainful employment in the United States.

state the occupation you intend to follow _____

APPENDIX 22, *cont.*

22. *(Complete this block only if you checked box A or D of block 1)*

☐ a. I have a priority on the consular waiting list at the American Consulate at_____as of_____
_____(City)_____(Date)

☐ b. A visa petition according me ☐ immediate relative ☐ preference status was approved by the district

director at_____on_____
_____(City and State)_____(Date)

☐ c. A visa petition has not been approved in my behalf but I claim eligibility for preference status because ☐ my spouse
☐ my parent is the beneficiary of a visa petition approved by the district director at_____
on_____(City and State)
_____(Date)

☐ d. I am claiming preference status as a refugee under the proviso to Section 203 (a)(7) of the Act who has been continuously physically
present in the United States for at least the past two years. *(If you check this item, you must execute and attach Form I–590A to this
application.)*

☐ e. Other *(Explain)*

---

23. *(Complete this block only if you checked Box E
or F of Block 1)*
A. I first arrived in the United States at (Port)

_____

on (Date)

_____

by means of (Name of vessel or other means of
travel)

_____

I ☐ was ☐ was not inspected by an immigration officer.

B. I entered the U.S. under the name *(Name at time
of entry)*

_____

and I was destined to (City and State)

_____

I was coming to join (Name and relationship)

C. Since my first entry I ☐ have ☐ have not been
absent from the United States. *(If you have been
absent, attach a separate statement listing the
port, date and means of each departure from and
return to the U.S.)*

24. ☐ Completed Form G–325A (Biographic Information) is
attached as part of this application. | Completed Form G–325A (Biographic Information) is not
attached as applicant is under 14 years of age.

25. IF YOUR NATIVE ALPHABET IS IN OTHER THAN ROMAN LETTERS,
WRITE YOUR NAME IN YOUR NATIVE ALPHABET BELOW: | Signature of Applicant:

Date of Signature:

26. *(Signature of person preparing form, if other than applicant.)* I declare that
this document was prepared by me at the request of the applicant and is
based on all information on which I have any knowledge. | Address of person preparing form, if other than applicant

Date: | Occupation:

(Application not to be signed below until applicant appears before an officer of the Immigration and Naturalization Service for examination)

I,_____, do swear (affirm) that I know the contents of this application subscribed by me
including the attached documents, that the same are true to the best of my knowledge, and that corrections numbered ( ) to ( ) were
made by me or at my request, and that this application was signed by me with my full, true name:

_____

(Complete and true signature of applicant)

Subscribed and sworn to before me by the above-named applicant at_____on_____
_____(Month)____(Day)____(Year)

_____

(Signature and title of officer)

(Page 3)

APPENDIX 23

Form ER-531

L-485 SUPPLEMENT FOR ISSUANCE OF I-551

ALIEN NUMBER	LAST NAME	FIRST NAME	MIDDLE NAME

ADDRESS

IN CARE OF

NUMBER/STREET

CITY | STATE | ZIP CODE

MOTHER'S FIRST NAME	FATHER'S FIRST NAME	CITY/TOWN/VILLAGE OF BIRTH

CITY OF RESIDENCE WHEN APPLYING FOR THIS STATUS	CITY OF DESTINATION AT TIME OF ORIGINAL ADMISSION TO THE UNITED STATES	LOCATION OF CONSULATE OR IMMIGRATION OFFICE WHERE ADJUSTED

DATE OF BIRTH	PORT OF ENTRY	DATE OF ENTRY OR ADJUSTMENT	COUNTRY OF BIRTH

COLOR PHOTOGRAPH SPECIFICATIONS

◀ SAMPLE PHOTOGRAPH

HEAD SIZE(INCLUDING HAIR) MUST FIT INSIDE OVAL ▶

29MM (1 1/8") CHIN TO TOP OF HAIR

22MM (7/8") HEAD WIDTH

SUBMIT **Two (2)** <u>COLOR</u> PHOTOS
MEETING THE FOLLOWING SPECIFICATIONS

● PHOTOGRAPH MUST SHOW THE SUBJECT IN A ¾ FRONTAL PORTRAIT AS SHOWN ABOVE

● RIGHT EAR MUST BE EXPOSED IN PHOTOGRAPH FOR ALL APPLICANTS, HATS MUST NOT BE WORN

● PHOTOGRAPH OUTER DIMENSION <u>MUST</u> BE LARGER THAN 1"ᵂ x 1"ᴴ, BUT HEAD SIZE (INCLUDING HAIR) <u>MUST</u> FIT WITHIN THE ILLUSTRATED OVAL (OUTER DIMENSION DOES NOT INCLUDE BORDER IF ONE IS USED)

● PHOTOGRAPH MUST BE COLOR WITH A WHITE BACKGROUND EQUAL IN REFLECTANCE TO BOND TYPING PAPER

● SURFACE OF THE PHOTOGRAPH <u>MUST BE GLOSSY</u>

● PHOTOGRAPH MUST NOT BE STAINED, CRACKED, OR MUTILATED, AND MUST LIE FLAT

● PHOTOGRAPHIC IMAGE MUST BE SHARP AND CORRECTLY EXPOSED, PHOTOGRAPH MUST BE UN-RETOUCHED

● PHOTOGRAPH MUST NOT BE PASTED ON CARDS OR MOUNTED IN ANY WAY

● **Two (2)** PHOTOGRAPHS OF EVERY APPLICANT, REGARDLESS OF AGE, MUST BE SUBMITTED

● PHOTOGRAPHS MUST BE TAKEN WITHIN THIRTY (30) DAYS OF APPLICATION DATE

● SNAPSHOTS, GROUP PICTURES, OR FULL LENGTH PORTRAITS <u>WILL NOT</u> BE ACCEPTED

● USING CRAYON OR FELT PEN, TO AVOID MUTILATION OF THE PHOTOGRAPHS, <u>LIGHTLY</u> PRINT YOUR NAME (AND ALIEN REGISTRATION RECEIPT NUMBER IF KNOWN) ON THE BACK OF ALL PHOTOGRAPHS

● <u>IMPORTANT NOTE</u> - FAILURE TO SUBMIT PHOTOGRAPHS IN COMPLIANCE WITH THESE SPECIFICATIONS WILL DELAY THE PROCESSING OF YOUR APPLICATION

ER 531   11-78(15)

APPENDIX 24

Fingerprint Chart

APPLICANT	LEAVE BLANK	TYPE OR PRINT ALL INFORMATION IN BLACK						FBI	LEAVE BLANK
		LAST NAME NAM FIRST NAME MIDDLE NAME							

SIGNATURE OF PERSON FINGERPRINTED

ALIASES AKA		O R I	NYINSNYOO USINS NEW YORK NY					

RESIDENCE OF PERSON FINGERPRINTED

DATE OF BIRTH DOB — Month Day Year

SIGNATURE OF OFFICIAL TAKING FINGERPRINTS

CITIZENSHIP CTZ	SEX	RACE	HGT.	WGT.	EYES	HAIR	PLACE OF BIRTH POB

EMPLOYER AND ADDRESS

YOUR NO. OCA	LEAVE BLANK
FBI NO. FBI	

REASON FINGERPRINTED

ARMED FORCES NO. MNU	CLASS _____
SOCIAL SECURITY NO. SOC	REF. _____
MISCELLANEOUS NO. MNU	

1. R. THUMB	2. R. INDEX	3. R. MIDDLE	4. R. RING	5. R. LITTLE

6. L. THUMB	7. L. INDEX	8. L. MIDDLE	9. L. RING	10. L. LITTLE

LEFT FOUR FINGERS TAKEN SIMULTANEOUSLY	L. THUMB	R. THUMB	RIGHT FOUR FINGERS TAKEN SIMULTANEOUSLY

APPENDIX 24, *cont.*

FEDERAL BUREAU OF INVESTIGATION
UNITED STATES DEPARTMENT OF JUSTICE
WASHINGTON, D.C. 20537

APPLICANT

1. LOOP

CENTER OF LOOP

DELTA

THE LINES BETWEEN CENTER OF LOOP AND DELTA MUST SHOW

2. WHORL

DELTAS

THESE LINES RUNNING BETWEEN DELTAS MUST BE CLEAR

3. ARCH

ARCHES HAVE NO DELTAS

FD-258 (REV. 12-29-82) ☆U.S. GOVERNMENT PRINTING OFFICE: 1983—385-983

TO OBTAIN CLASSIFIABLE FINGERPRINTS:

1. USE BLACK PRINTER'S INK.
2. DISTRIBUTE INK EVENLY ON INKING SLAB.
3. WASH AND DRY FINGERS THOROUGHLY.
4. ROLL FINGERS FROM NAIL TO NAIL, AND AVOID ALLOWING FINGERS TO SLIP.
5. BE SURE IMPRESSIONS ARE RECORDED IN CORRECT ORDER.
6. IF AN AMPUTATION OR DEFORMITY MAKES IT IMPOSSIBLE TO PRINT A FINGER, MAKE A NOTATION TO THAT EFFECT IN THE INDIVIDUAL FINGER BLOCK.
7. IF SOME PHYSICAL CONDITION MAKES IT IMPOSSIBLE TO OBTAIN PERFECT IMPRESSIONS, SUBMIT THE BEST THAT CAN BE OBTAINED WITH A MEMO STAPLED TO THE CARD EXPLAINING THE CIRCUMSTANCES.
8. EXAMINE THE COMPLETED PRINTS TO SEE IF THEY CAN BE CLASSIFIED, BEARING IN MIND THAT MOST FINGERPRINTS FALL INTO THE PATTERNS SHOWN ON THIS CARD (OTHER PATTERNS OCCUR INFREQUENTLY AND ARE NOT SHOWN HERE).

THIS CARD FOR USE BY:

1. LAW ENFORCEMENT AGENCIES IN FINGERPRINTING APPLICANTS FOR LAW ENFORCEMENT POSITIONS. *

2. OFFICIALS OF STATE AND LOCAL GOVERNMENTS FOR PURPOSES OF EMPLOYMENT, LICENSING, AND PERMITS, AS AUTHORIZED BY STATE STATUTES AND APPROVED BY THE ATTORNEY GENERAL OF THE UNITED STATES. LOCAL AND COUNTY ORDINANCES, UNLESS SPECIFICALLY BASED ON APPLICABLE STATE STATUTES DO NOT SATISFY THIS REQUIREMENT.*

3. U.S. GOVERNMENT AGENCIES AND OTHER ENTITIES REQUIRED BY FEDERAL LAW.**

4. OFFICIALS OF FEDERALLY CHARTERED OR INSURED BANKING INSTITUTIONS TO PROMOTE OR MAINTAIN THE SECURITY OF THOSE INSTITUTIONS.

INSTRUCTIONS:

*1. PRINTS MUST FIRST BE CHECKED THROUGH THE APPROPRIATE STATE IDENTIFICATION BUREAU, AND ONLY THOSE FINGERPRINTS FOR WHICH NO DISQUALIFYING RECORD HAS BEEN FOUND LOCALLY SHOULD BE SUBMITTED FOR FBI SEARCH.

2. PRIVACY ACT OF 1974 (P.L. 93-579) REQUIRES THAT FEDERAL, STATE, OR LOCAL AGENCIES INFORM INDIVIDUALS WHOSE SOCIAL SECURITY NUMBER IS REQUESTED WHETHER SUCH DISCLOSURE IS MANDATORY OR VOLUNTARY, BASIS OF AUTHORITY FOR SUCH SOLICITATION, AND USES WHICH WILL BE MADE OF IT.

**3. IDENTITY OF PRIVATE CONTRACTORS SHOULD BE SHOWN IN SPACE "EMPLOYER AND ADDRESS". THE CONTRIBUTOR IS THE NAME OF THE AGENCY SUBMITTING THE FINGERPRINT CARD TO THE FBI.

4. FBI NUMBER, IF KNOWN, SHOULD ALWAYS BE FURNISHED IN THE APPROPRIATE SPACE.

MISCELLANEOUS NO. - RECORD: OTHER ARMED FORCES NO., PASSPORT NO. (PP), ALIEN REGISTRATION NO. (AR), PORT SECURITY CARD NO. (PS), SELECTIVE SERVICE NO. (SS), VETERANS' ADMINISTRATION CLAIM NO. (VA).

LEAVE THIS SPACE BLANK

APPENDIX 25

Form I-601

UNITED STATES DEPARTMENT OF JUSTICE
IMMIGRATION AND NATURALIZATION SERVICE

FEE STAMP

APPLICATION FOR WAIVER
OF GROUNDS OF EXCLUDABILITY

(Pursuant to Section 212 (g), (h), or (i)
of the Immigration and Nationality Act)

SEE INSTRUCTIONS ON REVERSE – PLEASE TYPEWRITE OR PRINT PLAINLY WITH A BALLPOINT PEN.

NAME (Family Name in Capital Letters)	(First Name)	(Middle Name)	FILE NUMBER

PRESENT ADDRESS (Number and Street)	(City or Town)	(Country)	(Zip Code, If in U.S.)

DATE OF BIRTH	BIRTHPLACE (City or Town)	(Country)

APPLIED FOR A VISA AT THE AMERICAN CONSULATE AT	DATE OF VISA APPLICATION

WAS DECLARED INADMISSIBLE UNDER SECTION(S) (PLACE AN "X" IN THE APPROPRIATE BLOCK(S))

☐ 212(a) (1) ☐ 212(a) (3) ☐ 212(a) (6) ☐ 212(a) (9) ☐ 212(a) (10) ☐ 212(a) (12) ☐ 212(a) (19)

FOR THE FOLLOWING REASONS (List Acts, Convictions or Physical or Mental Conditions) (If alien has Tuberculosis, Active or suspected Tuberculosis the reverse of this page must be fully completed.)

PRINCIPAL RELATIVE IN THE UNITED STATES THROUGH WHOM I CLAIM ELIGIBILITY FOR WAIVER

NAME	ADDRESS	RELATIONSHIP	IMMIGRATION STATUS

I ALSO HAVE THE FOLLOWING RELATIVES WHO ARE CITIZENS OR LAWFUL PERMANENT RESIDENTS OF THE UNITED STATES:

NAME	ADDRESS	RELATIONSHIP	IMMIGRATION STATUS

WAS PREVIOUSLY IN THE UNITED STATES AT:

STREET ADDRESS	CITY AND STATE	FROM (DATE)	TO (DATE)	IMMIGRATION STATUS

SIGNATURE OF APPLICANT OR OF PERSON SUBMITTING APPLICATION IN BEHALF OF APPLICANT

SIGNATURE	RELATIONSHIP, IF ANY TO APPLICANT	DATE

SIGNATURE OF PERSON PREPARING FORM IF OTHER THAN APPLICANT

I declare that this document was prepared by me at the request of the applicant and is based on all information of which I have any knowledge.

SIGNATURE	ADDRESS	DATE

Form I-601
Rev. 1-1-76)N

RECEIVED	TRANS. IN	RET'D—TRANS. OUT	COMPLETED

APPENDIX 25, *cont.*

TO BE COMPLETED FOR APPLICANTS WITH ACTIVE
TUBERCULOSIS OR SUSPECTED TUBERCULOSIS

A. STATEMENT BY APPLICANT:
Upon admission to the United States I will go directly to the physician or health facility named in Section B; will present all X-rays used in the visa medical examination to substantiate diagnosis; will submit to such examinations, treatment, isolation, and medical regimen as may be required; and will remain under the prescribed treatment or observation, whether on inpatient or outpatient basis, until discharged.

Date	Signature of Applicant

APPLICANT'S SPONSOR IN U.S.: Arrange for medical care of the applicant and have the physician complete Section B.

B. STATEMENT BY PHYSICIAN OR HEALTH FACILITY (May be executed by a private physician, health department, other public or private health facility, or military hospital. NOTE: Upon arrival of the alien in the U.S., Form HSM 13.20 (CDC)—"Report on Alien with Tuberculosis Waiver"—will be sent to the address given below.)

I agree to supply any treatment or observation necessary for the proper management of the alien's tuberculous condition.

I agree to submit Form HSM 13.20 to the health officer* named below either (a) within 30 days of the alien's reporting for care, indicating presumptive diagnosis, test results, and plans for future care of the alien; or (b) 30 days after receiving Form HSM 13.20 if the alien has not reported.

Satisfactory financial arrangements have been made. (NOTE: This statement does not relieve alien of submitting such evidence as consul may require to establish that alien is not likely to become a public charge.)

I represent (enter X in the appropriate box and give complete name and address of facility):
1 ☐ Local Health Department Outpatient Clinic   3 ☐ Other Public or Private Health Facility
2 ☐ Military Hospital   4 ☐ Private Practice

Address (If military, enter name and address of receiving hospital)

*Military submits direct to Center for Disease Control, Atlanta, Ga. 30333	Date	Signature of Physician

APPLICANT'S SPONSOR IN U.S.: If medical care will be provided by a physician who checked box 3 or in Section B, have Section C completed by the Local or State Health Officer who has jurisdiction in the area where the applicant plans to reside in the U.S. Provide the Health Officer with the address at which the applicant plans to reside in the U.S.

C. ENDORSEMENT BY LOCAL OR STATE HEALTH OFFICER

Date	Endorsed by: Signature of Health Officer

Health Officer:
Endorsement signifies recognition of the physician or facility for the purpose of providing care for tuberculosis. If the facility or physician who signed in Section B is not in your health jurisdiction and is not familiar to you, you may wish to contact the health officer responsible for the jurisdiction of the facility physician prior to endorsing.

Enter name and address of the Local Health Department to which the "Notice of Arrival of Alien with Tuberculosis Waiver" should be sent when the alien arrives in the United States.

Local Health Department Address

APPENDIX 26

Form I-131

UNITED STATES DEPARTMENT OF JUSTICE
Immigration and Naturalization Service

Form approved.
OMB No. 43-R0052.

**APPLICATION FOR ISSUANCE OR EXTENSION
OF PERMIT TO REENTER THE UNITED STATES
as provided in section 223 of the
Immigration and Nationality Act**

Use typewriter or print in block letters with ball-point pen.

FEE STAMP

I hereby apply for (check one) ☐ issuance ☐ extension of Permit to Reenter the United States

1. YOUR NAME	FAMILY NAME (Capital Letters)	FIRST	MIDDLE	IMPORTANT: You must submit your Alien Registration Receipt Card with this application if you checked "Issuance" above. If you checked "Extension" you must submit the reentry permit you wish to have extended.
IN CARE OF	C/O			
MAILING ADDRESS IN U.S.	(No. and Street) (Apt. No.)			ALIEN REGISTRATION NUMBER A-
	(City)	(State)	(Zip Code)	

FILL IN ITEMS 2 THROUGH 6 ONLY IF APPLICATION IS FOR ISSUANCE OF REENTRY PERMIT

2. DATE OF BIRTH (Month, Day, Year)	COUNTRY OF BIRTH	COUNTRY OF CLAIMED NATIONALITY	COLOR OF EYES	COLOR OF HAIR

HEIGHT _____ FEET _____ INCHES | VISIBLE MARKS AND SCARS

3. FILL IN THE ITEMS IN THIS BLOCK AS TO *first* ARRIVAL IN UNITED STATES FOR PERMANENT RESIDENCE OR ADJUSTMENT TO PERMANENT RESIDENT STATUS.

NAME UNDER WHICH ADMITTED OR ADJUSTED	PORT OF ARRIVAL OR LOCATION OF IMMIGRATION OFFICE WHICH GRANTED ADJUSTMENT	DATE OF ARRIVAL OR DATE AS OF WHICH ADJUSTMENT OF STATUS WAS GRANTED

FILL IN REMAINING ITEMS IN THIS BLOCK ONLY IF YOU DID NOT ACQUIRE PERMANENT RESIDENCE THROUGH ADJUSTMENT.

MANNER OF FIRST ARRIVAL IN UNITED STATES FOR PERMANENT RESIDENCE (Name of Vessel, Airline, etc.)

FATHER'S NAME AT TIME OF YOUR ARRIVAL	MOTHER'S MAIDEN NAME

4. FILL IN THE ITEMS IN THIS BLOCK AS TO *last* ARRIVAL IN U.S. (Exclude any re-entry after an absence of less than six months in Canada or Mexico.)

NAME UNDER WHICH ADMITTED	PORT OF ARRIVAL	DATE OF ARRIVAL

NAME OF VESSEL, AIRLINE OR OTHER MEANS OF CONVEYANCE:

5. PORT OF *proposed* DEPARTURE FROM UNITED STATES | DATE OF *proposed* DEPARTURE | LENGTH OF INTENDED ABSENCE ABROAD

NAME OF TRANSPORTATION COMPANY | IF DEPARTURE IS TO BE BY VESSEL, GIVE NAME OF VESSEL

6. FILL IN ITEM 6 ONLY IF YOU HAVE PREVIOUSLY OBTAINED A PERMIT TO REENTER

ISSUANCE DATE OF LAST PERMIT	LOCATION OF IMMIGRATION AND NATURALIZATION OFFICE ISSUING LAST PERMIT (City and State)	MY LAST PERMIT ☐ IS ATTACHED ☐ IS NOT ATTACHED

IF THE PERMIT IS NOT ATTACHED, STATE REASON: | IF PERMIT IS ATTACHED, STATE EXPIRATION DATE

ALL APPLICANTS MUST FILL IN ITEMS 7 THROUGH 16, INCLUSIVE

7. PRESENT OCCUPATION: | NAME and ADDRESS OF EMPLOYER

SOCIAL SECURITY ACCOUNT NUMBER

8. MAILING ADDRESS ABROAD (Number and Street) | (City/Town) | (State/Province/District) | (Country)

9. REASONS FOR GOING ABROAD OR SEEKING EXTENSION (Be concise and complete):

FORM 1-131 (Rev. 10-25-79)N

OVER

RECEIVED	TRANS IN	RET'D-TRANS. OUT	COMPLETED

APPENDIX 26, *cont.*

10. I ☐ have ☐ have not engaged in business or employment outside the United States since I became a permanent resident of the United States. (If you have engaged therein, briefly describe and show periods of such employment or business activity.)

11. Since I became a permanent resident of the United States I ☐ have ☐ have not claimed nonresident alien status for Federal income purposes, either by filing no income tax return at all or by filing a return as a nonresident. (If such status was claimed by filing an income tax return as a nonresident alien, state the years for which you filed such a return, your address shown in each such return, and the location (City and State) of the Internal Revenue Service office with which you filed each such return; if you failed to file an income tax return at all because you regarded yourself as a nonresident alien for Federal income tax purposes, state the years for which you did not file a return for that reason.)

12. I ☐ do ☐ do not intend to return to the United States after my temporary visit abroad.

13. I ☐ do ☐ do not intend to retain my status as a lawful permanent resident.

14. CHECK ONE: ☐ My Alien Registration Receipt Card is attached.　☐ Application Form 1-90 for issuance of Alien Registration Receipt Card is attached.
☐ My Permit to Reenter, which I wish to have extended, is attached.

15. The Permit to Reenter, if issued or extended, and my Alien Registration Receipt Card if I submitted or applied for that card, should be forwarded to

☐ My address as shown in block # 1, on reverse.
☐ U.S. Embassy or Consulate at _____
☐ U.S. Immigration and Naturalization Office at _____
☐ Other (Specify) _____

16. If application is for **issuance** of a Permit to Reenter execute Block A of Item 17 only.
If application is for **extension** of a Permit to Reenter execute Block B of Item 17 only.
If application was completed by other than the applicant, that person must execute Item 18.

BLOCK A	BLOCK B
I do swear (affirm) that I know the contents of this application signed by me and that the statements herein are true and correct.	I certify that I know the contents of this application signed by me and that the statements herein are true and correct.
_____ (Signature of applicant) Subscribed and sworn to *(affirmed)* before me this _____ day of _____, 19_____ at _____ (SEAL) My commission expires _____ _____　_____ (Signature of officer administering oath)　(Title)	_____ (Signature of applicant) Date: _____　_____　_____ (Month)　(Day)　(Year)

17.　SIGNATURE OF PERSON PREPARING FORM, IF OTHER THAN APPLICANT

I declare that this document was prepared by me at the request of the applicant and is based on all information of which I have any knowledge.

_____　_____　_____
(Signature)　(Address)　(Date)

APPLICANT – DO NOT WRITE BELOW THIS LINE

Action with regard to Alien Registration Receipt Card	Action with regard to application for issuance or extension of Permit to Reenter
☐ I-151 or I-551 submitted by alien returned ☐ AR-103 or AR-3 submitted by alien returned ☐ New I-551 issued on basis of I-90	☐ DENIED *(See denial notice for reason(s)*. ☐ GRANTED Permit valid to _____ 　☐ Single entry　☐ Multiple entries Restriction on travel in following countries waived:

DATE OF ACTION	SERIAL NO. OF PERMIT ISSUED:	DELIVERY OF PERMIT ☐ BY MAIL ☐ TO APPLICANT PERSONALLY	INITIALS OF EMPLOYEE EFFECTING DELIVERY
OFFICE	OFFICE		DATE

APPENDIX 27

Form I-130

UNITED STATES DEPARTMENT OF JUSTICE

Immigration and Naturalization Service

Form Approved
OMB NO. 43—RO 401

PETITION TO CLASSIFY STATUS OF ALIEN RELATIVE FOR ISSUANCE OF IMMIGRANT VISA

PLEASE NOTE
YOU ARE THE PETITIONER
AND YOUR RELATIVE
IS THE
BENEFICIARY

Fee Stamp

1. Name of beneficiary (Last, in CAPS)   (First)   (Middle)

2. **Do Not Write In This Space**

3. Names, birthdates and countries of birth of beneficiary's children:

4. Other names used: (including maiden name if married)

5. Country of beneficiary's birth

6. Date of beneficiary's birth (Month, day, year)

7. My name is: (Last, in CAPS)   (First)   (Middle)

8. My phone number is:

9. Other names used: (including maiden name if married woman)

10. *Relationship of beneficiary to myself*

11. I was born: (Month)   (Day)   (Year)   in: (Town or city)   (State or Province)   (Country)

12. If you are a citizen of the United States, give the following:
   a. Citizenship was acquired: (Check one)

   ☐ *through birth in the U.S.*   ☐ *through parents*   ☐ *through naturalization*   ☐ *through marriage*

   (1) If acquired through naturalization, give name under which naturalized, number of naturalization certificate, and date and place of naturalization:

   (2) If known, my former alien registration was A _____

   (3) If acquired through parentage or marriage, have you obtained a certificate of citizenship in your own name? _____

   (a) If so, give number of certificate and date and place of issuance: _____

   (b) if not, submit evidence of citizenship in accordance with instruction 3 a (2)

13. If you are a lawful permanent resident alien of the United States, give the following:
   a. Alien Registration Number:

   A—

   b. Date, place, and means of admission for lawful permanent residence

14. Beneficiary's marital status:
   ☐ Married ☐ Widowed ☐ Divorced ☐ Single

15. Name of beneficiary's spouse, if married, and date and country of birth (Omit this item if petition is for your spouse)

16. Full address of beneficiary's spouse and children, if any (Omit this item if petition is for your spouse)

17. If this petition is for your spouse or child, give the following:

   a. Date and place of your present marriage

   b. Names of my prior spouses

   c. Names of spouse's prior spouses

18. Has this beneficiary ever been in the U.S.?
   ☐ YES   ☐ NO

19. Are beneficiary and petitioner related by adoption?
   ☐ YES   ☐ NO

—(CONTINUE WITH ITEM 20 ON REVERSE)—   *OATH OR AFFIRMATION OF PETITIONER*

I swear (affirm) that I know the contents of this petition signed by me and that the statements herein are true and correct.

Signature of petitioner (See Instruction No. 5) ....

Subscribed and sworn to (affirmed) before me this .... day of .... , 19 .... , at...

(SEAL) My commission expires ....

(SIGNATURE OF OFFICER ADMINISTERING OATH)   *(TITLE)*

SIGNATURE OF PERSON PREPARING FORM IF OTHER THAN PETITIONER

I declare that this document was prepared by me at the request of the petitioner and is based on all information of which I have any knowledge.

(SIGNATURE)   (ADDRESS)   (DATE)

FORM I—130
(Rev. 10-26-79) N

	RECEIVED	TRANS. IN	RET'D. TRANS. OUT	COMPLETED

APPENDIX 27, *cont.*

TO THE SECRETARY OF STATE:

The petition was filed on ....

The petition is approved for status under section:

SPOUSE,
☐ 201 (b) CHILD   ☐ 203 (a) (2)   DATE OF ACTION

☐ 201 (b) PARENT   ☐ 203 (a) (4)   DD

☐ 203 (a) (1)   ☐ 203 (a) (5)   DISTRICT

REMARKS
☐ PERSONAL INTERVIEW CONDUCTED
☐ DOCUMENT CHECK ONLY
☐ FIELD INVESTIGATION COMPLETED
☐ APPROVAL PREVIOUSLY FORWARDED

REMARKS *(Continued)*

(PETITIONER IS NOT TO WRITE ABOVE THIS LINE)

20. Check the appropriate box below and furnish the information required for the box checked.

☐ Beneficiary will apply for a visa abroad at the American Consulate in _____ *(CITY IN FOREIGN COUNTRY) (FOREIGN COUNTRY)*

☐ Beneficiary is in the United States and will apply for adjustment of status to that of a lawful permanent resident in the office of the Immigration and Naturalization Service at _____ *(CITY)* _____ *(STATE)*

If the application for adjustment of status is denied, the beneficiary will apply for a visa abroad at the American Consulate in

_____ *(CITY IN FOREIGN COUNTRY)* _____ *(FOREIGN COUNTRY)*

21. My residence in the United States is: *(C/O, if appropriate) (Apt. No.) (Number and Street) (Town or city) (State) (ZIP Code)*

22. My address abroad *(if any)* is: *(Number and street) (Town or city) (Province) (Country)*

23. Last address at which I and my spouse resided together *(Town or city) (State or Province) (Country) (Apt. No.) (Number and street)* From *(Month) (Year)* To *(Month) (Year)*

24. Address in the United States where beneficiary will reside *(City) (State)*

25. Address at which beneficiary is presently residing *(Apt. No.) (Number and street) (Town or city) (Province or State) (ZIP Code)*

26. (a) Beneficiary's address abroad *(if any)* is: *(Number and Street) (Town or City) (Province) (Country)*

  (b) If the beneficiary's native alphabet is other than Roman letters, write his/her name and address in the native alphabet: *(Name) (Number and Street) (Town or City) (Province) (Country)*

27. If this petition is for a child, *(a)*. is the child married? _____ *(b)*. is the child your adopted child? _____ if so, give the names, dates, and places of birth of all other children adopted by you. If none, so state.

28. If this petition is for a brother or sister, are both your parents the same as the alien's parents? _____ if not, submit a separate statement giving full details as to parentage, dates of marriage of parents, and the number of previous marriages of each parent.

29. If separate petitions are also being submitted for other relatives, give names of each and relationship to petitioner.

30. Have you ever filed a petition for this alien before? _____ If so, give place and date of filing and result.

31. If beneficiary is in the United States, give the following information concerning beneficiary:

  (a) Last arrived in U.S. as _____ *(Visitor, student, exchange alien, crewman, stowaway, etc.)* on *(Month) (Day) (Year)*   (b) Date beneficiary's stay expired or will expire as shown on his Form I-94 or I-95. *(Month) (Day) (Year)*   (c) Beneficiary's File number if any A-

  (d) Name and address of present employer   (e) Date alien began this employme

APPENDIX 28

Form I-140

FORM I-140
(Rev. 6-20-80) N

UNITED STATES DEPARTMENT OF JUSTICE

IMMIGRATION AND NATURALIZATION SERVICE

Form approved
OMB No. 43-R0418

PETITION TO CLASSIFY PREFERENCE STATUS OF ALIEN ON BASIS OF PROFESSION OR OCCUPATION

DATE RECEIVED	FEE STAMP

TO THE SECRETARY OF STATE

Petition was filed on _____

Beneficiary's file number: A _____

Petition is approved for status under section ☐ 203(a)(3).   ☐ 203(a)(6)

☐ Sec. 212(a)(14) certification attached.

☐ Blanket Sec. 212(a)(14) certification issued.

DATE OF ACTION	
DD	
DISTRICT	

REMARKS

PETITIONER IS NOT TO WRITE ABOVE THIS LINE

Read this form and the attached instructions carefully before filling in petition

Petition is hereby made to classify the status of the alien beneficiary named herein for issuance of an immigrant visa as ("X" one)

☐ A THIRD PREFERENCE IMMIGRANT — An alien who is a member of the professions, or who because of his exceptional ability in the sciences or arts will substantially benefit prospectively the national economy, cultural interests or welfare of the United States, and whose services are sought by an employer. (Sec. 203(a)(3), Immigration and Nationality Act, as amended.)

☐ A SIXTH PREFERENCE IMMIGRANT — An alien who is capable of performing skilled or unskilled labor, not of a temporary or seasonal nature, for which a shortage of employable and willing persons exists in the United States. (Sec. 203 (a) (6), Immigration and Nationality Act, as amended.)

(If you need more space to answer fully any questions on this form, use a separate sheet, identify each answer with the number of the corresponding question and sign and date each sheet.)

PART I— INFORMATION CONCERNING ALIEN BENEFICIARY

1. NAME (Last, in CAPS) (First) (Middle)	2. ALIEN REGISTRATION NO. (If any)	3. PROFESSION OR OCCUPATION
4. OTHER NAMES USED (Married woman give maiden name)	5. DO NOT WRITE IN THIS SPACE	6. DOES BENEFICIARY INTEND TO ENGAGE IN HIS/HER PROFESSION OR OCCUPATION IN THE UNITED STATES? ☐ YES ☐ NO. IF "NO," EXPLAIN.
7. PLACE OF BIRTH (Country)	8. DATE OF BIRTH (Month, day, year)	
9. NAME OF PETITIONER (Full name of organization; if petitioner is an individual give full name with last in capital letters)		10. NUMBER OF YEARS OF BENEFICIARY S EXPERIENCE (If none explain why.)
11. CITY AND STATE IN THE UNITED STATES WHERE ALIEN INTENDS TO RESIDE (City) (State)		
12. BENEFICIARY'S PRESENT ADDRESS (Number and street) (City or town) (State or province) (Country) (ZIP Code, if in U.S.)		

13. TO YOUR KNOWLEDGE, HAS A VISA PETITION EVER BEEN FILED BY OR ON BEHALF OF THIS BENEFICIARY BASED ON HIS/HER PROFESSION OR OCCUPATION? ☐ Yes ☐ No. If "Yes," give name of each petitioner and date and place of filing.

14. IF BENEFICIARY IS NOW IN THE U.S. (a) HE/SHE LAST ARRIVED ON _____

AS A _____   (Month) (Day) (Year)

(Visitor, student, exchange alien, temporary worker, crewman, stowaway, etc.) (b) SHOW DATE BENEFICIARY'S STAY EXPIRED OR W'LL EXPIRE AS SHOWN ON FORM I— 94 OR I— 95 (Show latest date)

15. BENEFICIARY'S SPOUSE (If Unmarried, State Unmarried)	NAME (Last name) (First name) (Middle name)			(Maiden name, if married woman)
	COUNTRY OF BIRTH	DATE OF BIRTH	PRESENT ADDRESS (No. and Street) (City or town) (State or Province) (Country)	

16. BENEFICIARY'S CHILDREN (If None State None)	NAME (Show M or S for married or single)	M.S.	BIRTHDATE	COUNTRY OF BIRTH	ADDRESS

RECEIVED	TRANS. IN	RET'D. TRANS OUT	COMPLETED

APPENDIX 28, *cont.*

17. "X" THE APPROPRIATE BOX BELOW AND FURNISH THE INFORMATION REQUIRED FOR THE BOX MARKED.

☐ Alien will apply for a visa abroad at the American Consulate in _____ (City in foreign country) _____ (Foreign country)

☐ Alien is in the United States and will apply for adjustment of status to that of a lawful permanent resident in the office of the immigration and Naturalization Service at _____ (City) _____ (State) If the application for adjustment of status is denied

the alien will apply for a visa abroad at the American Consulate in _____ (City in foreign country) _____ (Foreign country)

PART II—INFORMATION CONCERNING EMPLOYER AND POSITION

18. NAME OF PETITIONER (Full name of organization; if petitioner is an individual give full name with last in capital letters)

19. ADDRESS (Number and street) | (Town or city) | (State) | (ZIP code)

20. PETITIONER IS (X one) ☐ U.S. CITIZEN ☐ PERMANENT RESIDENT ALIEN ("A" NUMBER _____) ☐ NONIMMIGRANT ☐ ORGANIZATION

21. NET ANNUAL INCOME

22. WILL BENEFICIARY BE EMPLOYED AT THE ABOVE ADDRESS? WHERE THE ALIEN WILL WORK. ☐ YES ☐ NO IF "NO," GIVE ADDRESS

23. DO YOU DESIRE AND INTEND TO EMPLOY THE BENEFICIARY ☐ YES ☐ NO.

24. HAVE YOU EVER FILED A VISA PETITION FOR AN ALIEN BASED ON PROFESSION OR OCCUPATION? ☐ YES ☐ NO. IF "YES," HOW MANY SUCH PETITIONS HAVE YOU FILED?

25. ARE SEPARATE PETITIONS BEING SUBMITTED AT THIS TIME FOR OTHER ALIENS? ☐ YES ☐ NO. IF "YES," GIVE NAME OF EACH ALIEN.

26. THE FOLLOWING DOCUMENTS ARE SUBMITTED WITH THIS PETITION AND ARE MADE A PART THEREOF.

PART III—OATH OR AFFIRMATION OF PETITIONER OR AUTHORIZED REPRESENTATIVE

27. This petition was prepared by: ("X" one) ☐ the petitioner ☐ another person.
If petition was prepared by another person, Item 29 below must also be completed.
The petition may be subscribed and sworn to or affirmed only by the following persons:
In third preference cases — by the beneficiary or by the person filing the petition on the beneficiary's behalf. If the petition is being filed by a person on behalf of the alien beneficiary, Item 28 below must be completed by that person.
In sixth preference cases — by the employer who desires and intends to employ the beneficiary. If the employer is an organization, the petition must be signed, subscribed and sworn to or affirmed by a high level officer or employee of the organization.

I swear (affirm) that I have examined the contents on this petition and the accompanying documents and that the statements in this petition and the accompanying documents are true and correct to the best of my information and belief.

If petitioner is an organization, print full name and title of authorized official who is signing petition in behalf of organization:

SIGNATURE _____ (Petitioner's full, true, and correct name)

Name and Title _____

Subscribed and sworn to (affirmed) before me this _____ day of _____ 19___

at _____

[SEAL] . My commission expires _____ (Signature of officer administering oath) (Title)

28. DECLARATION OF PERSON FILING PETITION FOR THIRD PREFERENCE ON BEHALF OF ALIEN BENEFICIARY

I declare that I have been requested and authorized by the alien beneficiary to file this petition on his (her) behalf.

(Signature) (Address—Number, Street, City, State and ZIP Code) (Date)

29. SIGNATURE OF PERSON PREPARING FORM, IF OTHER THAN PETITIONER

I declare that this document was prepared by me at the request of the petitioner and is based on all information of which I have any knowledge.

(Signature) (Address—Number, Street, City, State and ZIP Code) (Date)

TO PETITIONER: DO NOT FILL IN THIS BLOCK — FOR USE OF IMMIGRATION OFFICER

a. Corrections numbered ( ) to ( ) were made by me or at my request. _____ (Date) _____ (City)

(Signature of petitioner or authorized member of petitioner's organization) (Title)

b. The person whose signature appears immediately above was interviewed under oath and affirmed all allegations contained herein.

(Date) (City) (Signature and Title)

APPENDIX 29

Schedule B: List of Occupations

Assemblers
Attendants, Parking Lot
Attendants (Service Workers such as Personal Service Attendants and Amusement and Recreation Service Attendants)
Automobile Service Station Attendants
Bartenders
Bookkeepers
Caretakers
Cashiers
Charworkers and Cleaners
Chauffeurs and Taxicab Drivers
Cleaners, Hotel and Motel
Clerks, General
Clerks, Hotel
Clerks and Checkers, Grocery Stores
Clerk-Typists
Cooks, Short-Order
Counter and Fountain Workers
Dining-Room Attendants
Electric-Truck Operators
Elevator Operators
Floorworkers
Groundskeepers
Guards
Helpers (for Any Industry)

Hotel Cleaners
Household Domestic Service Workers
Housekeepers
Janitors
Key Punch Operators
Kitchen Workers
Laborers, Common
Laborers, Farm
Laborers, Mine
Loopers and Toppers
Material Handlers
Nurses' Aides and Orderlies
Packers, Markers, Bottlers, and Workers in Related Industries
Porters
Receptionists
Sailors and Deck Hands
Sales Clerks, General
Sewing Machine Operators and Handstitchers
Stock Room and Warehouse Workers
Streetcar and Bus Conductors
Telephone Operators
Truck Drivers and Tractor Drivers
Typists, Lesser-Skilled
Ushers, Recreation and Amusement
Yard Workers

APPENDIX 30

Form I-590

<table>
<tr>
<td>

REGISTRATION FOR CLASSIFICATION AS REFUGEE
Section 207
Immigration and Nationality Act
</td>
<td align="center">

UNITED STATES DEPARTMENT OF JUSTICE
IMMIGRATION AND NATURALIZATION SERVICE
</td>
<td>

Form Approved
Budget Bureau No. 43-R0408

File No.

A
</td>
</tr>
</table>

REGISTRANT TO FURNISH THE FOLLOWING INFORMATION (READ INSTRUCTIONS ON REVERSE)

TYPE OR PRINT

1. My name is: First   Middle   Last

2. My present address is:

3. I was born on: (month)(day)(year)	Place of birth (city or town)	(Province)	(Country)	My present nationality is:

4. Height	Weight	Eyes	Hair	Complexion	Marks or Scars

5. I fled or was displaced from (Name of country)   On or about   (month)   (day)   (year)

6. Reasons: (State in detail)

7. My present immigration status in _____ is: _____
(Country in which residing)

The evidence of my immigration status in the country in which I am residing is:

(Describe)

8. My spouse's name is:	9. (His)(Her) present address is:	10. Spouse's nationality is:

11. My spouse ☐ will   ☐ will not   accompany me to the United States

12. Name of child(ren)	Date of birth	Place of birth	Present address

Place a mark (X) in front of name of each child who will accompany you to the United States

13. Schooling or Education

Name and location of school	Type	Dates attended	Title of Degree or Diploma

14. Military Service

Country	Branch and Organization	Dates	Serial No.	Rank Attained

Form I-590 (Rev. 5-1-80) N

APPENDIX 30, *cont.*

15. I list below all organizations, societies, clubs, and associations, past or present, in which I have held membership, and the periods and places of such membership. (If you have never been a member of any organization, state "None") _____

_____

16. I ☐ have ☐ have not been charged with a violation of law. (If you have ever been charged with a violation of law, give date and place and nature of each charge and the final result) _____

17. I ☐ have ☐ have not been in the United States. (If you have ever been in the United States, show the dates of entry and departure and the purpose of your entry. Visitor, permanent resident, student, seaman, etc.)

_____ File or Alien Registration number _____

18. I have the following close relatives in the United States:

| Names | Relationship | Present address |

19. I am being sponsored by (Give name and address of United States Sponsor)

| Date | Signature of registrant |

DO NOT WRITE BELOW THIS LINE

I, _____, do swear (affirm) that I know the contents of this registration subscribed by me including the attached documents, that the same are true to the best of my knowledge, and that corrections, numbered ( ) to ( ), were made by me or at my request, and that this registration was signed by me with my full, true name:

_____
(Complete and true signature of registrant)

Subscribed and sworn to before me by the above-named registrant at _____ on _____
(month)(day)(year)

_____
(Signature and title of officer)

INTERVIEW	APPROVED	
DATE	DATE	
AT		
Immigration Officer	Officer in Charge	

INSTRUCTIONS

This form should be executed, signed and submitted to the Officer-in-Charge of the nearest overseas office of the United States Immigration and Naturalization Service. When your name has been reached as a registrant you will be furnished additional instructions.

1. REGISTRATION - A separate Registration Form must be executed by each registrant and submitted in one copy. A Registration Form in behalf of a child under 14 years of age shall be executed by the parent or guardian.

2. ASSURANCES - Assurance Form I–591 executed by a United States sponsor will be required before your refugee status may be authorized but need not be submitted at this time.

APPENDIX 31

Form I-589

U.S. Department of Justice
Immigration and Naturalization Service

Form Approve
OMB No. 111?

REQUEST FOR ASYLUM IN THE UNITED STATES

INS Office:

Date:

1. Family Name	First	Middle Name	2. A number (if any or known)

All other names used at any time (include maiden name if married)

3. Sex
☐ Male
☐ Female

4. Marital status
☐ Single ☐ Divor
☐ Married ☐ Widov

I was born: (Month) (Day) (Year) in (Town or City) (State or Province) (Country)

Nationality — at birth | At present | Other nationalities

5. If stateless, how did you become stateless?

6. Ethnic group	7. Religion	8. Languages spoken

9. Address in United States (In care of, C/O, if appropriate)
(Number and street) (Apt. No.) (City or town) (State) (Zip Code)

10. Telephone number
(include area code)

11. Address abroad prior to coming to the United States
(Number and street) (City) (Province) (Country)

12. My last arrival in the U.S. occurred on: (Mo/Day/Yr)

As a ☐ Visitor ☐ Student ☐ Stowaway ☐ Crewman
☐ Other (Specify)

At the port of (City/State)

Means of arrival (Name of vessel or airline and flight number, etc.)

I ☐ was ☐ was not inspected

Date authorized stay expires (Mo/Day/Yr)

13. My nonimmigrant visa number is _____, it was issued by the U.S. Consul on_____
(If none, state "none") (Mo/Day/Yr)
at_____
(City, County)

14. Name and location of schools attended	Type of school	From Mo/Yr	To Mo/Yr	Highest grade completed	Title of degree or certification

15. What specific skills do you have?

16. Social Security No. (if any)

17. Name of husband or wife (wife's maiden name)

18. My husband or wife resides ☐ with me ☐ apart from me (if apart, explain why)

Address (Apt. No.) (No. and street) (Town or city) (Province or state) (Country)

Form I-589
(Rev. 3-1-81) N

(OVER)

RECEIVED	TRANS. IN	RET'D TRANS. OUT	COMPLE

APPENDIX 31, *cont.*

19. If in the U.S. is your spouse included in your request for asylum? ☐ Yes ☐ No (If not, explain why)

20. If in the U.S. is spouse making separate application for asylum? ☐ Yes ☐ No (If not, explain why)

21. If in the U.S. are children included in your request for asylum? ☐ Yes ☐ No (If not, explain why)

22. I have ——— sons or daughters as follows: (Complete all columns as to each son or daughter. If living with you state "with me" in last column; otherwise give city and state or foreign country of son's or daughter's residence).

Name	Sex	Place of birth	Date of birth	Now living at

23. Relatives in U.S. other than immediate family

Name	Address	Relationship	Immigration status

24. Other relatives who are refugees but outside the U.S.

Name	Relationship	Country where presently located

25. List all travel or identity documents such as national passport, refugee convention travel document or national identity card

Document type	Document number	Issuing country or authority	Date of issue	Date of expiration	Cost	Obtained by whom

Why did you obtain a U.S. visa?

If you did not apply for a U.S. visa, explain why not?

Date of departure from your country of nationality (Mo/Day/Yr)	29. Was exit permission required to leave your country? ☐ Yes ☐ No (If so, did you obtain exit permission ☐ Yes ☐ No (If not, explain why)

(2)

APPENDIX 31, *cont.*

30. Are you entitled to return to country of issuance of your passport ☐ Yes ☐ No Travel document ☐ Yes ☐ No Or other document ☐ Yes ☐ No (If not, explain why)

31. What do you think would happen to you if you returned? (Explain)

32. When you left your home country, to what country did you intend to go?

33. Would you return to your home country? ☐ Yes ☐ No (Explain)

34. Have you or any member of your immediate family ever belonged to any organization in your home country? ☐ Yes ☐ No. (If yes, provide the following information relating to each organization: Name of organization, dates of membership or affiliation, purpose of the organization, what, if any, were your official duties or responsibilities, and are you still an active member. (If not, explain)

35. Have you taken any action that you believe will result in persecution in your home country? ☐ Yes ☐ No (If yes, explain)

36. Have you ever been ☐ detained ☐ interrogated ☐ convicted and sentenced ☐ imprisoned in any country? ☐ Yes ☐ No (If yes, specify for each instance: what occurred and the circumstances, dates, location, duration of the detention or imprisonment, reason for the detention or conviction, what formal charges were placed against you, reason for the release, names and addresses of persons who could verify these statements. Attach documents referring to these incidents, if any).

37. If you base your claim for asylum on current conditions in your country, do these conditions affect your freedom more than the rest of that country's population? ☐ Yes ☐ No (If yes, explain)

38. Have you, or any member of your immediate family, ever been mistreated by the authorities of your home country/country of nationality ☐ Yes ☐ No. If yes, was mistreatment because of ☐ Race ☐ Religion ☐ Nationality ☐ Political opinion or ☐ Membership of a particular social group? Specify for each instance; what occurred and the circumstances, date, exact location, who took such action against you and what was his/her position in the government, reason why the incident occurred, names and addresses of people who witnessed these actions and who could verify these statements. Attach documents referring to these incidents.

39. After leaving your home country, have you traveled through (other than in transit) or resided in any other country before entering the U.S.? ☐ Yes ☐ No (If yes, identify each country, length of stay, purpose of stay, address, and reason for leaving, and whether you are entitled to return to that country for residence purposes.

40. Why did you continue traveling to the U.S.?

41. Did you apply for asylum in any other country? ☐ Yes—Give details ☐ No—Explain why not

(3)

APPENDIX 31, *cont.*

42. Have you been recognized as a refugee by another country or by the United Nations High Commissioner for Refugees? ☐ Yes ☐ No (If yes, where and when)

43. Are you registered with a consulate or any other authority of your home country abroad? ☐ Yes—Give details ☐ No—Explain why not

44. Is there any additional information not covered by the above questions? (If yes, explain)

45. Under penalties of perjury, I declare that the above and all accompanying documents are true and correct to the best of my knowledge and belief.

(Signature of Applicant)

(Date)

(Interviewing Officer)

ACTION BY ADJUDICATING OFFICER

(Date of Interview)

☐ GRANTED   ☐ DENIED

(Adjudicating Officer)

(Date)

Advisory opinion requested ☐

(Date)

(4)

APPENDIX 31, *cont.*

U.S. Department of Justice
Immigration and Naturalization Service

REQUEST FOR ASYLUM IN THE UNITED STATES

INSTRUCTIONS
READ ALL INSTRUCTIONS CAREFULLY BEFORE COMPLETING THIS FORM

1. General:

Use typewriter or print legibly in block letters with ballpoint pen.

DO NOT LEAVE ANY QUESTIONS UNANSWERED. Where appropriate insert "none" or "not applicable". If you need more space to fully answer any question, use a separate sheet of paper this size and identify each answer with the number of the corresponding question. One form may include an entire family (husband, wife, and children if they are also applying for asylum) except children over age 21 or married, who must file a separate form.

Each applicant age 14 or older must complete the Biographic Information Form G-325A and Fingerprint Chart FD-258.

2. SUBMISSION OF FORM:

Be sure to sign, mail or take this form to the Immigration and Naturalization Service having jurisdiction over your place of residence.

3. FINGERPRINTS:

Fingerprint cards with instructions for their completion are available at the office of the Immigration and Naturalization Service where you intend to file your application. You may have your fingerprints recorded on Form FD-258 at an office of the Immigration and Naturalization Service, other Law Enforcement Offices, Immigration and Naturalization Service Outreach Centers, Charitable and Voluntary Agencies. The card must be signed by you in the presence of the individual taking your prints, who must then sign his name and enter the date in the spaces provided. It is important to furnish all the information called for on the card.

4. PASSPORT INFORMATION:

You will be notified to appear for an interview with an Immigration Officer within 45 days after your form is received. You must bring your passport with you to this interview. If other members of your family are included in your form, they must also appear for the interview and bring their passports.

An immigration officer will interview you regarding asylum and make an evaluation of the propriety of the claim.

You may remain in the United States until a final decision is made on your case (or you are notified otherwise by this Service).

5. UNITED NATIONS:

You may, if you wish, forward a copy of your form and other supporting documents to the: Regional Representative of the United Nations, High Commissioner for Refugees, United Nations, 1785 Massachusetts Ave. N.W. Washington, D.C. 20036.

6. SUPPORTING DOCUMENTS:

Background materials, such as newspaper articles, affidavits of witnesses or experts, periodicals, journals, books, photographs, official documents, your own statements, etc., must include explanations from you of their relevance to your personal case and situation. Give full citation of your sources, dates, pages, etc.

The burden of proof is upon you to establish that you have a wellfounded fear of persecution on account of your race, religion, nationality, membership in a particular social group or political opinion, and for this reason you are unwilling or unable to return to your country of last residence. To persecute is defined as: "to pursue; to harass in a manner designed to injure, grieve or afflict; to oppress; specifically, to cause to suffer or put to death because of belief".

Answer all questions on this form as to "when", "where", "how", "who", and "why" relating to your claim of persecution.

Attach as many sheets and explanations as necessary to fully explain the basis of your claim.

7. TRANSLATION:

Any document in a foreign language must be accompanied by a translation in English. The translator must certify that he or she is competent to translate and that the translation is accurate.

FORM-I-589
(Rev. 3-1-81) N   (Tear off this instruction sheet before submitting application)

APPENDIX 31, *cont.*

8. WORK AUTHORIZATION:

You may request permission to work while your asylum form is pending. Submit a written statement with this form explaining your reasons and include the original Form I-94 ARRIVAL AND DEPARTURE RECORD of each person seeking work.

Generally, work authorization, if granted, will be valid during the pendency of the form.

9. PENALTY:

Title 18, United States Code, section 1546, provides, "whoever knowingly makes under oath any false statement with respect to a material fact in any application, affidavit, or other document required by the immigration laws or regulations prescribed thereunder, or knowingly presents any such application, affidavit or other document containing any such false statement, shall be fined not more than $2,000 or imprisoned not more than 5 years or both."

APPENDIX 32

Form N-400

UNITED STATES DEPARTMENT OF JUSTICE
IMMIGRATION AND NATURALIZATION SERVICE

Form Approved
OMB NO. 43-R0079

FEE STAMP

APPLICATION TO FILE PETITION FOR NATURALIZATION

Mail or take to:

IMMIGRATION AND NATURALIZATION SERVICE

ALIEN REGISTRATION
(Show the exact spelling of your name as it appears on your alien registration receipt card, and the number of your card. If you did not register, so state.)

(See INSTRUCTIONS. BE SURE YOU UNDERSTAND EACH QUESTION BEFORE YOU ANSWER IT. PLEASE PRINT OR TYPE.)

Name ....

No. ....

Section of Law ....
(Leave Blank)

Date: ....

(1) My full true and correct name is ....
(Full true name without abbreviations)

(2) I now live at ....
(Number and street,)

....
(City, county, state, zip code)

(3) I was born on .... in ....
(Month) (Day) (Year)   (City or town)   (County, province, or state)   (Country)

(4) I request that my name be changed to ....

(5) Other names I have used are: ....
(Include maiden name)   Sex: ☐ Male   ☐ Female

(6) Was your father or mother ever a United States citizen? .... ☐ Yes ☐ No
(If "Yes", explain fully)

(7) Can you read and write English? .... ☐ Yes ☐ No

(8) Can you speak English? .... ☐ Yes ☐ No

(9) Can you sign your name in English? .... ☐ Yes ☐ No

(10) My lawful admission for permanent residence was on .... under the name of
(Month)   (Day)   (Year)
.... at ....
(City)   (State)

(11) Since that date I have resided continuously in the United States and continuously in the State of .... where I now live since .... During the last five years I have been physically present in the United States for a total of .... months

(12) Do you intend to reside permanently in the United States? ☐ Yes ☐ No If "No," explain:

(13) In what places in the United States have you lived during the last 5 years? List present address FIRST.

From ·	To ·	STREET ADDRESS	CITY AND STATE
(a) ...., 19......	PRESENT TIME		
(b) ...., 19......	.........., 19......		
(c) ...., 19......	.........., 19......		
(d) ...., 19......	.........., 19......		

(14) (a) Have you been out of the United States since your lawful admission as a permanent resident? .... ☐ Yes ☐ No
If "Yes" fill in the following information for every absence of *less than 6 months*, no matter how short it was.

DATE DEPARTED	DATE RETURNED	NAME OF SHIP, OR OF AIRLINE, RAILROAD COMPANY, BUS COMPANY, OR OTHER MEANS USED TO RETURN TO THE UNITED STATES	PLACE OR PORT OF ENTRY THROUGH WHICH YOU RETURNED TO THE UNITED STATES

(b) Since your lawful admission, have you been out of the United States for a period of *6 months or longer?* .... ☐ Yes ☐ No
If "No", state "None"; If "Yes", fill in following information for every absence of more than 6 months.

DATE DEPARTED	DATE RETURNED	NAME OF SHIP OR OF AIRLINE, RAILROAD COMPANY, BUS COMPANY, OR OTHER MEANS USED TO RETURN TO THE UNITED STATES	PLACE OR PORT OF ENTRY THROUGH WHICH YOU RETURNED TO THE UNITED STATES

Form N–400 (Rev. 11–26–79)N

(OVE

(1)

APPENDIX 32, *cont.*

(2)

(15) The law provides that you may not be regarded as qualified for naturalization, if you knowingly committed certain offenses or crimes, even though you may not have been arrested. Have you ever, in or outside the United States:

   (*a*) knowingly committed any crime for which you have not been arrested?..☐ Yes ☐ No

   (*b*) been arrested, cited, charged, indicted, convicted, fined or imprisoned for breaking or violating any law or ordinance, including traffic regulations?..☐ Yes ☐ No

   If you answer "Yes" to (*a*) or (*b*), give the following information as to each incident.

WHEN	WHERE	(City)	(State)	(Country)	NATURE OF OFFENSE	OUTCOME OF CASE, IF ANY
(*a*)						
(*b*)						
(*c*)						
(*d*)						
(*e*)						

(16) List your present and past membership in or affiliation with every organization, association, fund, foundation, party, club, society or similar group in the United States or in any other country or place, and your foreign military service. (If none, write "None.")

(*a*) ....

(*b*) ...., 19........ to 19........

(*c*) ...., 19........ to 19........

(*d*) ...., 19........ to 19........

(*e*) ...., 19........ to 19........

(*f*) ...., 19........ to 19........

(*g*) ...., 19........ to 19........

(17) (*a*) Are you now, or have you ever, in the United States or in any other place, been a member of, or in any other way connected or associated with the Communist Party? (If "Yes", attach full explanation) ....☐ Yes ☐ No

   (*b*) Have you ever knowingly aided or supported the Communist Party directly, or indirectly through another organization, group or person? (If "Yes", attach full explanation) ....☐ Yes ☐ No

   (*c*) Do you now or have you ever advocated, taught, believed in, or knowingly supported or furthered the interests of Communism? (If "Yes", attach full explanation) ....☐ Yes ☐ No

(18) Have you borne any hereditary title or have you been of any order of nobility in any foreign state? ....☐ Yes ☐ No

(19) **Have you ever been declared legally incompetent or have you ever been confined as a patient in a mental institution?** ·······☐ Yes ☐ No

(20) Are deportation proceedings pending against you, or have you ever been deported or ordered deported, or have you ever applied for suspension of deportation? ....☐ Yes ☐ No

(21) (*a*) My last Federal income tax return was filed........................... (year) Do you owe any Federal taxes? ....☐ Yes ☐ No

   (*b*) Since becoming a permanent resident of the United States, have you:

     —filed an income tax return as a nonresident? ....☐ Yes ☐ No

     —failed to file an income tax return because you regarded yourself as a nonresident? ....☐ Yes ☐ No

   (If you answer "Yes" to (*a*) or (*b*) explain fully.)

(22) Have you ever claimed in writing, or in any other way, to be a United States citizen? ....☐ Yes ☐ No

(23) (*a*) Have you ever deserted from the military, air, or naval forces of the United States? ....☐ Yes ☐ No

   (*b*) If male, have you ever left the United States to avoid being drafted into the Armed Forces of the United States? .....☐ Yes ☐ No

(24) The law provides that you may not be regarded as qualified for naturalization if, at *any* time during the period for which you are required to prove good moral character, you have been a habitual drunkard; committed adultery; advocated or practiced polygamy; have been a prostitute or procured anyone for prostitution; have knowingly and for gain helped any alien to enter the United States illegally; have been an illicit trafficker in narcotic drugs or marijuana; have received your income mostly from illegal gambling, or have given false testimony for the purpose of obtaining any benefits under this Act. Have you ever, *anywhere*, been such a person or committed any of these acts? (If you answer yes to any of these, attach full explanation.) ....☐ Yes ☐ No

(25) Do you believe in the Constitution and form of government of the United States? ....☐ Yes ☐ No

(26) Are you willing to take the full oath of allegiance to the United States? (See Instructions) ....☐ Yes ☐ No

(27) If the law requires it, are you willing:

   (*a*) to bear arms on behalf of the United States? (If "No", attach full explanation) ....☐ Yes ☐ No

   (*b*) to perform noncombatant services in the Armed Forces of the United States? (If "No", attach full explanation) ....☐ Yes ☐ No

   (*c*) to perform work of national importance under civilian direction? (If "No", attach full explanation) ....☐ Yes ☐ No

(28) (*a*) If male, did you ever register under United States Selective Service laws or draft laws? ....☐ Yes ☐ No

   If "Yes" give date............; Selective Service No....................; Local Board No..................; Present classification............

   (*b*) Did you ever apply for exemption from military service because of alienage, conscientious objections, or other reasons? ☐ Yes ☐ No

   If "Yes," explain fully...

(29) If serving or ever served in the Armed Forces of the United States, give branch...;

from............................, 19........ to ...., 19........, and from...................... 19........ to .... 19........;

☐ inducted or ☐ enlisted at..; Service No................................

type of discharge...; ....; rank at discharge....................................;

       (Honorable, Dishonorable, etc.)

reason for discharge...

                 (alienage, conscientious objector, other)

☐ Reserve or ☐ National Guard from...19........ to.....................

APPENDIX 32, *cont.*

(30) My occupation is...

List the names, addresses, and occupations (or types of business) of your employers during the last 5 years? (If none, write "None.")

List present employment FIRST.

From -	To-	EMPLOYER'S NAME	ADDRESS	OCCUPATION OR TYPE OF BUSINESS
(*a*) ...., 19........	PRESENT TIME..........			
(*b*) ...., 19........	..............., 19........			
(*c*) ...., 19........	..............., 19........			
(*d*) ...., 19........	..............., 19........			

(31) **Complete this block if you are or have been married.**

I am.. The first name of my husband or wife is (was)............................
    (Single, married, divorced, widowed)

We were married on............................ at............................ He or she was born at............................

.... on............................ He or she entered the United States at (place)............................

.... on (date)............................ for permanent residence and now resides ☐ with me

☐ apart from me at ....
    (Show full address if not living with you.)

He or she was naturalized on............................ at............................; Certificate No............................

or became a citizen by .... His or her alien Registration No. is............................

(32) How many times have you been married?............ How many times has your husband or wife been married?............ If either of you has been married more than once, fill in the following information for each previous marriage.

DATE MARRIED	DATE MARRIAGE ENDED	NAME OF PERSON TO WHOM MARRIED	SEX	*(Check One)* PERSON MARRIED WAS CITIZEN ☐ ALIEN ☐	HOW MARRIAGE ENDED
(*a*)				☐........ ☐	
(*b*)				☐........ ☐	
(*c*)				☐........ ☐	
(*d*)				☐........ ☐	

(33) I have............children: (Complete columns (a) to (h) as to each child. If child lives with you, state "with me" in column (h), other-
  (Number)   wise give city and State of child's residence.)

(a) Given Names	(b) Sex	(c) Place Born (Country)	(d) Date Born	(e) Date of Entry	(f) Port of Entry	(g) Alien Registration No.	(h) Now Living at -

(34) **READ INSTRUCTION NO. 6 BEFORE ANSWERING QUESTION (36)**

I............................want certificates of citizenship for those of my children who are in the U.S. and are under age 18 years that are named below
  (Do) (Do Not)

(Enclose $15 for each child for whom you want certificates, otherwise, send no money with this application.)

....
    (Write names of children under age 18 years and who are in the U.S. for whom you want certificates)

If present spouse is not the parent of the children named above, give parent's name, date and place of naturalization, and number of marriage

APPENDIX 33

Form N-470

UNITED STATES DEPARTMENT OF JUSTICE
Immigration and Naturalization Service

Form approved.
OMB No. 43–R0098

**APPLICATION TO PRESERVE RESIDENCE
FOR NATURALIZATION PURPOSES**
(Under Section 316(b) or 317, Immigration and Nationality Act)

(Please read instructions on reverse)

Take or mail to:

IMMIGRATION AND NATURALIZATION SERVICE

Fee Stamp

Alien Registration No.

1. My full true name is ....

2. My home address in the United States is ....
(Number and street)

.... (City or town) .... (State) .... (ZIP code)

My foreign address (☐ is, ☐ will be) ....
(Number and street)

.... (City or town) .... (State)

3. I am an alien. I was lawfully admitted to the United States for permanent residence at ....

.... (Port of entry) .... under the name of ....

on .... (Month) .... (Day) .... (Year) .... on the vessel .... (If otherwise than vessel show manner of arrival)

I have resided in and have been physically present in the United States for an uninterrupted period of at least .... year(s) since such lawful entry. Since the date of my lawful entry, I have been absent from the United States as follows (include date of last departure if now abroad, and if necessary attach an additional sheet to show all absences):

Date of departure	Date and port of return	Name of vessel	Purpose of trip

4. Since becoming a permanent resident, have you ever filed an income tax return as a nonresident alien or otherwise claimed or received benefits as a nonresident alien under the income tax laws? ☐ Yes ☐ No

5. I (☐ am, ☐ will be, ☐ was) employed as, or under contract as, ...

by ....
(Name of employer)

address .... (Number and street) .... (City or town) .... (State) .... (ZIP code)

Such employment of contract {necessitates / will necessitate / necessitated} my presence in ....
(Country or countries)

from .... (Month) ...... (Day) ...... (Year) .... to .... (Month) ...... (Day) ...... (Year)

6. My absence from the United States for such periods (☐ is, ☐ will be, ☐ was):

☐ on behalf of the United States Government.
☐ for the purpose of carrying on scientific research on behalf of an American institution of research.
☐ for the purpose of engaging in the development of foreign trade and commerce of the United States on behalf of an American firm or corporation or a subsidiary thereof engaged in the development of such trade and commerce.
☐ necessary to the protection of the property rights abroad of an American firm or corporation engaged in the development of foreign trade and commerce of the United States.
☐ on behalf of a public international organization of which the United States is a member, by which I was first employed on
...., 19......
☐ solely in my capacity as a ☐ clergyman, ☐ missionary, ☐ brother, ☐ nun, or ☐ sister.

7. In support of the foregoing statement of facts I submit the following documents ....

....
(See instructions)

8. I respectfully request that you find my absence under the above-stated conditions to be in compliance with the provisions of Sec. 316(b) or 317 of the Immigration and Nationality Act.

Signature of Person Preparing Form, If Other Than Applicant	**Signature of Applicant**
I declare that this document was prepared by me at the request of the applicant, and is based on all information of which I have any knowledge.	I certify that the above statements are true and correct to the best of my knowledge and behalf.
SIGNATURE	COMPLETE SIGNATURE OF APPLICANT
ADDRESS — DATE	MAILING ADDRESS- Number, street, city, State, and ZIP code — DATE

Form N–470 (Rev. 1–22–73) N

INDEX

ANTHONY SAMPSON

THE MONEY SPINNERS

THE MONEY SPINNERS reveals for the first time the power, the workings and the personalities of the money men who make the world go round:

The Superbankers – including Chase's David Rocke-feller, Citibank's Walter Wriston, Lloyd's Sir Jeremy Morse and Robert McNamara.

The debt-ridden regimes of Poland and Iran, Brazil, Zaire and Pakistan.

The Medicis, the Rothschilds, the Barings, the Barclays whose banks have transformed the economic map of the world.

THE MONEY LENDERS tells the full story of the world banking crisis: as *The Guardian* review confirmed 'Anthony Sampson has said it all. There's nothing else to say'

ALSO AVAILABLE FROM CORONET

WINSTON FLETCHER

☐ 36376 2   Meetings, Meetings   £1.95

ANTHONY SAMPSON

☐ 21323 X   The Seven Sisters   £2.75
☐ 18284 9   The Sovereign State   £2.25
☐ 22594 7   The Arms Bazaar   £2.50
☐ 28771 3   The Money Lenders   £2.50
☐ 28434 X   The Changing Anatomy Of Britain   £3.95

ROBERT TOWNSEND

☐ 14986 8   Up The Organisation   £1.95

All these books are available at your local bookshop or newsagent, or can be ordered direct from the publisher. Just tick the titles you want and fill in the form below.

Prices and availability subject to change without notice.

CORONET BOOKS, P.O. Box 11, Falmouth, Cornwall.

Please send cheque or postal order, and allow the following for postage and packing:

U.K.—55p for one book, plus 22p for the second book, and 14p for each additional book ordered up to a £1.75 maximum.

B.F.P.O. and EIRE—55p for the first book, plus 22p for the second book, and 14p per copy for the next 7 books, 8p per book thereafter.

OTHER OVERSEAS CUSTOMERS—£1.00 for the first book, plus 25p per copy for each additional book.

Name ....

Address...

....